POETS
ON
POETRY

Edited by HOWARD NEMEROV

BASIC BOOKS, Inc., Publishers

New York   *London*

Second Printing

© 1966 by Howard Nemerov

Library of Congress Catalog Card Number: 65-27338

Manufactured in the United States of America

POETS
ON
POETRY

Edited by HOWARD NEMEROV

BASIC BOOKS, Inc., PUBLISHERS
New York   *London*

Second Printing
© 1966 by Howard Nemerov
Library of Congress Catalog Card Number: 65-27338
Manufactured in the United States of America

Contributors

CONRAD AIKEN, poet, critic, and novelist, was a contributing editor of *The Dial;* American correspondent for *The Athenaeum,* London, and *The London Mercury;* and London correspondent for *The New Yorker.*

BEN BELITT, poet and translator, is a member of the Faculty of Literature and Languages, Bennington College. Former Assistant Literary Editor of *The Nation,* his achievements have merited the Shelley Memorial Award, a Guggenheim Fellowship, two awards from *Poetry* magazine, a National Institute of Arts and Letters grant; and a Brandeis Creative Arts Award.

JOHN BERRYMAN, poet, literary critic, fiction writer, and biographer, is Professor of Humanities, University of Minnesota. For his poetic contributions, he was elected to membership in the National Institute of Arts and Letters and has received a Shelley Memorial Award, a Harriet Monroe Memorial Award, and a Pulitzer Prize.

JOHN MALCOLM BRINNIN, critic and biographer, currently teaches at the University of Connecticut. Former Director of the Poetry Center in New York City, Mr. Brinnin was the 1955 recipient of the Poetry Society of America's Gold Medal for distinguished service in poetry.

GREGORY CORSO, one of the inner circle of the "Beat Generation" writers, is an original voice in American poetry. He won the Longview Award in 1959 for his poem, "Marriage."

J. V. CUNNINGHAM, poet and critic, is currently Professor of English at Brandeis University. Pursuing his literary interests in the academic setting, he has held positions at a number of leading American universities and is the recipient of a National Institute of Arts and Letters grant.

JAMES DICKEY, poet and critic, is current Poet in Residence at the San Fernando Valley State College, California. He has been the recipient of a Guggenheim Fellowship.

ROBERT DUNCAN, poet and educator, was Assistant Director of the Poetry Center at San Francisco State College.

v

RICHARD EBERHART, Professor of English and Poet in Residence at Dartmouth College, has held several academic positions. His numerous accolades include Yale's Bollingen Prize, appointments as Consultant in Poetry and Honorary Consultant in American Letters at The Library of Congress, and membership in the National Institute of Arts and Letters and the Advisory Committee on the Arts for the National Cultural Center in Washington, D.C., under the Eisenhower administration.

JACK GILBERT, who has taught poetry courses at San Francisco State College and the University of California, Berkeley, received the Yale Series of Younger Poets Award in 1961 for his lyric work, *Views of Jeopardy*.

BARBARA HOWES, poet and translator, has been the recipient of two prizes from *Poetry* magazine, a Brandeis University Creative Arts Award in Poetry for 1958, and a Guggenheim Fellowship.

VASSAR MILLER, poet, received prizes from *Poetry* magazine for 1957 and 1961.

MARIANNE MOORE, America's outstanding woman poet, was a former editor of *The Dial*. Her honors include membership in the American Academy of Arts and Sciences and the National Institute of Arts and Letters.

HOWARD NEMEROV, novelist, essayist, and poet, is currently a member of the Faculty of Literature and Languages at Bennington College. Former Consultant in Poetry at The Library of Congress, he is a member of the National Institute of Arts and Letters and a Fellow in the American Academy of Arts and Sciences.

WILLIAM JAY SMITH, poet, translator, and prose writer, is Poet in Residence at Williams College. A former member of the Vermont House of Delegates, he has been awarded Washington University's alumni citation for his poetic achievements.

MAY SWENSON, poet, editor, and former newspaperwoman, has been the recipient of a Guggenheim Fellowship, a National Institute of Arts and Letters Award, an Amy Lowell Traveling Scholarship, a Robert Frost Fellowship, and a Ford Foundation Poet-Theater grant.

THEODORE WEISS, publisher and editor of the *Quarterly Review of Literature* at Bard College, is an honorary Fellow of Ezra Stiles College, Yale University. He is the recipient of a

Ford Fellowship and a first-prize winner of the Wallace Stevens Award.

REED WHITTEMORE, essayist, editor, and poet, was Consultant in Poetry at The Library of Congress for 1964–1965. He is editor of *The Carleton Miscellany* and is a founder of the Association of Literary Magazines of America.

RICHARD WILBUR, educator, critic, translator, and poet, is Professor of English at Wesleyan University and editor of The Laurel Poetry Series of Dell Books. His translation of Molière's *Tartuffe* has been produced by the Lincoln Center Repertory Theater.

Preface

At the time that I agreed to serve as coordinator of these discussions, I was Consultant in Poetry to The Library of Congress. I was therefore at least in the right position, if not necessarily in possession of the right talents.

But selection is always an invidious business; it just is, and there is no way around it. For a week, I sat at my desk drawing up lists of poets. I never knew that there were so many of us. And, since perhaps no more than three turned down the invitation, it is plain that the responsibility for selection is altogether mine. I do not think that this requires much justification beyond the obvious observation that another editor might have made a substantially different set of choices and come up with a list of contributors as gifted as those presented here. But I should perhaps add that, though I did not go out of my way to avoid choosing friends and acquaintances just because they were friends and acquaintances, I did try to give fair representation to as many tendencies or "schools" as I thought I saw on the contemporary scene. This was a somewhat difficult matter, because a poet is first of all himself and only secondarily of interest as illustrating or representing this or that belief about the nature of the art. For the quality of my judgment in this matter I may not speak, though the beauty and force of the essays as they came in pleased me a great deal; but I did keep in mind the object of showing as well as possible the variety of work that is available.

With the idea of making some sort of center to the discussion, I proposed four questions to the contributors, explaining, however, that these were to be taken mainly as stimulus or even irritant and need not be regarded at all if the writer's interests took him along some other path. As I might have expected, few set themselves to answer directly; some paid the questions no heed whatever; whereas others, perhaps a majority, wrote essays in which the substance of the questions is obliquely reflected. For this reason, though the questions do appear here and there throughout the text, it may be convenient for the reader to have them listed.

1. Do you see your work as having essentially changed in character or style since you began?

2. Is there, has there been, was there ever, a "revolution" in poetry, or is all that a matter of a few sleazy technical tricks? What is the relation of your work to this question, if there is a relation? Otherwise put: do you respond to such notions as The New Poetry, An American Language Distinct from English, The Collapse of Prosody, No Thoughts but in Things, The Battle between Academics and—What?—Others (A Fair Field Full of Mostly Corpses)?

3. Does the question whether the world has changed during this century preoccupy you in poetry? Does your work appear to you to envision the appearance of a new human nature, for better or worse, or does it view the many and obvious changes as essentially technological?

4. What is the proper function of criticism? Is there a species of it that you admire (are able to get along with)?

Though this book cannot be regarded as formally responsive to that interrogation, which in retrospect appears to me to be indeed somewhat nosey, I think that there has come together here a happier result than such a response would have been: a good many examples of candid reflection and personal observation of the poetic art by some of its present adepts whose essays offer a fair conspectus of the range, achievement, and objects of American poetry now.

It remains to record my gratitude for the steady help and friendship of the Voice of America Forum Series editors, Max R. Grossman and Theodore A. Wertime; of their assistant, Miss Joy MacFadyen; and of Miss Phyllis Armstrong at The Library of Congress. Finally, I thank the contributors for the courtesy and patience with which they met my bumblings about in the realm of the muse's administration.

HOWARD NEMEROV

Bennington College
October 1965

Contents

POETS ON POETRY

1 POETRY AND THE MIND OF MODERN MAN

Conrad Aiken

As a regular and energetic critic of American poetry from 1915 on, contributing editor of *The Dial*, American correspondent for the *Athenaeum* in London and *The London Mercury*, and editor of three anthologies of American poetry, it will be clear that from very early in this century I had to take sides and to make up my mind not only where poetry should go, but where I, too, as a poet, should go. In my first volume of criticism, published in 1919, I discussed this involvement with considerable candor in a preface called "Apologia Pro Specie Sua." In sum, I argued that each of us was trying to urge poetry in a direction favorable to himself and that dispassionate judgment was a chimera. This was, of course, the period when the so-called New American Poetry was emerging in the persons of Frost, Robinson, Masters, the Imagists, Pound, Eliot, the Vorticists, and the groups in New York known as "the Others." My own position in this melee was, I would say, a shade to the left of center, if we take Robinson as the center. I was opposed to the extremes of fragmentation advocated by the Imagists and the Others and argued, in my review in 1917, that Eliot's rhymed free verse, which was not really free verse at all but a highly controlled and very subtly modulated medium, was probably the best signpost available as to the direction in which the form and tone of poetry might most adventurously go.

This precocious judgment has, I think, been proved true by time. A great deal of the "newest" of the so-called new poetry has now either become dated or disappeared, and, in the perspective we have since gained, we can see that there was never any real revolution in American poetry, in the true sense of an overturning, but rather an orderly and quite logical development from the past, both American and European. It is true that, as James said earlier in his study of Hawthorne, we were aware of a meagerness in our past, or, at any rate, of a lack of richness in it, or at least some of us thought so; this accounts but only partly for the remarkable exodus of young American writers to Europe after World War I. It accounts, too, for the fact that Eliot and myself, who were friends at Harvard College from 1908 on, discussed this need for a richer chemical solution in which to swim and breathe, a more sustaining *ambiente* than our own then appeared to be. What could be done about it? Eliot, as we all know, elected France and what was then "modern" French poetry and got this creative venom into his veins before the fortunes of World War I settled him in England. I myself preferred the English tradition and lived there many years because that seemed to me what I needed. Later, the fortunes of another war sent me back to America, where I found that my ancestral roots claimed me; I should have remained there all the time.

And the truth is that James was wrong, and so were Eliot and myself and all the others, in thinking that there was an insufficient cultural inheritance in this country; it was there, but neither our teachers nor ourselves were yet aware of it. In Whitman, Melville, Dickinson, Mark Twain, Emerson, Thoreau, Hawthorne, Poe, and James himself, what more could the ripening consciousness of this country, which in a curious way was both old and young, demand? It was enough, if only someone had pointed it out to us; but it remained for *ourselves* to make the discovery. As it was left for me, for example, to make the "discovery" of Emily Dickinson—which was disapproved of by both Pound and Eliot—in an essay on her and a selection of her poems published in England in 1924.

Anyway, there it all was, waiting for us; and I think we can now see that it was at just about this point, in the early 1920's, that we can be said to have first taken possession of it and that this possession began to be manifest in our work. We could see our roots in Whitman and Emerson and Dickinson and then, in the forgotten figure of Trumbull Stickney, the link between them and us, the first sounding of the "modern" note, the abandonment of the oratorical or grandiose for a more flexible and colloquial tone of voice, which nevertheless, when occasion demanded, could rise to the full *vox humana* of the highest poetic speech. We were quite conscious of our search for this medium. Eliot found it in Vildrac and Laforgue, even in Henley's *Sunday up the River*, while I found it in Stickney, John Masefield, and in some of Francis Thompson. As early as 1911, in a composition course at Harvard, I produced a longish narrative poem, called "The Clerk's Journal," which deliberately eschewed "poetic" words and tried to emphasize the telephone wires and cobblestones, not to mention the lunch counters and coffee cups.

This was one side of the poetic experiment in which we were all engaged, the linguistic and tonal side; but in my own case it was made more complicated by the fact that at this time two other influences were brought to bear on me. Music was one of these, in particular that of Richard Strauss in the tone poems and the symphonies and quartets of Beethoven; and this was to lead me pretty far afield. An early poem of this period was subtitled "A Tone Poem." This was followed by a group of sonatas and nocturnes, very bad indeed, and then by the group of "symphonies" which now compose the book called *The Divine Pilgrim*. Admittedly, this preoccupation led to considerable diffuseness, which I was, myself, the first to acknowledge; but I defended it, too, and not without ingenuity, and I think these poems still have their virtues.

But, if they have, it is largely because of the *other* influence— both had really begun at Harvard—and this was my interest in the then "new" psychology of Freud and in the notion, learned from Santayana in his lectures on *Three Philosophical Poets*— Lucretius, Dante, and Goethe—that poetry at its best and broadest must be philosophical, must have at its center some sort of world view, or *weltanschauung*. But how, in the fragmented world of the psychologists—not only Freud, but Jung, Adler, Ferenczi, Holt, and all the rest—was one to shape this? The symphonies of *The Divine Pilgrim* sought it in an over-all solipsism, but with increasing accent on the disintegration of the ego, the disappearance of the self into series, like the vaudeville actors who come and go on the stage. The two interests do, I think, hold the book together and give it an aim. If it is certainly no *Faust*, it at least

3

belongs to that category. And its final section, "Changing Mind," written a little later than the others and which takes as its theme the complete breakdown of personality into its components of heredity and sex, signals, I think, the moment of change-over from the earlier and more deliberately musical style to the later, which is more condensed, analytic, and even at times *preceptual*.

But before I go into that, let us pause at this moment, which is 1925, and look round at what the other poets are up to. As a matter of fact, it is one of the most brilliant moments for poetry in the century. Stevens had just published *Harmonium*, probably his best book, with all his characteristics fully developed, but with the form in tight and delicious control and the humor and metaphysics going hand in hand. Eliot had stunned us all with *The Waste Land*. Robinson, now for a moment neglected, was at his apogee in that extraordinary sequence of Arthurian romances, *Merlin* and the others, which can only be likened, psychologically, to Henry James. And, if Masters had come and gone, leaving behind him little more than *Spoon River*, Frost was at the top of his form and Cummings, Marianne Moore, and William Carlos Williams were coming importantly on stage. Sandburg was having his greatest success; Jeffers and MacLeish were emerging. On the whole, I think it can be said that at this point and for the next thirty years the best poetry written in English was American. In fact, I think it has remained so since. English poetry, in a sense, had moved to America.

But with complications. For this galaxy of poets was seldom agreed on anything. Each had to go his own way. It was in some respects a kind of quiet—and sometimes not so quiet—gang warfare. And I think we all realized this—it was kill or be killed; it was the normal evolutionary process and involved, quite rightly, the survival of the fittest; it was poetry, as the vanguard of man's consciousness, as it always has been, once again, by trial and loss, finding out its own way, or trying to, to bring into consciousness every scrap of knowledge, from whatever field and no matter how uncompromisingly unpoetic or antipoetic it might seem to be.

And it was toward this concept of poetry that I, myself, now began more and more deliberately to move, and in this I think it can be said that, although my later poetry *looks* different or *sounds* different, nevertheless this basic direction can be seen in

4

it all. What begins with the musical fragmentation of *The Jig of Forslin* and *The House of Dust* or the animist dissociations and reassociations of the consciousness of Senlin in "Senlin: A Biography," turns more and more, by degrees, into a preoccupation with the very nature of consciousness itself, that evanescent bubble of awareness which is all that we know of ourselves. This, of course, is my answer to the question asked me by the editor of this series, namely, whether the change in man's world during this century has preoccupied me. And how could it not? With Darwin, Nietzsche, and Freud behind us, where were the comfortable values to which we had been born? Perhaps this fact was brought home to me earlier than to most of my generation, for I inherited this sort of liberalism and agnosticism from my grandfather, William James Potter, who was one of the great liberal Unitarians of the nineteenth century, had adapted himself by midcentury to *The Origin of Species,* studied with Humboldt, and was one of the founders and later president of the Free Religious Association. I was brought up with no beliefs, or none of a dogmatic sort. Wasn't it enough that the world was beautiful, terrible, astonishing, even incredible? One could, if one liked, call it divine or conceive of a god in various forms, as my Festus does, to amuse himself, in "The Pilgrimage of Festus." But more important, it seemed to me, was to take the *next* step, and analyze the world in the only terms we had any genuine knowledge of, to wit, ourselves. One must be as conscious of this as possible, if only as a preliminary step to anything else; and this endeavor seemed to involve another possible concept—that in the *evolution of consciousness* man was already embarked, willy-nilly, on a perhaps divine pilgrimage of his own.

I do not want to be and cannot be too precise about all this or the timing of it; who of us can possibly remember the exact point at which he became finally conscious of the compass of his mind and the relation of this compass to his body, the whole psychosomatic machine? Like everything else, this knowledge comes in fractions, is a series, an accretion. One observes, as a child, the wasp stinging the locust to death, then dragging away the locust to its underground nest. And to bring this observation into association with the small boy's experience of urinating into a bowl and there, by himself, creating an entire cosmos of bubbles, and of an extraordinary beauty, is to realize how early in life one begins this attempt at a correlation of the mysteries, apparently inexplicable, with one's own unexplainable existence at the very center of it. Who am I? We inevitably get back to that fundamental question. And how did I come by it? And what should I do with it?

Well, those have been my preoccupations, and they have allowed me a quite considerable range. As for form, here again I have always maintained that, as poetry is an art, and perhaps the highest, it should use every prosodic and linguistic device at its disposal; I cannot subscribe to the theory that a mere counting of syllables can be substituted for verse. And the form must be suited to the theme. In the two series of "Preludes," which I think are the center of my work, I did not hesitate to mix a sort of organic free verse with the most formal of lyrics. As for another poem, "The Kid," a poem that deals with the pioneers of America, those of the mind as well as of the broadax, I didn't hesitate to use a kind of ballad form, a folk doggerel, in couplets, which nevertheless, when necessary, could become pure seventeenth-century severity. And again, for such longer philosophical meditations as "A Letter from Li-Po" or "The Crystal" I found a free blank verse most suitable. In short, the theme will almost invariably, left to itself, call the tune.

The poet is only the medium.

Finally, I would like to repeat something I said thirty years ago about poetry in general and its function.

Poetry has always kept easily abreast with the utmost man can do in extending the horizon of his consciousness, whether outward or inward. It has always been the most flexible, the most comprehensive, the most farseeing, and hence the most successful, of the modes by which he has accepted the new in experience, realized it, and adjusted himself to it. Whether it is a change in his conception of the heavens, or of the law of gravity, or of morality, or of the nature of consciousness, it has always at last been in poetry that man has given his thought its supreme expression—which is to say that most of all, in this, he succeeds in making real for himself the profound myth of personal existence and experience.

But if poetry is to accomplish this, in any age, it must think;

6

it must embody the full consciousness of man at that given moment. It cannot afford to lag behind the explorations of knowledge, whether of the inner or outer worlds; these it is its business to absorb and transmute. What made Elizabethan poetry great, above all, was the fearlessness with which it plunged into the problem of consciousness itself. No item of man's awareness was too trivial to be noted, too terrifying to be plumbed. Shakespeare's poetry is everywhere vascular with this rich consciousness of self, thought being carried bodily into the realm of feeling, and feeling as boldly carried into the realm of thought. This was no mere decorative toy, no amusement or anodyne for women; it was the advance guard in man's conquest of the knowable. It was a portrait of man with the sweat on his brow, the blood on his hands, the agony in his heart; with his gaieties, his absurdities, his obscenities; his beliefs and his doubts. No poetry since has been so great, for none has been either so comprehensive or so truthful. The fashions changed, the "idea" of poetry changed, the novel absorbed a part of its province—one could multiply indefinitely the reasons for it. But today, as I have suggested, the signs are not wanting that poetry may again occupy its own province, may again speak with full-voiced gusto of the horrors and subtleties and magnificences of the great myth in which we find ourselves the bewildered actors.

And I would like to say again what I said in 1948, in one of the prefaces to my collection of symphonies, that in the evolution of man's consciousness, ever widening and deepening and subtilizing his awareness, and in the dedication of himself to this supreme task, man possesses all that he could possibly require in the way of a religious credo; when the half-gods go, the gods arrive; he can, if he only will, become divine.

2 SOME ANSWERS TO QUESTIONS POSED BY HOWARD NEMEROV

Marianne Moore

I

Do you see your work as having essentially changed in character or style since you began?

No, except that rhythm was my prime objective. If I succeeded in embodying a rhythm that preoccupied me, I was satisfied.

Uniform line length seemed to me essential as accrediting the satisfactory model stanza and I sometimes ended a line with a hyphen, expecting the reader to maintain the line unbroken (disregarding the hyphen). I have found readers misled by the hyphen, mistaking it as an arcane form of emphasis, so I seldom use it today.

I am today much aware of the world's dilemma. People's effect on other people results, it seems to me, in an enforced sense of responsibility—a compulsory obligation to participate in others' problems.

II

Is there, has there been, was there ever, a "revolution" in poetry, or is all that a matter of a few sleazy technical tricks? What is the relation of your work to this question, if there is a relation? Otherwise put: do you respond to such notions as The New Poetry, An American Language Distinct from English, The

Editor's Note: Miss Moore in this lecture goes at once to the questions posed. These questions, herewith repeated in each case before Miss Moore's answers, seek to call forth the author's own recollection of the growth of her art and to relate that art to the social and literary movements of the period.

Collapse of Prosody, No Thoughts but in Things, The Battle between Academics and—What?—Others (A Fair Field Full of Mostly Corpses)?

The individuality and emotions of the writer should transcend modes. I recall feeling oversolitary occasionally (say in 1912)—in reflecting no "influences"; in not being able to be called an "Imagist"—but determined to put the emphasis on what mattered most to me, in a manner natural to me. I like end-stopped lines and depend on rhyme, but my rhymes are often hidden and, in being inconspicuous, escape detection. When I began writing verse, I regarded flowing continuity as indispensable.

A Jellyfish[1]

Visible, invisible,
a fluctuating charm
an amber-tinctured amethyst
inhabits it, your arm
approaches and it opens
and it closes; you had meant
to catch it and it quivers;
you abandon your intent.

Then when I came on Charles Sorley's "The Idea" (probably in *The Egoist,* London)—

It was all my own;
I have guarded it well from
the winds that have blown
too bitterly

—I recognized the unaccented syllable (the light rhyme) as means for me, as in "The Jerboa":[2]

---

[1] From Marianne Moore, *O to Be a Dragon* (New York: The Viking Press, 1956). All rights reserved; reprinted by permission of The Viking Press, Inc.

[2] Reprinted with permission of The Macmillan Company from *Collected Poems* by Marianne Moore. Copyright 1935 Marianne Moore; renewed 1963 Marianne Moore and T. S. Eliot.

> . . . one would not be he
> who has nothing but plenty.

> . . . closed upper paws seeming one with the fur
> in its flight from a danger.

Having written the last stanza first, I had to duplicate it, progressing backward.

> Its leaps should be set
> to the flageolet;
>   pillar body erect
>   on a three-cornered smooth-working Chippendale
>   claw—propped on hind legs, and tail as third toe
>   between leaps to its burrow.

In "Occasionem Cognosce,"[3] the light rhyme is upside down:

> . . . "Atlas"
> (pressed glass)

> looks best
> embossed.

Poetry is a magic of pauses, as a dog-valentine contrasting "pawses" and "pauses"—sent me from Harvard where I had been discussing pauses—reminded me. I do not know what syllabic verse is. I find no appropriate application for it.

Might I say of the light rhyme that T. S. Eliot's phrase, "the greatest living master of the light rhyme," in his Introduction to my *Selected Poems*—suggesting conscious proficiency or at most a regulator art on my part, hardly deserves the term. Conscious writing can be the death of poetry.

3 From *The Lowell House Chronicle*, May 30, 1963. "Occasionem Cognosce," by Marianne Moore, first appeared as a Lowell House separatum designed by Eric Martin and Laurence Scott in honor of Elliott and Mary Perkins and printed in an edition of 75 copies by the Stinehour Press, Lunenburg, Vermont, May 1, 1963. Reprinted with the permission of The Master and Tutors of Lowell House, Harvard University.

For me, what W. H. Auden says in the Preface to his *Collected Shorter Poems* is true:

> In the eyes of every author, I fancy, his own past work falls into four classes. First, the pure rubbish which he regrets ever having conceived; second—for him the most painful—the good ideas which his incompetence or impatience prevented from coming to much ("The Orators" seems to me such a case of the fair notion fatally injured); third, the pieces he has nothing against except their lack of importance; these must inevitably form the bulk of any collection since, were he to limit it to the fourth class alone, to those poems for which he is honestly grateful, his volume would be too depressingly slim. The slim, seldom pieces are like a Gravenstein of the Hesperides, certainly, or a Sir Philip Sidney "medicine of cherries."

I should like to exonerate Mr. Auden of having selected me as a suitable translator of the La Fontaine *Fables*. Chivalry seems to have deterred him from flatly denying that he recommended me. He did approve, as advisor to a publisher, a retranslation of the La Fontaine *Fables* and, perhaps under extortion to name a specific translator, may tentatively have named me. Never have axioms seemed to me to have a more ever-current life than the morals of La Fontaine; and, of all the lessons taught, the most valuable for me has been this one with wide application, from "The Rabbits":[4]

> When fables allure
> Rest assured that they are short.

"Strangeness is a quality," Howard Nemerov says, "belonging inseparably to language and vision" and (quoting Conrad): " 'It is above all, in the first place, to make you see,' said Joseph Conrad of the object of art; and he said again, more formally, that the writer's object is 'to render the highest kind of justice to the visible world.' Seeing and saying—language is a special extension of the power of seeing, inasmuch as it can make visible not only the already visible world, but through it the invisible world of relations and affinities." The world of the soul? As diffi-

[4] From Jean de La Fontaine, *Fables,* trans. Marianne Moore (New York: The Viking Press, 1954).

cult as it is to define the soul, is "creativeness" perhaps as near a definition as we can get? I am recalling the statement made in a sermon by Mr. Stanley Taylor, Co-ordinator of Inter-Urban Affairs of Protestant Churches in the Presbytery of Brooklyn-Nassau.

To sum up: poetry is not a thing of tunes, but of heightened consciousness—as in these lines, say, by Eric Schroeder about the sea:

Element IV[5]

Haste waste and Haste the horror of the sea
Downfall and trampling and swift yeasty reach,
retreat, hoar tyranny-rearing dream, height, curling
toppling, to another Hopeless Hurling
Crashing and crawling
warning
the froth scuds
the sky spatters
the spume flies
And a bird comes downwind, rocking down the wind,
struggles, recovers, and sails and away goes
wavering down the wind and away

Is not Professor I. A. Richards always "new," as in this "Alpine Sketch"?[6]

. . . Swift flows the race,
Old Overshot wheels glittering o'er;
With no ill grace
The log draws through the saw;

His "Not No"[7] being electric with spontaneity?

[5] *Visions of Elements and Other Poems* (Freeport, Maine: The Bond Wheelwright Company, 1963).
[6] *Good-bye Earth and Other Poems* (New York: Harcourt, Brace & Company, 1958).
[7] *Good-bye Earth and Other Poems* (New York: Harcourt, Brace & Company, 1958).

Ha, Skater on the Brink
           Come whence
                     Where go?

Anywhere
      Elsewhere
           Where I would not know
Not mine, not mine, all this lived through in me.

Who asks? Who answers? What ventriloquy!

George Herbert's untampered-with-by-vanity "Heaven's Echo"
also eludes vanity:

> O who will show me those delights on
>   high? *I.*
> Thou, echo, thou art mortal, all men
>   know. *No.*
> Then tell me what is that supreme delight?
>   *Light.*
> Light to the mind: what shall the will
>   enjoy? *Joy.*
> But are there cares and business with the
>   Pleasure? *Leisure.*
> Light, joy and leisure; but shall they per-
>   sever? *Ever.*

Lastly, John Bunyan's prestatement about *The Pilgrim's
Progress* provides us with manner-without-manner's true model:

> I did not think
> To show the world my pen and ink.
> Nor did I undertake
> Thereby to please my neighbor; no, not I,
> I did it mine own self to gratifie.

"Perhaps the last English book written without thought of a
review," T. B. Fowler says ("even of a possible reader," said
Bunyan himself):

Over 100,000 copies were sold in his lifetime. Between 1678 and 1778, thirty-three editions of Part One and fifty-nine editions of Parts One and Two together. Then the publisher stopped counting.[8]

The Elegy for Mr. Valiant-for-Truth

When Mr. Valiant "had this for a token that the summons was true, . . . that his pitcher was broken at the fountain. . . . Then said he, . . . 'though with great difficulty I have got hither, yet now I do not repent me of all the trouble I have been at to arrive where I am. My sword I give to him that shall succeed me in my pilgrimage, and my courage and skill to him that can get it. My marks and scars I carry with me, to be a witness for me that I have fought His battles who now will be my rewarder.' . . . When the day that he must go hence was come, many accompanied him to the river-side, into which, as he went, he said, 'Death, where is thy sting?' And as he went down deeper, he said, 'Grave, where is thy victory?' So he passed over, and all the trumpets sounded on the other side."

In the phases of creativeness presented, we have maximum impact, it seems to me, unblurred and innate.

I see no revolution in the springs of what results in "poetry." No revolution in creativeness. Irrepressible emotion, joy, grief, desperation, triumph—inward forces which resulted in the Book of Job, Dante (the *Vita Nuova, Inferno*), Chaucer, Shakespeare— are the same forces which result in poetry today. "Endless curiosity, observation, research, and a great amount of joy in the thing," George Grosz, the caricaturist said, explaining his art. These account for many other forms of art, I should say.

One's manner of objectifying feeling has many variants, of course. Governance of the emotions and impassioned perceptiveness seem to me "the artist." Thoreau said, "A true account of action is the rarest poetry." Flaubert's "Describe a tree so no other tree could be mistaken for it" is basic, as exemplified by Leonardo da Vinci in his every sketch. Mannerism and pedantry have no place in art. Ezra Pound excludes much trivia when he

---

8 *The English-Speaking World,* August 1938.

says, "Use no word that under stress of emotion you could not actually say."

I do not make a distinction between the American and the English language.

I find that modern society becomes more and more concise— takes for granted more and more as not needing to be explained.

III

Does the question whether the world has changed during this century preoccupy you in poetry? Does your work appear to you to envision the appearance of a new human nature, for better or worse, or does it view the many and obvious changes as essentially technological?

It preoccupies me, not as timely topics, but fundamentally and continuously. Every day it is borne in on us that we need rigor— better governance of the emotions. We behave like the companions of Ulysses who, "thinking that license emancipates one, Were slaves whom they themselves had bound"; like the rout in *The Green Pastures*—like the people of Sodom, causing God to repent of having created man and to consider destroying mankind, so that the angel Gabriel says, "Do dat Lawd, and start a new animal."

I think I see the beginning of a common understanding—some sincerity about "justice for all."

Considering "the bomb," General Eisenhower and David Lilienthal remind us that "anxiety and imminent danger have been man's constant companion in many periods of history." As Adolf Berle says, "Let us all go to work in the little and in the greater affairs with which we have contact, putting potential danger out of the mind . . . dealing with situations which are within our grasp."

IV

What is the proper function of criticism? Is there a species of it that you admire (are able to get along with)?

Criticism should stimulate an improved understanding of the subject discussed—"with a truce to politeness," as Montaigne says; unmannered and "without the pestilent filth of ambition."

Certain reviews of my work have been indispensable to me, not only in correcting uninitiate errors and affording information, but as models of writing. Dr. Johnson's critical observations and didacticisms throw light or stimulate resistance. Emerson's "Representative Men," fearless in appraisal and comparisons, aid one in being affirmative yet not invariably encomiastic. Sir Kenneth Clark seems to me the ideal expositor—enabled to speak extempore safely because of knowledge that is objective. He says, "Landscape painting must express conviction," and "In art you can not achieve naturalness without emotion." There is an integrity of performance.

In his careful reasoning, Kenneth Burke demonstrates that it is well to take time if one wants results, lending emphasis to the axiom by noting that what to some authors are difficulties the artist welcomes as opportunities.

Ford Madox Ford's book reviews in the *English Review* (1908 to 1912) were of inestimable value to me, as method. Wyndham Lewis, in *Blast*, by his "heat" (massive energy) and skill, was instructive.

Criticism should animate the imagination, should afford comparisons one had not thought of, should be affirmative, with unequivocal gusto—like that of Ezra Pound in *The Spirit of Romance*.

3 HOW I WRITE POETRY

Richard Eberhart

I began writing poetry when I was about fifteen as a high school boy in Austin, Minnesota. I had a native facility with words and could write many poems with ease and with the greatest pleasure. My verbal imagination seemed at odds with a mathematical one. I was from the beginning noticeably better at verse than at figures. My mother loved poetry. On our library table was a leatherbound copy of Tennyson. I still have this copy with her name in it. Tennyson was the first poet I read in depth. He became my model. I admired his almost perfect blending of sound and sense; but of course my early exercises were derivative.

However, one poem, quite un-Tennysonian, survives from my high school days. It was written when I was sixteen, entitled "Indian Pipe," discovered many years later in its small school notebook and published in 1953 when I was forty-nine. It is about the partial death of a whole race, the race of American Indians. I used to see Indian Pipes in the woods near home. Later, I was pleased to learn that Emily Dickinson particularly liked them. They were embossed on covers of her posthumous books. Its three stanzas seemed to have a classic elegance when discovered all those years later and to give off a delicate, somewhat wistful, poetic charge.

Here is the poem "Indian Pipe":[1]

> Searching once I found a flower
> By a sluggish stream.
> Waxy white, a stealthy tower

> To an Indian's dream.
> This its life supreme.
>
> Blood red winds the sallow creek
>   Draining as it flows.
> Left the flower all white and sleek,
>   Fainting in repose.
>   Gentler than a rose.
>
> Red man's pipe is now a ghost
>   Whispering to beware.
> Hinting of the savage host
>   Once that travelled there.
>   Perfume frail as air.

As a student at Dartmouth, I recall Housman as our favorite poet, but I in no way imitated him. We assumed something of his intellectual attitudes, however. Robert Frost was the first poet to mention a poem of mine in print, in a small book entitled *The Arts Anthology,* 1925, for which he wrote an introduction. Presently, Harriet Monroe published a group of my poems in *Poetry,* "A Magazine of Verse." But it was not until my Cambridge University years, 1927–1929, that I felt I was arriving at a style to command and pursue. I. A. Richards took interest in every line of mine and helped me to get my first book published. This was a long poem, *A Bravery of Earth,* on which I worked for months under the spell of Wordsworth, whose portrait by Pickering I sat beneath in hall at St. John's College. Cambridge poetry was lively then. William Empson, Kathleen Raine, Hugh Sykes-Davies, Ronald Bottrall, T. H. White, J. Bronowski, J. L. Sweeney, and others made it so.

Besides Wordsworth, the poet who influenced me, probably to a deeper extent, was William Blake, with whom critics for decades noticed an affinity. I was also much moved by Hopkins when I first encountered him at Cambridge. Critics noted traces of his style in mine for a few years, but this did not persist. I probably cannot claim progenitors besides Wordsworth, Blake, and Hopkins, although critics have also adduced Whitman. I had the fortune not to feel any urge to imitate Eliot, Pound, or Yeats.

I would like to tell my readers something of how I have written certain poems through three decades and longer of writing poetry. I should like to present the poems and give commentaries. It would seem reasonable to employ here poems which have been more used, known, and discussed than others of mine less noticed. There must be some significance in acceptance and use of poems over decades. The poems which are kept in the minds of readers through anthologies and textbooks must represent the taste of the times in a closer fashion than poems which may conceivably be better, but due to difficulty, to complexity, to some impenetrable strangeness, or to some other factor are not accepted. There is the possibility that these known and well-used poems are absolutely better than others. It is for the critics to bring out their absolute values. Time winnows away the bad poems; the true grain is in poems that have a certain timeless quality, yet this is relative. I have felt that everything about poetry is relative rather than absolute. Coleridge's relativist statement, "Poetry gives most pleasure when only generally and not perfectly understood," appeals to me as one of the truest statements about poetry, leaving as it does room for individual differences. Yet the oldest or most nearly timeless poems are not necessarily the best or better than the best contemporary poems.

Two theories about the complex and ancient art of poetry have specially impressed me. They are opposite, yet each seems true, and I can subscribe to both. One is that poetry comes from an excess of *élan vital*. It is an overflowing of powerful feelings from a healthy psyche. A poet is a normal man with superabundant creative powers. The other is that poetry comes from a sick soul and is to heal or make up for psychic deficiencies. One can name poets in either category. I can never find one theory or definition sufficient for all of poetry and have felt both these points of view as realities within myself, as well as many realities in between.

The problem of time in poetry has always fascinated me. Does a poet mate with his times or transcend his times? What are, or can be, his principles when writing? It would seem that a poet, even the greatest, speaks for a few decades, maybe only one or two. I have the idea of a time-spirit in the air which the poet seizes, mysteriously, out of the air to give his truth to the world. Each time-spirit differs from every other. The 1920's differed

19

from the 1930's, the 1930's from the 1940's, the 1940's from the 1950's, and so on, using decades as arbitrary markers. A poet may be prophetic, as was Hopkins, who mates with our times, which would have seemed an improbable future when he was writing in the nineteenth century, his poetry known only to a few persons.

One had to live beyond a decade to see its limitations. Poets of the Depression years in the 1930's who wrote of contemporary events fared less well than poets whose realities transcended the immediate. Each poet was struggling with the real, yet only poems which had a reality beyond the concerns of the time survive. These surviving poems must have something of the timeless in them. "Timeless" is itself a relative term. I suppose that, if a poem lasts for three or four hundred years, we can call it, but not accurately, timeless. We think of Shakespeare's sonnets as timeless. And, if a poem is read for thirty years, I suppose that it is more nearly timeless than if it is forgotten after ten years. What makes poems survive, what unique qualities poems which survive possess, are matters of the deepest interest to truth-seeking critics. In the final analysis, although there is no final analysis, the deepest things about poetry seem to me to be mysterious. They go beyond the mind into the vast reservoir and region of the spirit and appear to be not entirely accountable to reason. I cannot go so far as to say that the deepest things about poetry are irrational, but I would include irrational perception and components in my view of poetry. Poetry is a confrontation of the whole being with reality. It is a basic struggle of the soul, the mind, and the body to comprehend life; to bring order to chaos or to phenomena; and by will and insight to create communicable verbal forms for the pleasure of mankind.

Here is an early poem.

For a Lamb[2]

I saw on a slant hill a putrid lamb,
Propped with daisies. The sleep looked deep,
The face nudged in the green pillow
But the guts were out for crows to eat.

2 From Richard Eberhart, *Collected Poems 1930–1960* (New York: Oxford University Press, 1960; London: Chatto & Windus, Ltd., 1960). © 1960 by Richard Eberhart; reprinted by permission of Oxford University Press, Inc.

Where's the lamb? whose tender plaint
Said all for the mute breezes.
Say he's in the wind somewhere,
Say, there's a lamb in the daisies.

"For a Lamb" was written after seeing a dead lamb among
daisies in a field near Cambridge, England, in 1928. It is a metaphysical poem based on the proposition that things are not what
they seem. It can be read as straight description or as a transcendental poem. Its connotations invite transcendental considerations. The ending is ambiguous.

Here is a more complex but in some ways similar poem.

The Groundhog[3]

In June, amid the golden fields,
I saw a groundhog lying dead.
Dead lay he; my senses shook,
And mind outshot our naked frailty.
There lowly in the vigorous summer
His form began its senseless change,
And made my senses waver dim
Seeing nature ferocious in him.
Inspecting close his maggots' might
And seething cauldron of his being,
Half with loathing, half with a strange love,
I poked him with an angry stick.
The fever arose, became a flame
And Vigour circumscribed the skies,
Immense energy in the sun,
And through my frame a sunless trembling.
My stick had done nor good nor harm.
Then stood I silent in the day
Watching the object, as before;
And kept my reverence for knowledge
Trying for control, to be still,

3 From Richard Eberhart, *Collected Poems 1930–1960* (New York: Oxford
University Press, 1960; London: Chatto & Windus, Ltd., 1960). © 1960 by
Richard Eberhart; reprinted by permission of Oxford University Press, Inc.

21

To quell the passion of the blood;
Until I had bent down on my knees
Praying for joy in the sight of decay.
And so I left; and I returned
In Autumn strict of eye, to see
The sap gone out of the groundhog,
But the bony sodden hulk remained.
But the year had lost its meaning,
And in intellectual chains
I lost both love and loathing,
Mured up in the wall of wisdom.
Another summer took the fields again
Massive and burning, full of life,
But when I chanced upon the spot
There was only a little hair left,
And bones bleaching in the sunlight
Beautiful as architecture;
I watched them like a geometer,
And cut a walking stick from a birch.
It has been three years, now.
There is no sign of the groundhog.
I stood there in the whirling summer,
My hand capped a withered heart,
And thought of China and of Greece,
Of Alexander in his tent,
Of Montaigne in his tower,
Of Saint Theresa in her wild lament.

I wrote this poem in a high state of awareness, in a total charge
and commitment of the whole being in about twenty minutes, I
think in the fall of 1933 in my master's quarters, Dormitory E,
at St. Mark's School, Southborough, Massachusetts. By an ironic
turn of fate the manuscript remains unfound. I remember having
to change only a word or two. Of many of my manuscripts, I
would like to view this one particularly to see if I could learn
anything of my state of mind from the orthography.

The vision of the groundhog was had some time earlier (maybe
two years earlier) at Broadwater Farm, near Phoenixville,
Pennsylvania, the estate of the father of my Dartmouth friend

Andrew B. Foster, who read History at St. John's College, Cambridge, when I was there. The spot where I saw the dead animal seething with maggots was a few hundred feet from the Game Room, in full summer.

It may have been, however, that the poem was written in late summer. I distinctly recall writing four poems that summer, all at about the same time, and thinking that they were all equally good. I could not distinguish one from another, which may say something about the purity of the creative impulse.

Only one of the others, "In a Hard Intellectual Light," has been reprinted in anthologies and is known to some readers. Yet "The Groundhog" has had an active poetical life now for thirty years. The other two poems are unused. When I had the vision of the groundhog he seemed to have more life in his maggot-seething body than if he were alive and running along a field. It was the paradox of life in death. The poem arises to a unified view of history.

I have always been bemused by the fact that when I wrote the four poems I could not tell the difference in their value. From a creative point of view my effort was equal, yet the results were markedly different. Poems which endure must possess some universality of meaning.

The writing of "The Groundhog" is an example of a theory I have that poetry is a gift of the gods. It cannot be had only by taking thought. The process is ultimately mysterious, involving a total thrust of the whole being, some kind of magical power. When a poem is ready to be born it will be born whole, without the need to change a word, or perhaps with the need to change only a word or two. I thus go back to an ancient theory of inspiration. It must suggest strong, active memory and an instantaneous synthesizing power when the whole being, not the mind alone, or the senses or the will alone, can come to bear on life with significance. Probably more than half of my best-known poems have come to me in this way, when the being was a seemingly passive vehicle for the overwhelming dominance of the poem, which was then put down with ease, immediacy, fluency, and comprehensive order.

Here is another early poem, "If I Could Only Live at the Pitch That Is Near Madness."

If I Could Only Live at the Pitch That Is Near Madness[4]

If I could only live at the pitch that is near madness
When everything is as it was in my childhood
Violent, vivid, and of infinite possibility:
That the sun and the moon broke over my head.

Then I cast time out of the trees and fields,
Then I stood immaculate in the Ego;
Then I eyed the world with all delight,
Reality was the perfection of my sight.

And time has big handles on the hands,
Fields and trees a way of being themselves.
I saw battalions of the race of mankind
Standing stolid, demanding a moral answer.

I gave the moral answer and I died
And into a realm of complexity came
Where nothing is possible but necessity
And the truth wailing there like a red babe.

This poem in retrospect epitomizes the 1930's, for me at least. It was my answer, or one answer, to the severity of the times. It was written early in the second half of the decade. Perhaps if it had not been for the breakdown in our society in the Depression this poem would not have been written. The times forced me to a deep inward look and threw me back on the past conceived as better than the present. The poem owes something to Wordsworth's "Ode on the Intimations of Immortality Recollected from Early Childhood." My poem goes back to a vision of perfection in childhood, from which we are fallen away in maturity. The poem ends by facing a complex world of mature reality in a resolution between becomingness and the become. In the title line I do not intend pathological madness, but rather the "divine madness" of the Greeks, their famous free spirit and play of imagination at the intensest level of consciousness. This is a

4 From Richard Eberhart, *Collected Poems 1930–1960* (New York: Oxford University Press, 1960; London: Chatto & Windus, Ltd., 1960). © 1960 by Richard Eberhart; reprinted by permission of Oxford University Press, Inc.

Platonic poem. I think of Plato's world soul as an amorphous cloud hanging in the heavens. When we are born a portion of the world soul is joined to our bodies. They stay in mysterious relationship until the body dies and the soul goes back to the world soul. It is a pre-Christian notion. Wordsworth particularized Plato's idea. My poem holds to the immaculate quality of the ego in childhood, the early perfection of life, but recognizes the changes of time, man's inevitable confrontation of complexity, with the resolution as a tension of opposites.

Here is "New Hampshire, February," a poem dating from the end of the 1930's. I was as yet unmarried and had been given a cabin in Kensington, New Hampshire, near Exeter, during the winter vacation. The only heat was from the kitchen stove. I read philosophy and wrote poetry. One day some wasps fell through the roof onto the stove. They were numb but moved toward the center, getting more lively all the time. Recognizing a threat, I pushed them to the outside where they grew slower immediately. I first did this innocently, by instinct. However, I had early read much Schopenhauer and Hardy and soon decided to play with these creatures as the instrument of their fate, "malice prepense." I would push them toward the center of the stove. They would become lively, buzzing their wings, able to sting. Then I would immediately move them toward the outer edge of the stove where they would quickly become gelid. I manipulated them at will. The philosophical implications of this in the relation of ourselves to God, were immediately to hand and I wrote the following poem, with changes from the above facts which you will see. For instance, I use my breath instead of my hand as agent. There is an allusion to and reminder of "God touching his finger to Adam" from Michelangelo's Sistine painting.

New Hampshire, February[5]

Nature has made them hide in crevices,
Two wasps so cold they looked like bark.

[5] From Richard Eberhart, *Collected Poems 1930–1960* (New York: Oxford University Press, 1960; London: Chatto & Windus, Ltd., 1960). © 1960 by Richard Eberhart; reprinted by permission of Oxford University Press, Inc.

Why I do not know, but I took them
And I put them
In a metal pan, both day and dark.

Like God touching his finger to Adam
I felt, and thought of Michelangelo,
For whenever I breathed on them,
The slightest breath,
They leaped, and preened as if to go.

My breath controlled them always quite.
More sensitive than electric sparks
They came into life
Or they withdrew to ice,
While I watched, suspending remarks.

Then one in a blind career got out,
And fell to the kitchen floor. I
Crushed him with my cold ski boot,
By accident. The other
Had not the wit to try or die.

And so the other is still my pet.
The moral of this is plain.
But I will shirk it.
You will not like it. And
God does not live to explain.

Of the several war poems I wrote during World War II, "The
Fury of Aerial Bombardment" has been most studied. It was
written in Dam Neck, Virginia, in the summer of 1944 while I
was stationed there as a Naval Reserve officer teaching aerial free
gunnery. I taught tens of thousands of young Americans to shoot
the .50-caliber Browning machine gun from aircraft. The subject
was called Sighting. All too soon their names would come back
in the death lists. This depressed me so much that one time I
was sitting on a barracks steps at the end of the day and felt the
ruthlessness and senselessness of war so acutely that I wrote the
first three stanzas of the poem, which are in effect a kind of
prayer. I put it away. Some time later I felt it needed something

added to it. Maybe the interval was a week or two. With an analytical mind, quite removed from the passionate one of the first three stanzas, I composed the last four lines. It is said that these in relation to the others make this a particularly modern poem. Indeed, if I had not added the last stanza, perhaps the poem would remain unused. This is an example of a certain fortuitous quality determining the fate of a poem.

The Fury of Aerial Bombardment[6]

You would think the fury of aerial bombardment
Would rouse God to relent; the infinite spaces
Are still silent. He looks on shock-pried faces.
History, even, does not know what is meant.

You would feel that after so many centuries
God would give man to repent; yet he can kill
As Cain could, but with multitudinous will,
No farther advanced than in his ancient furies.

Was man made stupid to see his own stupidity?
Is God by definition indifferent, beyond us all?
Is the eternal truth man's fighting soul
Wherein the Beast ravens in its own avidity?

Of Van Wettering I speak, and Averill,
Names on a list, whose faces I do not recall
But they are gone to early death, who late in school
Distinguished the belt feed lever from the belt holding pawl.

After the War, I was in business in Boston for six years. "The Horse Chestnut Tree" is from this time, written in 1948. The actual tree stands in the garden of my father-in-law, now deceased, at 117 Lake View Avenue, Cambridge. The poem is based on a true incident. As with many of my poems, it came not immediately upon the experience, but welled into being some time later. Sometimes the interval would be months, sometimes years. This is another case of a poem being a "gift of the gods." When it was ready to come it was born whole, with the need to alter only one, or possibly two words, as I recall. Thus, I theorize that poetry may come into being in a state of contemplation, where memory must be operant, when the mind and being have a grasp of more than usual order and one is able to project and execute a poem easily with total authority.

Every fall a group of wild Irish boys would troop down the street and enter my father-in-law's garden to break down the horse chestnut tree with sticks and stones to get the nuts. They were about sixteen to eighteen, very hardy types. My father-in-law was getting old and could not cope with them. They had no respect for private property or for capitalism. I was feeling very strong and capable and one fall said I would take over the situation.

When the molesting boys came into the garden I felt I had the situation perfectly in hand. I knew precisely what I would do and had every right to do it. I rushed out with perfect confidence and grabbed one of the tough youths by the shoulder, whereupon he immediately yelled "Police! Police!" and I was so startled that I confess I let go and ran back into the house. Could it be that they were in cahoots with the police? O the high-spirited, undaunted Irish! (My middle name is Ghormley.) In a hundred years they had taken over Boston and would soon have a President in the White House. I had my revenge, of a sort, on the boy whose name I will never know, by writing the poem. It may be that some day the unwitting protagonist or one of his band will read it.

I perceived that these ruffians were actually Plato's lovers of the beautiful. They perceived, although they could not verbalize it, that beauty is useless. They only wanted to hold a shiny chestnut in their hands or in their pockets. They were, in effect, aestheticians and lovers of the good. I empathized with them for I had also loved and enjoyed the shiny feel of chestnuts in my youth. When the poem came to be written I understood certain relationships between the desires of man and his limitations, which are in the poem. A lawless act brought me to the laws and order of the poem.

The Horse Chestnut Tree[7]

Boys in sporadic but tenacious droves
Come with sticks, as certainly as Autumn,
To assault the great horse chestnut tree.

There is a law governs their lawlessness.
Desire is in them for a shining amulet
And the best are those that are highest up.

They will not pick them easily from the ground.
With shrill arms they fling to the higher branches,
To hurry the work of nature for their pleasure.

I have seen them trooping down the street
Their pockets stuffed with chestnuts shucked, unshucked.
It is only evening keeps them from their wish.

Sometimes I run out in a kind of rage
To chase the boys away: I catch an arm,
Maybe, and laugh to think of being the lawgiver.

I was once such a young sprout myself
And fingered in my pocket the prize and trophy.
But I still moralize upon the day

And see that we, outlaws on God's property,
Fling out imagination beyond the skies,
Wishing a tangible good from the unknown.

And likewise death will drive us from the scene
With the great flowering world unbroken yet,
Which we held in idea, a little handful.

Also from this period is one of the few pieces I have written immediately upon the experience which caused the poem. This is "The Cancer Cells." I was a fatigued salesman at the end of a

7 From Richard Eberhart, *Collected Poems 1930–1960* (New York: Oxford University Press, 1960; London: Chatto & Windus, Ltd., 1960). © 1960 by Richard Eberhart; reprinted by permission of Oxford University Press, Inc.

hot day in August and found myself in Newark, New Jersey. I took a room at the "Military Park Hotel," curiously amused at the odd name since I was so exhausted. I bought a copy of *Life* magazine. When I entered my room, fatigued, I opened the magazine accidentally to a two-page spread of the spiky shapes of cancer cells leaping out of test tubes. The vision startled me; it aroused me to an immediate perception of the hostility and beauty of these strange forms, the lethal and the beautiful simultaneously understood, death in life. I am sure the vision would not have struck me so hard if I had not been so tired. I happened to have a pencil and an envelope in my coat pocket and wrote the poem immediately on the back of a letter just as it stands. The form of poems seems to be natural corollary to what is being said.

The Cancer Cells[8]

Today I saw a picture of the cancer cells,
Sinister shapes with menacing attitudes.
They looked like art itself, like the artist's mind,
Sinister shapes with menacing attitudes,
Into a world beyond, a virulent laughing gang.
They looked like art itself, like the artist's mind,
Powerful shaker, and the taker of new forms.
Some are revulsed to see these spiky shapes;
It is the world of the future too come to.
Nothing could be more vivid than their language,
Lethal, sparkling and irregular stars,
The murderous design of the universe,
The hectic dance of the passionate cancer cells.
O just phenomena to the calculating eye,
Originals of imagination. I flew
With them in a piled exuberance of time,
My own malignance in their racy, beautiful gestures
Quick and lean: and in their riot too
I saw the stance of the artist's make,
The fixed form in the massive fluxion.

8 From Richard Eberhart, *Collected Poems 1930–1960* (New York: Oxford University Press, 1960; London: Chatto & Windus, Ltd., 1960). © 1960 by Richard Eberhart; reprinted by permission of Oxford University Press, Inc.

I think Leonardo would have in his disinterest
Enjoyed them precisely with a sharp pencil.

After World War II we went every summer to Cape Rosier on
the coast of Maine. The sea gave me several poems. One is called
"Seals, Terns, Time." When I had the experience of it I was not
thinking of poetry. This is an example of a poem being born
when ready long after the event, probably half a year later. In a
contemplative state, in winter, in my study, memory and imagination arose to the consciousness from which came literary execu-
tion.

The facts were these. I was alone in a skiff a mile off shore at
midday in high summer at the westward end of Pond Island, facing Green Ledges, which has a flashing light. The boat had an
outboard but I was using oars. I was lolling in a large, still pool
of water. Seals would come up around the boat, curious and play-
ful, but they would never get closer than about twenty feet. By
remaining as still as possible they could be coaxed quite near.
Perhaps there were a dozen seals in this pack. Their great eyes
reminded me of Hart Crane's line "The seal's wide spindrift gaze
toward Paradise."

If I had only seen the seals I do not think there would have
been a poem. Suddenly overhead, as if a silk scarf were drawn
swiftly across the heavens, there flashed by, only a couple of
hundred feet up, a flight of fork-tailed terns, curveting and
flashing, close together, the sun catching their underbodies in a
breathless vision as they wheeled from sight.

If I had seen only the terns that day I do not think there would
have been a poem.

Usually when we have experiences these seem to be self-suffi-
cient. They are part of the phenomena of life. I had no idea of
"making anything" of the experience of the seals, and sufficient
unto the terns was the glory of their instantaneous, unexpected
vision. One lived in nature and was part of nature.

When the poem came, relationships were seen which I had not
felt when enjoying the raw, disparate experiences of the poem.
The significance of the events was held in the imagination and
synthesized into a comprehensive view; control was laid on ex-

perience; life was ordered to a whole view of truth, within the limits of the experience and of the poem.

Man was seen (not thought of when I was sitting in the boat) as "A gauze and spindrift of the world," a delicately balanced creature, on a frail integument, the boat a cockle shell on the vastness of the ocean, man a precarious creature of short duration seen against the vastness of time and eternity. In the poem man is posed as a balanced object on the sea, under him the seals, symbols of our animal nature going back to the beginning of evolution, over him the wheeling birds, symbols of our spiritual nature. The birds are enticing us to "the release of the sky." Man is in between flesh and spirit, partaking of both. He is related to both in his short duration "balanced on the sea" of meaning.

Seals, Terns, Time[9]

The seals at play off Western Isle
In the loose flowing of the summer tide
And burden of our strange estate—

Resting on the oar and lolling on the sea,
I saw their curious images,
Hypnotic, sympathetic eyes

As the deep elapses of the soul.
O ancient blood, O blurred kind forms
That rise and peer from elemental water:

I loll upon the oar, I think upon the day,
Drawn by strong, by the animal soft bonds
Back to a dim pre-history;

While off the point of Jagged Light
In hundreds, gracefully, the fork-tailed terns
Draw swift esprits across the sky.

Their aspirations dip in mine,
The quick order of their changing spirit,
More freedom than the eye can see.

[9] From Richard Eberhart, *Collected Poems 1930–1960* (New York: Oxford University Press, 1960; London: Chatto & Windus, Ltd., 1960). © 1960 by Richard Eberhart; reprinted by permission of Oxford University Press, Inc.

Resting lightly on the oarlocks,
Pondering, and balanced on the sea,
A gauze and spindrift of the world,

I am in compulsion hid and thwarted,
Pulled back in the mammal water,
Enticed to the release of the sky.

Another poem of about the same time came while we were driving across the country to Seattle in 1952 and stopped to see Cousin Florence, a woman of powerful mind and character, then over ninety, in the hospital. She had broken her hip but was undaunted in spirit. Again, I was not thinking of a poem during our visit. During our conversation she opened a drawer, took out a hand-sized piece of marble, and handed it to me. She said, "Richard, I want you to have this. It is a piece of the Parthenon. I got it when I was young. One picked up souvenirs in those days when there were no police around." It wasn't until long afterward, quite a few months I seem to recall, and, as it happened, after her death, that the poem grew in the imagination and was set down. I perceived the analogy of the laying on of hands, the handing down of religious traditions in the church, and the transferring of her cultural realizations from her generation to mine through the symbol of the marble.

My admiration for her was so great that in this poem character is recognized as superior to art, although we often think of art as superior to character and nature, as lasting longer than the flesh. This poem, though, holds that life itself, live acts of love, are preferable to art. The spirit is even deeper than beautiful works of "leaping marble." It is a belief not popular (accredited) in these times.

Cousin Florence[10]

There it is, a block of leaping marble
Given to me by an ancestor.

[10] From Richard Eberhart, *Collected Poems 1930–1960* (New York: Oxford University Press, 1960; London: Chatto & Windus, Ltd., 1960). © 1960 by Richard Eberhart; reprinted by permission of Oxford University Press, Inc.

The hands that passed it held down ninety years.
She got it in the love-time of Swinburne.

This woman with her stalwart mien,
More like a Roman than a Greek,
Fumbled among old bags of rubble
For something indomitable that she could seek.

She saw the light of ancient days around her,
Calling in the hip-cracked hospital.
She chose at last. Then the clear light
Of reason stood up strong and tall.

With a pure, commanding grace
She handed me a piece of the Parthenon,
Saying, this I broke with my own hands,
And gave me the imagination of the Greeks.

I thought the spirit of this woman
The tallest that I had ever seen,
Stronger than the marble that I have,
Who was herself imagination's dream

By the moment of such sacrament,
A pure force transmitting love,
Endurance, steadfastness, her calm,
Her Roman heart, to mine, of dream.

I would rather keep her noble acts,
The blood of her powerful character, a mind
As good as any of her time, than search
My upward years for such a stone that leaps.

Another poem from the coast of Maine, from the mid-1950's,
is "A Ship Burning/And a Comet All in One Day." This was
based on a real experience. The first boat we ever had larger than
a skiff, when it was laid up one fall, elicited the statement from
its caretaker that we were lucky to be alive: he could put his fist
through the side. We placed the hulk on Grandma's lawn before
the sea, put flowers in it, and offered it to the children to play in.

Grandma's brother, now in his seventies, had been in the Naval
Academy. He argued that just as we would not leave a corpse

above ground and just as men love boats—as is seen in their giving them the names of women—we should give the boat decent burial. We should burn the vessel. A family argument ensued all winter. Our Annapolis relative won and the following August we had an ancient ceremony.

Timothy Rhodes, from Beach Island several miles down Penobscot Bay, determined when the tide would be at dead low. About sixty persons from surrounding cottages came in the late afternoon. About six of the men pulled the old hulk with a long line off the bank, down the shingle, to the edge of the sea. There was a sense of excitement and ceremony. The notion of a ship burning fires the imagination, taking us back to ancient Greece or perhaps to similar ceremonies in the time of Beowulf. Somebody brought red glass cups to the spectators and these were heaped with spirits—actually whiskey I am delighted to report.

A helper poured kerosene fore and aft. As the flames began I stepped amidships and raised a toast to the vessel. I remember becoming so enthusiastic and elated that I made up a spontaneous prayer, inventing on the spot a phrase which got into the poem when I consigned her "to immortal transubstantiation."

When the vessel was consumed down to the last debris the ending of the poem actually happened, strange as it may seem. It was like a benediction. A great comet appeared in the sky, but stranger still, at the end of its long tail, in the middle, a star was set, making the whole appearance jewel-like and marvelous.

A Ship Burning
And a Comet All in One Day[11]

When the tide was out
And the sea was quiet,
We hauled the boat to the edge,
On a fair day in August,
As who, all believing,
Would give decent burial
To the life of a used boat,
Not leave a corpse above ground.

11 From Richard Eberhart, *Collected Poems 1930–1960* (New York: Oxford University Press, 1960; London: Chatto & Windus, Ltd., 1960). © 1960 by Richard Eberhart; reprinted by permission of Oxford University Press, Inc.

And some, setting fires
On the old and broken deck,
Poured on the kerosene
With a stately quietude,
Measuring out departure,
And others brought libations
In red glasses to the sea's edge,
And all held one in hand.

Then the Captain arose
And poured spirit over the prow
And the sparks flew upward
And consigned her with fierce
Cry and fervent prayer
To immortal transubstantiation.
And the pure nature of air
Received her grace and charm.

And evening came on the sea
As the whole company
Sat upon the harsh rocks
Watching the tide come in
And take the last debris,
And when it became dark
A great comet appeared in the sky
With a star in its nether tail.

A poem from the mid-1950's which, like "The Cancer Cells," was written immediately upon having the experience which resulted in the poem, is "On a Squirrel Crossing the Road/In Autumn, in New England." I was alone in my car when a squirrel dashed out and apparently ran under it. I pulled immediately to the right and came to a stop in a ditch. I saw I had not hit the squirrel. Then I experienced a few minutes of high nervous awareness during which I felt clairvoyant. I felt I knew every relationship between the small creature, myself as a slightly larger animal, and the immense idea of God. I was an instrument of fate. I pulled out an envelope and a pencil and wrote down the poem just as it is.

The wit of the last half-line increases the meaning of the poem by affording connotations which otherwise would not obtain. My British publishers suggested that I leave the irregular last half-line out. I said I would entertain the notion in proof, knowing full well that this ending was crucial to the poem.

On a Squirrel Crossing the Road
In Autumn, in New England[12]

It is what he does not know,
Crossing the road under the elm trees,
About the mechanism of my car,
About the Commonwealth of Massachusetts,
About Mozart, India, Arcturus,

That wins my praise. I engage
At once in whirling squirrel-praise.

He obeys the orders of nature
Without knowing them.
It is what he does not know
That makes him beautiful.
Such a knot of little purposeful nature!

I who can see him as he cannot see himself
Repose in the ignorance that is his blessing.

It is what man does not know of God
Composes the visible poem of the world.

.. Just missed him!

The last poem I should like to discuss is "Am I My Neighbor's Keeper?" written January 5, 1962. The poem was begun after reading a newspaper account of a murder which occurred several years ago in the part of New England in which I live. The mur-

---

12 From Richard Eberhart, *Collected Poems 1930–1960* (New York: Oxford University Press, 1960; London: Chatto & Windus, Ltd., 1960). © 1960 by Richard Eberhart; reprinted by permission of Oxford University Press, Inc.

derer or murderers were never discovered or brought to trial. All the powers of the law were of no avail to bring about justice.

Whereas I believe in a theory of inspiration and think that some of my best poems have come spontaneously, this poem was written by the rational use of the will. Perhaps Keats's Negative Capability was at work. If Positive Capability would be purposive action impinging on the world, Negative Capability could stand for a surrogate for positive action, pen or pencil on paper creating a work of art.

I began with Keats's first line from "On the Grasshopper and Cricket," dated December 30, 1816, "the poetry of earth is never dead." This line had stayed with me all my life. I wanted something sterner, not only pleasant, and emended it to read "The poetry of tragedy is never dead."

When I began the poem I did not know it was going to be a sonnet, but this form soon developed, although I wrote two spaced quatrains before fixing on the form. These present generalizations, abstract realizations of the matter at hand. The sestet particularizes, giving graphic details of a tragedy in real life. The poem suggests that the deepest things in life are ultimately mysterious. In this case, the murder is irremediable, unsolved, and unredeemed. The statement at the end, which secretes a pun on the word damn, not only announces the final bleakness of the tragic situation but has an overtone perhaps, that if the murdered man could speak he would do so, although he could only do so now in the mute form of a corpse. The poem suggests universal guilt. The irony here is that society protected the definitely guilty from coming to justice.

Am I My Neighbor's Keeper?[13]

The poetry of tragedy is never dead.
If it were not so I would not dream
On principles so deep they have no ending,
Nor on the ambiguity of what things ever seem.

[13] From Richard Eberhart, *The Quarry* (New York: Oxford University Press, 1964; London: Chatto & Windus, Ltd., 1964). © 1964 by Richard Eberhart; reprinted by permission of Oxford University Press, Inc.

The truth is hid and shaped in veils of error
Rich, unanswerable, the profound caught in plain air.
Centuries after tragedy sought out Socrates
Its inexplicable essence visits us in our lair,

Say here, on a remote New Hampshire farm.
The taciturn farmer disappeared in pre-dawn.
He had beaten his handyman, but no great harm.
Light spoke vengeance and bloodstains on the lawn.
His trussed corpse later under the dam
Gives to this day no answer, says I am.

While this poem is an example of the rational use of the intellect, as I view the writing of my own poetry since my youth, roughly over a period of forty years, I admire Plato's idea in the *Ion* when he says, "For the poet is a light and winged and holy thing, and there is no invention in him until he has been inspired and is out of his senses, and the mind is no longer in him: when he has not attained to this state, he is powerless and is unable to utter his oracles." I respect this theory of inspiration because it is beyond and above conscious will. A poem composed as the reception of a "gift of the gods" would seem to be of a higher origin and nature than a poem composed by taking thought and then by taking care.

Some of my poems which I think of as coming under this theory of creation are "Now Is the World Made of Chiming Bells," "If I Could Only Live at the Pitch That Is Near Madness," "1934," "Go to the Shine That's on a Tree," "Only in the Dream," and possibly also, but less purely, poems like "Maze," "For a Lamb," "The Groundhog," "In a Hard Intellectual Light," "In Prisons of Established Craze," "Light from Above," and "Vast Light."

On the other hand, a poem like "Am I My Neighbor's Keeper?" has the impurity, as does most poetry in comparison with Plato's ideal, of the whole warring and loving human nature of man.

4 SEVERAL KINDS OF SHORT POEM

J. V. Cunningham

Poetry may be thought of in various ways, and the way one habitually thinks of it will qualify the poetry he writes. For definition is not subsequent to action but precedes it; it is not gathered from the result but shapes the result. I do not, for example, ordinarily think of poetry as vision, although I know it sometimes is, and so I have no vision. I have no intuition into the heart of things; I have no special way of seeing. I think of poetry as a way of speaking, a special way of speaking. As a poet I speak in meter, and sometimes in rhyme; I speak in lines. It follows naturally that I am a formalist and that anything that can be said in metrical lines is subject for poetry, even vision, and that anything worth saying should sometime be said. This last adds a principle of value, the principle of what is worth saying as distinguished from what is not. And to this, formalism adds another principle of value, for the aim of the formal is the definitive. A poem, then, on this view is metrical speech, and a good poem is the definitive statement in meter of something worth saying.

Such a view of poetry, if we do not take it too loosely, will somewhat narrow the kinds of poetry one writes. Some poems, for instance, are not in any ordinary sense of the term statements. They are constructs, fiction, things made up. I have written a few such—one, for example, on that mythical bird, "The Phoenix."[1]

> More than the ash stays you from nothingness!
> Nor here nor there is a consuming pyre!

[1] From J. V. Cunningham, *The Exclusions of a Rhyme*, "Poems and Epigrams" (Denver: Alan Swallow, 1960). "The Phoenix" is reprinted by permission of the publisher, Alan Swallow; copyright 1960 by J. V. Cunningham.

Your essence is in infinite regress
That burns with varying consistent fire,
Mythical bird that bears in burying!

I have not found you in exhausted breath
That carves its image on the Northern air,
I have not found you on the glass of death
Though I am told that I shall find you there,
Imperturbable in the final cold,

There where the North wind shapes white cenotaphs,
There where snowdrifts cover the fathers' mound,
Unmarked but for these wintry epitaphs,
Still are you singing there without sound,
Your mute voice on the crystal embers flinging.

But this is not my characteristic mode. Of such a poem one does not say that it is definitive or not, but that it is just right or it is not.

Other poems aim at recording a real or imagined personal experience; they are memoir. In such poems, if one has a partiality toward the definitive, the attitude is directed not so much toward the statement as toward the experience. The aim becomes not so much definitive statement as the asseveration under oath that this is exactly the way it was, in fact and feeling. The poems toward the end of this essay illustrate this aim, if not its accomplishment.

The characteristic poem motivated by a concern for definitive statement, however, will be the poem that explains—an expository poem, a statement in the ordinary sense of that word. And it will be short, for the concern for definitiveness is a prejudice for brevity. If one has said something definitively he will not be impelled to amplify, to say it again undefinitively. So the poet who holds this view becomes an epigrammatist. He writes:

When I shall be without regret
And shall mortality forget,
When I shall die who lived for this,
I shall not miss the things I miss.

41

> And you who notice where I lie
> Ask not my name. It is not I.

or

> In whose will is our peace? Thou happiness,
> Thou ghostly promise, to thee I confess
> Neither in thine nor love's nor in that form
> Disquiet hints at have I yet been warm;
> And if I rest not till I rest in thee
> Cold as thy grace, whose hand shall comfort me?

or

> And what is love? Misunderstanding, pain,
> Delusion, or retreat? It is in truth
> Like an old brandy after a long rain,
> Distinguished, and familiar, and aloof.[2]

But the short poem in isolation has the defect of brevity; it comes naked to the reader without a locating context. It cannot build its own world, as *The Faerie Queene* and *The Prelude* do. And so one thinks, if he is committed by temperament and habit to the shorter poem, how he can make it longer.

There are two ways—perhaps there are more, but two I shall speak of here—by which a group of shorter poems can be aggrandized into a work of greater length. Length, however, is only a means; what one wants is a situation in which the several items can lend each other context, reference, and resonance, in which this short poem will be something more than it would be in isolation by belonging to a whole. The first method is an ancient one, invented, we are told, in Rome at the time of Vergil: one sets the poems in a matrix of relevant prose. The most famous and most influential, work exemplifying this method is Boethius' *The Consolation of Philosophy*. It is the method of Dante's *The New Life*. And in both these works the poems gain stature from the surrounding prose. And, indeed, it is a matter of common observation that the poem we encounter in the course of reading a

2 From J. V. Cunningham, *The Exclusions of a Rhyme*, "Poems and Epigrams" (Denver: Alan Swallow, 1960), pp. 45, 74, 86, 101. Reprinted by permission of the publisher, Alan Swallow; copyright 1960 by J. V. Cunningham.

novel or an essay is more likely to stay in our memory than one read among other poems, for we come to it in a relevant context. Some fifteen to twenty years ago I used this method myself in a little work called *The Quest of the Opal.* There I surrounded a group of my early poems with prose commentary and paraphrase.

There is, however, a problem in the marriage of prose and verse that arises from an ambiguity of attitude on the part of audiences. On the one hand, the audience for poetry is willing, and sometimes eager, to hear the poet speak of his own work, as I am doing now, especially if he can adjoin to the work some anecdotal richness or give some hints of insight into the creative process. Yet the same audience on another occasion will feel, and sometimes strongly, that the poem should not need prose, that it should stand by itself unexplained, that the intrusion of commentary is a confession of failure. There is, then, both an appetite for commentary and a superiority to it, and what at one time is gratefully welcomed, at another is regarded with embarrassment.

There is an alternative way of aggrandizing a group of shorter poems into a work of greater length, and that is the poetic sequence. The sequence is a series of short poems in whose succession there is an implicit structure—in the case I have in mind, a narrative structure. The ancient precedent for the poetic sequence is the *Cynthia* of Propertius, a contemporary of Vergil. It consists of twenty-two or so elegies, what the Germans have called subjective erotic elegies, but though there are narrative elements in that sequence there is no story-line; the several poems are merely related to an established narrative context, and this is also the case with such a Renaissance sonnet sequence as Sir Philip Sidney's *Astrophil and Stella.* The particular form of sequence I have here in mind was invented, I believe, by Tennyson. It is likely that he discovered the form in the process of composing *In Memoriam,* for that sequence began apparently as a series of journal entries, acts of memoir, and was then developed within a structure of ideas and an implicit narrative structure, the Christmas poems marking off the years. Subsequently, he wrote *Maud,* a fictional narrative with primary attention to the emotional aspects, in which the narrative is implicit in the sequence of lyrics. It is an interesting form, though *Maud* is a bad poem.

An interest in a form is an invitation to attempt to realize it. I had entertained the general notion of such a sequence for many years and had designated the areas of experience that would be involved. The poems would deal with the American West, that vast spiritual region from Great Falls, Montana, to El Paso, Texas; from Fort Riley, Kansas, to the sinks of Nevada; and with the California Coast, another and perhaps less spiritual region. And the poems would relate some sort of illicit and finally terminated love affair. And there would be a fusion of the feeling in the personal relationship and the feeling for the West and the Coast. But nothing happened for eight or nine years until a few years ago, driving west through the Dakotas to Sheridan, Wyoming, I composed in memory these four lines:

> I drive Westward. Tumble and loco weed
> Persist. And in the vacancies of need,
> The leisure of desire, whirlwinds a face
> As luminous as love, lost as this place.

This was clearly the beginning of the sequence.

I turn now to the sequence in its final form, and say no more of the accidents of composition. It is entitled *To What Strangers? What Welcome?*, and consists of an epigraph and fifteen poems. They are of various sorts, in the tradition of *Maud:* epigram, lyric, discourse; construct, memoir or purported memoir, and statement. They are in various formal patterns, some traditional and some as untraditional as octosyllabic blank verse and syllabic meters. Consequently, the unity of the sequence, if it has unity, will not depend on a formal consistency, as in a sonnet sequence, but on the story that is implied. It is, as it must be, a simple story, so common that any audience can supply what must be said between one poem and the next. A traveler drives west; he falls in love; he comes home. The conclusion is anticipated by the epigraph, which consists of some lines from Edwin Arlington Robinson's long Arthurian poem, *Merlin*. It is one of Robinson's finest passages. Merlin is speaking, having just returned to Camelot after three years in Broceliande with the Lady Vivian; he says if he does not go back to her the Lady Vivian will remember him, and say:

I knew him when his heart was young,
Though I have lost him now. Time called him home,
And that was as it was. . . .[3]

The sequence proper opens with "I drive Westward," with its
intimation of a face "As luminous as love, lost as this place."
There follows:

On either side of the white line
The emblems of a life appear
In turn: purpose like lodgepole pine
Competitive and thin, and fear

Agile as aspen in a storm.
And then the twilit harboring
In a small park. The room is warm.
And by the ache of traveling

Removed from all immediacy,
From all time, I as time grows late
Sense in disordered fantasy
The sound and smell of love and hate.

And then an unsent letter, meditated at midnight, to no one at
all, of which this is the central stanza:

I'll not summon you, or feel
In the alert dream the give
And stay of flesh, the tactile
Conspiracy.

The snow falls
With its inveterate meaning,
And I follow the barbed wire
To trough, to barn, to the house,
To what strangers, what welcome
In the late blizzard of time.

3 From *Collected Poems* (New York: Macmillan). "Merlin" is copyright 1917
by Edwin Arlington Robinson, renewed 1945 by Ruth Nivison. Reprinted
with permission of The Macmillan Company.

After certain unrewarding adventures, a pick-up at one time, at
another a stripper in Las Vegas, the traveler comes to the Pacific:

> the surf breaking,
> Repetitive and varied as love
> Enacted, and inevitably
> The last rim of sunset on the sea.

He has an apartment on the beach.

> The night is still. The unfailing surf
> In passion and subsidence moves
> As at a distance. The glass walls,
> And redwood, are my utmost being.
> And is there there in the last shadow,
> There in the final privacies
> Of unaccosted grace,—is there,
> Gracing the tedium to death,
> An intimation? Something much
> Like love, like loneliness adrowse
> In states more primitive than peace,
> In the warm wonder of winter sun.

The intimation becomes reality:

> A half hour for coffee, and at night
> An hour or so of unspoken speech,
> Hemming a summer dress as the tide
> Turns at the right time.

> Must it be sin
> This consummation of who knows what?
> This sharp cry at entrance, once, and twice?
> This unfulfilled fulfilment?

> Something
> That happens because it must happen.
> We live in the given. Consequence,

And lack of consequence, both fail us.
Good is what we can do with evil.

At this point "Time called him home, And that was as it was":

I drive Eastward. The ethics of return,
Like the night sound of coyotes on a hill
Heard in eroded canyons of concern,
Disposes what has happened, and what will.

There is the long drive back across the continent, over the high
desert, through the central plains, to the stone walls of New
England:

Absence, my angel, presence at my side,
I know you as an article of faith
By desert, prairie, and this stonewalled road—
As much my own as is the thought of death.

There in the last warmth of a New England autumn the story
comes to an end, and the traveler addresses himself:

Identity, that spectator
Of what he calls himself, that net
And aggregate of energies
In transient combinations—some
So marginal are they mine? Or is
There mine? I sit in the last warmth
Of a New England fall, and I?
A premise of identity
Where the lost hurries to be lost,
Both in its own best interests
And in the interests of life.[4]

4 From J. V. Cunningham, *To What Strangers, What Welcome* (Denver:
Alan Swallow, 1964). Reprinted by permission of the publisher, Alan Swallow.
Copyright 1964 by J. V. Cunningham.

5 IN SEARCH OF THE AMERICAN SCENE

Ben Belitt

I hear America singing
—WALT WHITMAN

American poets since Whitman have reason to wonder what Whitman heard when he "heard America singing." Presumably, they were singing on key and in perfect American, and left their mark on both the language and prosody of the poet and his vision of a national scene. In the poem named, Whitman, as it happens, is more concerned with the proletarian diversity of the singers—carpenters, masons, shoemakers, ploughboys—than with the American matrix of their song. Significantly, he omits the poets; but elsewhere he singles out "poets to come" with benevolent pugnacity as a "new brood, native, athletic, continental," answerable for "the substance of an artist's mood" and the "singing that belongs to him." He then withdraws, with the tact of a favorite uncle demurely schooled in the self-help of an enlightened psychology:

> I am a man who, sauntering along without fully stopping,
>   turns a casual look upon you, and then averts his face,
> Leaving it to you to prove and define it,
> Expecting the main things from you.

As a "native" American singer who feels neither "new" nor "athletic" nor "continental"—and would rather choose the adjectives for himself—I admit to some uneasiness. If "poets of the

Modern" have had to "prove and define," rather than to postulate, their claim to the "ensemble" of American song since *Leaves
of Grass*, it is due largely to the aggressive cast of Whitman's
evangelism. Countercharges of chauvinism are a fastidious im-
pertinence in this case, since they do scant justice to the depth
and perspective of Whitman's genius and blink aside an in-
corrigible hunch that America, after all, *ought* to be there.
"Agents" must have their "scenes," as Kenneth Burke would say;
and though Dante was not preoccupied with the specifically Ital-
ian inflection of his *Divine Comedy*, or Milton with a premise of
British supremacy in Eden, or Homer with a prosody for militant
Greeks—Italy, England, and Ilium are there, with their gods and
cosmologies.

The "vista" for American poets, then, is a "democratic" one—
but the "politics of vision" has proved more mischievous than
Whitman imagined. It was possible in 1959 for a major American
talent of the 1940's to repudiate the manifest diversity of two
decades—Eliot, Stevens, Marianne Moore, Ezra Pound, among
others—as a "diseased" and "academic" art, and proscribe T. E.
Hulme's *Speculations* (1924) as "the *Mein Kampf* of modern
criticism."[1] The mischief touched chaos a year later when a slate
of forty-four "new American poets"[2] with "their own tradition,
their own press, and their public" was thrown up like a barricade
between 1945 and the present, in a war of anthologies and in-
centive to insure the purity of poetry in our time. Thus it is that
the bucket of William Carlos Williams goes down into the American Dream and the bucket of T. S. Eliot comes up; and "the
abounding, glittering jet" of Yeats's vision is nowhere in sight.
The vista is no longer "democratic" but oligarchic; and the poets
are the orphans of Whitman, rather than his "*élèves*."

Let us grant, nevertheless, that we would all like to be as
American as Coca Cola or pumpkin pie. We would like to enlist
among Whitman's "indigenous rhapsodes," "native authors and
literatuses" flooding themselves "with the immediate age as with

1 Karl Shapiro, "What's the Matter with Poetry?" (*The New York Times
Book Review*, December 13, 1959).
2 Donald M. Allen, ed., *The New American Poetry 1945-1960* (New York:
Grove Press, 1960).

vast oceanic tides,"—with "spinal, modern, germinal subjects," "tonic and alfresco physiology," "rude, rasping, taunting, contradictory tones," "vista, music, half-tints," "a new literature, a new metaphysics, a new poetry." We would like, in short—the language is still Whitman's—to negotiate for "the Yankee swap." Others will claim, as their American due, total access to "the free channel of ourselves,"—Whitman's words—"significant only because of the Me in the center," and defend their option with peyote and lysergic acid. Most plaintively of all, they would like, in this nineteen-hundred-and-sixty-fourth year of our neo-Faustian era, to have a real, right, disestablished, demoniacal, intuitional experience.

Obviously, all these satisfactions are not forthcoming as inalienable aspects of the American scene, and must eventually be appraised in terms of what they displace in the economy of American letters. In my own case, I prefer to dwell on the poet's traditional commitment to his conscience and his medium as "the main thing," rather than bow to the avuncular ultimatums of a giant. I prefer to dwell, not on a platform for hearty Americans, nor on an American aesthetic emergency, but on the facts of an imaginative venture as reflected in a first volume of poems published in 1938—in itself no monument of contemporary letters, but symptomatic, I think, of the poet's quest for the American scene in that decade. I choose a tone of wonder, because I find myself genuinely curious, dubious, and ungainly in the public scrutiny of processes and motivations which I have habitually resolved as *poems*, rather than as tactics for poets or patriots.

Prefaces to first volumes are rare since the hortatory days of the founding Romantics, but are occasionally infiltrated in the guise of copyright acknowledgments. My first volume, published in 1938 under the title of *The Five-Fold Mesh*, carried a prefatory note which I now read with some puzzlement:

> In making this selection of poems written over a period of eight years, it has been my hope to suggest a discipline of integration, rather than a series of isolated poetic comments . . . to state a problem in orientation . . . in an expanding record of change. What has been sought, in a word, is an effect of se-

quence—a sequence which, beginning with simple responses to the natural world, moves on to an awareness of the personal identity, and attempts finally to establish usable relationships between the personal and contemporary world.

In comparison with Whitman's bristling resolution to "cheer up slaves and horrify despots," the language seems subdued: indeed, there were many to remind me that the program had long served first volumes from the time of the Psalmist to the present, and need hardly be made a matter of public record. The concern with contemporaneity, however, with poetry as a "discipline of integration," an "expanding record of change" with "usable relationships," a "problem in orientation," may help to suggest the predicament of the poet who, engaging his "scene" for the first time, discovers that *place* is not given him ready made as a datum of "the American imagination," and that the American identity is the most elusive chimera of them all.

Rereading the earlier lyrics of *The Five-Fold Mesh,* I find all the categories and permutations of Polonius: lyrics tragical, tragical-comical, tragical-comical-pastoral, tragical-comical-pastoral-historical—but little that shows the cut and thrust of the American scene. The tragical-pastoral predominates, in the guise of poems which seek enigmatically to blend some undivulged personal quarrel with suitable staples of landscape: fields cloven and left fallow, fountainheads, March cardinals, primroses, woodbine, laurel, hawks, berries, violets. The tone is one of stoical and sententious ambiguity, with ominous allusions to the majesty and the ironies of unreflective self-denial: "Lay not your shoulder to this rock/Good Jacob: this is bitter water"; "Never mind, never mind/The uncloven field, the unheaped rafter"; "No hand in the indignant hour/May move to comfort or to curb:/The strength shall vanish from the flower/The healing wither in the herb"; and (I thought climactically): "Now it were valor to unbend the flesh/Burst the bright harness of dissembling sense,/The fine and five-fold mesh,/And loose the inward wound to bleed afresh." A single example will suggest the outcome of this vague and hermetic strategy for eluding two landscapes, one inner and the other outer, and erecting in their place the literary pathos of the *Minnesinger:*

From Towers of Grass[3]

Long enmity of part and part,
Of strict mind, mutinous under steel,
Has leaned this spear upon my heart
And clapped this armor at my heel—
Some difference, wanting not for fuel
Of trickster blood and warlike bone,
Nursing a sword's point, blue and cruel,
On some primordial whetting-stone.

Useless to cry the shape of laurel,
The lilac star and June cockade:
Grow strong against this mortal quarrel
And heap a summer palisade—
Seal, seal the green, ephemeral tower
That keeps me hostage here, who know
How I am succored with a flower,
How done to death with snow.

The result here is not a scene, or an identity, but a pastoral compromise. The "place" is nowhere, or inside the compounding defenses of the quatrain or the sonnet, like a maze without a minotaur; and the hoped-for "record of change" is not yet apparent.

Yet "agent" and "scene," I would contend, are there, as shaping forces in a drama of conscience; and one need not labor the patriotic casuistries of Whitman to assume that they are American, rather than Roman or Alexandrian. What bemuses me now and was not apparent to me in 1938 as a poet preoccupied with his craft, is the total absence of place names—the direct confrontation of geographical fact as a cartographer or a naturalist might view it—in all but a handful of the poems. Whitman, on the contrary, creates the American opportunity at once by "Starting from Paumanok" (the red man's word for Long Island) which he sees like the mapmaker, from above, as a "fish-shape"

3 From Ben Belitt, *The Five-Fold Mesh* (New York: Alfred A. Knopf, Inc., 1938). "From Towers of Grass" is copyright 1933 by Ben Belitt; reprinted by permission of Alfred A. Knopf, Inc.

island, and then appropriates the whole of Mannahatta (talking Indian). He finds nothing antipoetic in a place name like Brooklyn (talking Danish)—now a formula of condescension among fastidious Americans; and he has "endless announcements" for Ontario, Erie, Huron, Connecticut, Massachusetts, Chicago, and points east, west, north, and south, which he transforms into a kind of Pindaric formula for exultation. Similarly, Emily Dickinson, in her own view of things, was seeing "New Englandly" behind the hedgerows and sherry glasses of Amherst, and was avidly geographical; William Carlos Williams sought to "induce his bones to rise into a scene" of Paterson, New Jersey, whose squalors and incongruities rival Brooklyn's; Hart Crane waited under the shadows of Brooklyn Bridge and toiled toward redemption in Key West, "drinking Bacardi and talking U.S.A." Robert Frost mended wall north of Boston and hunted witches in New Hampshire and Vermont; Wallace Stevens looked away from the marzipan world of Oxidia, "banal suburb," to "An Ordinary Evening in New Haven."

I do not propose to suggest by this that the American scene is a kind of gerrymander—a good American word for the unnatural division of place for political advantage—in which the poet stakes out his "territory" and sings out his stations like a portable loudspeaker. Indeed, I assume that the dangers of this point of view are already apparent to all: that the poet aggressively committed to the American inflection of his "scene" and his language may reveal nothing but the persistence of the colonial mentality. He may exchange the historical sanity of Whitman's contention that "the English language befriends the grand American expression," for the idiocy of William Carlos Williams': "We poets have to talk a language which is not English." In his programmatic rejection of the feudal, he may invite the platitudes of the capitalist, and in his rejection of the European, he may entrench himself like a troll or a tick in the "folklore" of a region.

The American perspective, then, is not the province (I use the word narrowly) of the tactical ethnologist, the historian, the patriot, or the visiting Frenchmen; but the "poetry of place" does offer clues to the quality and depth of the poet's engrossment in the American scene. If we are to talk about creation at all, we must talk about names, habitations, worlds—usually

those we are born into; and it is significant that Book Three of
W. C. Williams' *Paterson* bears the epigraph of a citizen of the
world who liked to regard himself as "The Last Puritan":

> Cities are a second body for the human mind, a second organ-
> ism, more rational, permanent, and decorative than the animal
> organism of flesh and bone: a work of natural yet moral art,
> where the soul sets up her trophies of action and instruments
> of pleasure.
>
> —GEORGE SANTAYANA

I find this combination of geography and "psychology" a promising one; and I therefore reread with pleasure two poems from
The Five-Fold Mesh which name names and appoint hours, as
if for a duel or an assignation. One, a poem about a charwoman
who regularly appeared with mop, pail, and goiter in the corridors of 20 Vesey Street, where I worked for some months as
editorial assistant on *The Nation,* bears the signature of a time
and a place as indispensable facts of the imaginative occasion:
it is, without seeking to be so, an "American" poem. Let me cite
it in its entirety:

Charwoman
(Lower Manhattan: 6:00 P.M.)[4]

Clapping the door to, in the little light,
In the stair-fall's deepening plunge,
I see, in the slate dark, the lumped form, like a sponge,
Striking a rote erasure in the night—

And keep that figure; while a watery arc
Trembles and wanes in wetted tile, as if
It wrote all darkness down in hieroglyph
And spoke vendetta with a watermark.

That shadowy flare shall presently define
A scuffed and hazardous wrist, a ruined jaw
Packed into goiter like a pigeon's craw,
A bitten elbow webbed with a naphtha line;

---

4 From *The Five-Fold Mesh* (New York: Alfred A. Knopf, 1938). "Charwoman" is copyright 1938 by Ben Belitt; reprinted by permission of Alfred
A. Knopf, Inc.

While light shall lessen, blunting, by brute degrees,
The world's waste scanted to a personal sin,
Till all is darkness where her brush has been
And blinds the blackening marble by her knees.

* * *

I mark what way the dropping shaft-light went;
It flung the day's drowned faces out, and fell
Hasped like a coffin, down a darkening well:

And poise on the shaftway for my own descent.

The other, by far the most ambitious piece in *The Five-Fold Mesh,* is in three parts and bears the name of "Battery Park: High Noon"—again a symptomatic, and perhaps an "American" commitment to punctuality and place. The poem is too long to be presented in its entirety; but, like "Charwoman," it is bounded by the geography of lower New York and the schedule of *The Nation* magazine: in this case, the lunch hour, when it was possible on fine afternoons to walk toward the geographical spur of Whitman's Mannahatta, through the Wall Street crevasses, to the Old Trinity Churchyard, the Aquarium, the Park which gives the poem its name, and finally, the pleasure-boats leaving for the Statue of Liberty and the brilliant expanse of the harbor. The opening section should suggest both the style and the psychological occasion of the poem—which is a curious transposition of two places, in which, by a trick of vision, an afterimage of my Virginian childhood was superimposed for a moment on the fact of my residence in New York City.

Battery Park: High Noon[5]

Suddenly, the old fancy has me!
                                                            Suddenly,
Between flint and glitter, the leant leaf,
The formal blueness blooming over slate,

5 From Ben Belitt, *The Five-Fold Mesh* (New York: Alfred A. Knopf, 1938). "Battery Park: High Noon" is copyright 1938 by Ben Belitt; reprinted by permission of Alfred A. Knopf, Inc.

> Struck into glass and plate,
> The public tulips treading meridian glare
> In bronze and whalebone by the statue-bases—
> Elude the Battery Square,
> Turn, with a southern gesture, in remembered air
> And claim a loved identity, like faces. . . .

Two matters concern me in each of the two poems named: one, the startling increase in specificity and power which flows from the *total* commitment to "place"—specificity of rhythm, form, language, and self-knowledge, as well as particulars of the American scene; and the other, the deepening of the imaginative occasion by a contradictory shift from the theme of place to the theme of *dis*placement. In the "Charwoman," for example, the poet's quarrel with himself, vaguely disposed of in an earlier poem as "some difference, wanting not for fuel/Of trickster blood and warlike bone" is given a protagonist—the charwoman—and explores a cause: the haunting complicity that the young and the sound may feel in the presence of the maimed and the aging, the political and moral enigma of "the world's waste scanted to a personal sin" for which nothing stands ready to atone.

I note also that, with the increasing proximities of the scene, the imaginative particulars of the poem have been brought optically and intellectually into closer range of both the poet and his reader. The fact of goiter is confronted with pity and terror in the "ruined jaw/Packed into goiter like a pigeon's craw"; the occupational marks of the charwoman are clinically incised in a manner which one critic has called Flemish: by a composite of highlight and chiaroscuro which focuses painfully on "A bitten elbow, webbed with a naphtha line, like a cartoon etched in detergents." Similarly, in "Battery Park" the metropolitan landscape and statuary are ironically and substantively seen, as the Virginia landscapes were not: "The public tulips treading meridian glare/In bronze and whalebone by the statue-bases" are both actual and submerged. They stand memorially against their midcity background of "flint and glitter," "glass and plate," "pigeons and peanut shells" and reject all pastoral compromise. To the extent that they do so, the poem, the lighting, and the scene are not "Flemish," or impressionistic, actually, but "American."

It is this engagement of curiosity with the actual—to the point at which, in Hopkins' words, "whatever you look hard at, seems to look hard at you—" that I find crucial to the poetry of place and the criteria of "American" song. With more time, I might go on to illustrate how in the two collections which have followed— *Wilderness Stair* (1955) and *The Enemy Joy* (1964)—the geographical fact has constantly enlarged itself to toughen my idiom and refine my sense of "vista" as a poet writing democratically in "American." I would dwell on the circumstance by which the theme of place and displacement leads the poet by inevitable stages to the timeless themes of reality and appearance, permanence and change, being and nonbeing, as they led Whitman: to the *myth*, as well as the fact, of departure, and the possibility that all places are actually one place and all poetries one poetry, and that one travels, as the dancer moves, in order to "reach the still point where the dance is."

It is the same point which Whitman sought on the furthest perspectives of his art when, in *Passage to India* he invoked the "aged, fierce enigmas" "below the Sanskrit and the Vedas." It was the vision which was uppermost in my own mind when I concluded a section of "Battery Park" with an exhortation which has since carried me into many Americas, inner, outer, and continental, and led to new scenes and displacements:

> Bend then to seaward. The element you ask
> Rarer than sea is, wantoner than time:
> You bear it on you, strangely, like a mask,
> And dream the sailing in a pantomime.
>
> *The element is blood.* Tired voyager, turn:
> The reckoning you take is yet to learn.
> Somber, at fullest flood, the continents ride
> And break their beaches in a sleeper's side.

6 A VIEW OF POETRY

Barbara Howes

It is difficult to write about one's own poetry—difficult, perhaps, to make it interesting—but one does at least have a close relationship to it, a friendly feeling toward its ups and downs, its moderate successes and its failures. And also a poet knows that his own work has a connection with other people's, for we are all living at the same time, and most of the major events of this century touch us all in some way.

The twentieth century has produced a fine flowering of poetry written in English, and that language has been worked on, added to, stretched, and at times sadly misused during these sixty-five years, which is, after all, nearly two-thirds of the century. But there has been a great deal of energy put into the writing of poetry over these years and the body of good work that has been built up will, I think, for the most part stand.

In spite of the chaos and waste of World Wars I and II, in spite of the increased tempo at which one lives, I think fundamentally that the climate for poetry is good. Now with the greater availability of verse due to paperback publication, records, and the prevalence of poetry readings, good (and atrocious) writing is at hand. There is also a greater accessibility to the work of writers in other countries. Nowadays it is not hard to become acquainted with writers of talent in England, or in Australia, for that matter; in Canada, New Zealand, the Caribbean, and English-speaking parts of Africa. There is thus, one might say, a sort of United Nations' attitude open to those of us whose language is English; no country anymore need think it has cornered this special poetic market. That is no longer so.

And this is all very much to the good, for the over-all body of the English language is greatly enriched by idioms from individual countries; thus the elevated speech of writers from England has had to brush elbows with Dylan Thomas' Welsh choral organ-tones, with peculiarities of the American language produced in this great melting pot of races, and also with the strange and vigorous words with which the Australians stud their pages. As well as words, new rhythms which have grown out of specific aspects of the national character have been added: for instance, the pioneering hard-driving or jogging ballad rhythms that must have come out of the Australian's century-old struggle with the "outback." In this country, rhythms have come into being from folk songs and jazz; poems have been written which could easily be sung; others narrate some epic effort to come to grips with this huge, varied, and busy land that stretches from sunrise to sunset, from winter to summer, and which includes glacier and bald cypress, the Grand Canyon and the canyons of Wall Street, the assembly line and the chain gang.

The English language has, I think, gained in vitality in this century as a result of these and other factors, and is certainly a language offering inexhaustible opportunities to poets fortunate enough to be blessed by those basic requisites: talent, a good ear, and a desire to work. The resources of this language of ours are very great: made up principally of the two great strains of Anglo-Saxon and Latin, it has been added to from all over the world. Its galleons, one might say, have returned with riches of rhythm and imagery, of vigor and nuance, with idioms as exotic as spices from the Orient, with usages of language, to draw on Gerard Manley Hopkins in "Pied Beauty": ". . . counter, original, spare, strange"; with formal elegance and every sort of colloquialism. It is a language in which poetry *should* flourish.

To move on to more specific matters which affect individual poets, I would like to begin with the concept of Time. I think of aspects of this problem of Time very often, in connection with my work, for it is constantly having an effect on my writing. I read somewhere that Time is merely a device to keep everything from happening at once, and this possibly superficial remark impressed me. A poem, after all, is a measure of time, both as to the length of time it takes to read it, the far greater length it takes to understand it, and the generally very much longer period involved in its composition. The poem also must in some way *embody* the passage of time, for it must move from one experience to another, from one mood to a conflicting mood, on to some sort of resolution. Very few poems could balance on the head of a pin, as they are only very rarely made up of one intimation; they must move on, turn a corner, change into something else.

The writing of a poem indeed involves time, for often a short poem may be worked and reworked over a period of years; occasionally, again, some experience that took long in the living can be got down on paper in one fortunate hour. But fundamentally it is one of the great wonders of poetry that its small size, its small duration—a stanza or four or five—can embrace such long stretches of experience, stories that took, "in life," days and years to work themselves out.

A poem is something made, put together, constructed. As Professor H. D. F. Kitto has written: "Such, after all, is the very meaning of the Greek word . . . *poiesis*, which has become our word 'poetry'; quite literally it means 'construction.' " Aristotle understood it in this way, and Dryden wrote: "A poet is a maker, as the word signifies." One really does construct a poem out of time, the time given to it, and the time included within it, and also there are all those years in which one was learning how to put a poem together.

The following poem of mine, written in an old French form, the rondeau, is about time—about a lifetime, really, compressed into the perception of a moment:

Death of a Vermont Farm Woman[1]

Is it time now to go away?
July is nearly over; hay
Fattens the barn, the herds are strong,
Our old fields prosper; these long
Green evenings will keep death at bay.

[1] From Barbara Howes, *Light and Dark* (Middletown, Conn.: Wesleyan University Press, 1959). "Death of a Vermont Farm Woman" is © 1959 by Barbara Howes.

Last winter lingered; it was May
Before a flowering lilac spray
Barred cold for ever. I was wrong
                       Is it time now?

Six decades vanished in a day!
I bore four sons: one lives; they
Were all good men; three dying young
Was hard on us. I have looked long
For these hills to show me where peace lay . . .
                       Is it time now?

Another concept, which is far from being merely "abstract," that also has great influence on poets of our day is *place*. Modern American writers are much concerned with where they come from, where they may be going, or with the fact that they do not seem to belong in any special part of the country at all. Americans, one often reads, are always on the move—eternal migrants out after new lives, new jobs, new experience. Aside from the many poets whose interest in travel stems partly from their knowledge of their own homeland, we have also had lately a rash of hitchhiker poets, whose aim, perhaps, is to seem continually on the move, rather than ever to arrive anywhere. But it is true that we are a very mobile nation, and individuals and families are continually being excised from the places they know, and removed to different scenes and activities.

Fundamentally, however, a place one knows—one whose hills or the angle of whose apartment house one feels utterly familiar with—is, as Eudora Welty wrote, one's own: "place is where he has his roots, place is where he stands; in his experience out of which he writes it provides the base of reference, in his work the point of view."

This is a very important ingredient in the work of the major poets of this century, as one can easily see. Robert Frost, Edwin Arlington Robinson, Edna St. Vincent Millay, in their different styles, were all New Englanders. Allen Tate and John Crowe Ransom are clearly Southerners; Robinson Jeffers and Ezra Pound come from the West. One does not necessarily belong

where one was born and brought up, but one does belong somewhere; there is some section that one fits into without having
constantly to translate the language of the nature surrounding
one or the speech and behavior of the inhabitants back into one's
own language in order to feel at home.

A number of poets, of course, have made a larger move, from
their background to one more satisfying, by becoming expatriates,
as Mr. Eliot has done. But though he has lived most of his life in
England, he is still open to the middle-Western and New England
influences of his youth. What I am saying is that the important
thing about place for a poet is that he be aware of "his" place;
then he can go forth from there and visit the world.

I have been so fortunate as to live for a year or two in Italy
and for briefer periods in the south of France and in Haiti. It
came to me very sharply that one of the great values of these experiences was that things happened to me in another country
that would not have happened at home. There is a certain mysterious influence at work in another land, made up of its history,
its landscape, the psychology of its people; and so one sees and
feels and goes through special happenings that are marked with
the mark of that specific part of the world. Images, moods, words
that one would never have known, come to one after one has
been steeped for a long enough period in some other place. And
sometimes one feels one has come to know the special beneficent
or demonic presence—the *genius loci,* or familiar spirit, of that
section.

It is quite true that I could not have written the following
poem if it had not been for a fairly thorough acquaintance with
the wet, dark, winter streets of Florence, and the sun-drenched,
narrow lanes ascending so sharply up away from that city.

Primavera[2]

The horse with consumption coughed like the end of the world.
We heard its temblors echo in that dry bark,
But on our carriage rolled; we minted miles,
Like hoops our coined wheels rolled until the dark

2 From Barbara Howes, *Light and Dark* (Middletown, Conn.: Wesleyan
University Press, 1959). "Primavera" is © 1954 by Barbara Howes.

Came down upon the city, and grey shade
Merged all the cathedral's zebra stripes; the park
Recessed for night, vendors' flags, bird-wings furled.

Onward and on we rode until the dawn.
From jeweled opera-box and catacomb
We summoned up the past: released, the ghosts
Came forth in cloth of gold and tilting heaume
In every city street and hornèd lane
Whose flowers pell-mell hung down, geranium foam
From walls all staunch with red, red staunched by stone.

And on and on; where would the journey end?
Giotto conceived a tower in pure air,
Heraldic rainbow; balanced on her shell
All beauty woke in Aphrodite fair
As history's fairest. Now to trespassers
On the volcano's flank the tocsins blare:
Our mare's obsidian hooves foreknelled the end.

Or, to use a more exotic example:

Dead Toucan: Guadeloupe[3]

Down like the oval fall of a hammer
The great bill went,
Trailed by its feather-duster body
Splat on cement.
His mates fell out of countenance,
All listened, shivering in the sun,
For what was off, amiss:
In his pretend haven under a flame tree
The agouti crouched, chewed on his spittle, shook,
The porcupine rolled in his box, the parakeets
Chattered regrets,
Knowing something was wrong in their hot Eden;
That their King had followed his heavy fate to earth;
And his superb
Accomplishment,

3 From *The Atlantic Monthly* (September 1964). "Dead Toucan: Guadeloupe" is © 1964 by the Atlantic Monthly Company, Boston, Massachusetts.

His miracle of balance,
Had come to nothing, nothing. . . .
A beak with a panache
Chucked like an old shell back to the Caribbean.

The whole question of the origin of a poem is of course a large and vague one. Who can tell? Who knows what trivial impression, stored up for years, may not suddenly, on coming up against some new impression, suddenly produce an image, an idea, a poem? But to be overprecise about what may have brought about a poem would be foolhardy. For after all, no poet is completely in the know about the source or sources of his work, or even how he may have managed to improve it. He sees certain things, he cuts what is clearly bad and tries to repair the weak points, but he can hardly pretend to complete critical good sense, quite simply because no one has it.

Perhaps I can illustrate this by an example which also connects up with the influence of place:

Mirror Image: Port-au-Prince[4]

Au petit
Salon de Coiffeur
Monique's / hands fork
like lightning, like a baton
rise / to lead her client's hair
in *repassage:* she irons out the kinks.
Madame's brown cheek / is dusted over with a
paler shade / of costly powder. Nails and lips are red.

Her matching lips and nails incarnadined, / in the
next booth Madam consults her face / imprisoned
in the glass. Her lovely tan / is almost
gone. Oh, watch Yvonne's astute
conductor fingers set the
permanent, / *In little*
Drawing-room of
Hairdresser!

4 From Barbara Howes, *Light and Dark* (Middletown, Conn.: Wesleyan University Press, 1959). "Mirror Image: Port-au-Prince" is © 1954 by Barbara Howes.

This poem derived from a number of impressions gathered during our four-month sojourn in the town of Pétionville, three or four miles up the road from the capital city of Haiti in the West Indies. I had occasion, of course, to go to the hairdresser, and could not help but notice that the process took rather longer than it does at home; and this was due quite simply to the fact that the operator had to go against her usual practice by trying to insert some curl into my straight locks, while ordinarily she used her skill to smooth them out. I felt rather keenly the ironies of life on noticing this, and then for some reason recalled pictures I used to draw again and again as a child. One "sameby" was a rabbit: long ears, short tail, a jacket and tie and belt. The other "sameby," a squirrel: short ears, bushy long tail, jacket, belt, and tie. Well, thinking of my interest in a good wave and a proper tan, I found myself playing further with the idea and felt that there must be a poem somewhere in this subject for me. On the way up by bus to our house, there was a sign tacked to a tree with the words: "*Au petit salon de coiffeur.*" I had a starting-point.

It then came to me that the question of the form of this poem would be important and I suddenly saw how form in this special case could be employed in the aid of meaning. I arranged the poem on the page so that it looks like two triangles, the bottom one pointing downward; the whole is thus shaped like a diamond, with a space cutting it in half. The mirror is the line drawn between the two verses, but perhaps really it is not a mirror at all, but a piece of glass, and the two female figures sitting there on each side look through it, and believe that the other's state is more desirable. It is perfection that one wants to see in a mirror: but life does not always allow this.

To return to the matter of a poem's origins: I do believe that the entire explanation of the creative act will never be given, however hard the literary critic may try. One can fill in with some useful facts here and there; one can learn this, that, and the other about the workings of a poet's mind or about his habits, but something will always remain hidden. So many different streams, some amounting to no more than nuance, have fed into any given poem that no one should possibly expect to analyze them out with accuracy. The imagination has its own rules and its own modesty, and for readers of poetry to understand this is of the deepest importance.

Another question that readers of prose or verse must ask is, how do the vast changes in the "outside" world affect a writer's work? Does the latter change along with change, does it keep pace with the upheavals, experiments, and catastrophes of our time?

The answer to this, I should think, would be that the work changes as the writer does, and as we do live in this world we are affected more acutely or less so by what concerns everyone else. And this basic reality—that one lives in a vast and extremely complex world—affects any poet of sensitivity and stature. Hopkins wrote, in "Spring and Fall," about "autumn leaves," but he wrote in depth, about the condition of man.

A poet, though, is not editing a newspaper, and so do not ask of him any up-to-the-minute response to the news-of-the-day. He will take his own time and find his own occasion. It may be years before the poem out of November 22nd, 1963, will be written; it may by then be so worked and altered as not to be recognizable. But the writer who went through that experience will never lose it; it happened to him and it will always be there.

So, changes in the world change me. But just how this may affect my work over the next years, I do not know; we shall have to find out.

Sometimes, though, one does write an "occasional" poem, a poem done for a special occasion:

To W. H. Auden
on His Fiftieth Birthday[5]

> Books collide—
> Or books in a library do:
> Marlowe by Charlotte Mew,
> Sir Horace Walpole by Hugh;
> The most unlikely writers stand shoulder to shoulder;
> One studies incongruity as one grows older.

5 From Barbara Howes, *Light and Dark* (Middletown, Conn.: Wesleyan University Press, 1959). "To W. H. Auden on His Fiftieth Birthday" is © 1957 by Barbara Howes.

Symbols collide—
Signs of the zodiac
Range the celestial track,
Pisces has now swung back
Into the lead: we learn to recognize
Each fleck for what it is in our mackerel skies.

Ideas collide—
As words in a poem can
The poet, Promethean,
Strikes fire in a single line,
Form glows in the far reaches of his brain;
Poets who travel will come home again.

Feeling collides—
Lying for years in wait,
May grope or hesitate.
Now let us celebrate
Feeling, ideas, symbols, books which can
Meet with greatness here within one man.

Another way in which the poet of these times is influenced by the world he inhabits is that while he has a far greater idea of its vastness and complexity, he also can circle round it in a matter of hours. One can fly from Sydney to Los Angeles and then, having forgotten a luncheon engagement in Honolulu, retrace one's steps and very likely be scarcely late at all. Daedalus captured the imagination of men for centuries by his foolhardy journey up toward the sun. Now we are faced with the realities of John Glenn and the other astronauts, whizzing at unbelievable speeds around the entire globe. The imagination, I think, can much better come to terms with Daedalus; but somehow we will have to try and absorb these astral journeys and fit them into our everyday point of view. I tried to write something about an aspect of this racing through space: what a paradox it is to be in one way so close to an individual or to a country, even though at the same time one is so extremely far.

A Short Way by Air[6]

Between now and the moment when you touch
Down at the end of your trip, so much
Will happen. Before you lies
A legendary fairground, whose size
Measures the days ahead; a carrousel
Swings round and round, its bright mounts fall
And rise as did our breathing—carrying
The scenes and persons of your travelling,
Each for a moment outlined legibly
Against a mulberry sky
That fades to dawn or ripens into night.

                 The light
Brushes tower after tower, or swaying
Into the past a palace topples, as round again
The equestrian hours throng. . . . I look far out
Over what lies before me—a prospect
Of absence, whose extent I shall
Count over; the everyday is genial
Enough, but there was never such
Warmth, for me, as when we are in touch.

All serious poets are constantly testing out new happenings, new knowledge, in their work. W. H. Auden, for instance, has been unusually courageous in his use of words out of everyday life, out of mechanics, out of slang—words that a few years ago would have been thought utterly "unpoetic"; but the really powerful and flexible poetic mind can cope with subway tie-ups or malaria control, as it must with life and death. There is really no limit to subject matter; the only limitation is in a writer's ability to make something out of it. Understanding this has, I think, given modern poets a greater confidence; they have a large, in fact an unlimited, field of material before them; what is closed

6 From *The New Republic* (June 1962). © 1962 Harrison-Blaine of New Jersey, Inc.

or hidden is only what they do not understand. And this is challenging to the imagination too; it is as simple as this: one can write about absolutely anything, *if one is able to*.

To mention another problem that besets the poet is to turn the other way and concentrate on the great difficulties of writing. I have noticed that one is often defeated in bringing off a line, merely by accident. Sometimes the very word that seems to be best in a line turns out, through bad luck, to have been used already a line or so back; or one finds that what seem the sharpest and most accurate words for a stanza have nearly all the same first letter; or perhaps too many of them accidentally rhyme. Then one must cast around and work and rework the poem, in the hope that there is really a *better* word or phrase, or at least something as good, which will remove the curse of overalliteration or repetitiousness. In a great poem, it looks as if every word were just *right*, and that not one could be changed except for the worse; it is hard for the layman to realize what hard work, and also to some extent what luck, have gone into that poem for it to come together so perfectly.

Luck, too, one finds in coming upon a subject. Very often the slightest of impressions will set one off; very often, too, one pays no attention, and the poem-that-might-have-been is lost. Poets do not go about most of the time with great thoughts seething in their brains; so much of the time it is the most delicate of experiences that touches them, giving them that curious feeling that they must look into the matter further: dream about it, let their mind wander over it till they find out what was at the bottom of the original impression—a dog slipping on ice; a goldfinch, that bright gold and black bird, which skims over the roadside as if scooping the air out of its path; the noise of a far-off train whistle. Sounds and sights that seem quite ordinary, that one has noticed or half-noticed a thousand times, one day may pierce one through with a sense of meaning and then one must try to find out, through a poem, what that meaning really is.

I had a powerful impression, of evil almost, one day walking home from the village of Le Lavandou in the south of France. Or at least trying to walk home. The wind, the Mistral, was blowing so strongly I could scarcely make my way along. Here was something one could feel but not see, that was turning life in that countryside upside down. The force of the impression from the force of the wind was so strong that I started even as I pushed my way through it to make up some lines.

Mistral[7]

Percussive, furious, this wind
Sweeps down the mountain, and
Under its pennon of skirling air
Blows through each red-tiled house as if
Nothing were there: Mistral
Quartz-clear, spread-eagle,
Falls on the sea.
Gust after gust batters
The surface—darkening blue—
Into a thousand scalloped fans. Where
Shall our noontime friends,
Cicada, hummingbird,
Who stitched the air with sound and speed,
Now hide? All rocks, islands, peninsulas
Draw near, hitch up their chairs,
Companions in this clearer, clean
Air, while inland fields are stripped of soil.
As I start home, a coven
Of winds is let loose at every corner;
Alone in a howling
Waste, figurehead sculptured in air,
Bent low, deafened, I plunge
On, blind in the eye of the storm.

To end on a more familiar note, I shall include a poem which is done in the old French form of the triolet. It is a difficult form, as the frequent repetition of lines gives one very little leeway for getting on with the subject. It is, however, a good thing to attempt, for the fascination of form is endless.

7 From Barbara Howes, *Light and Dark* (Middletown, Conn.: Wesleyan University Press, 1959). "Mistral" is © 1957 by Barbara Howes.

Early Supper[8]

Laughter of children brings
 The kitchen down with laughter.
While the old kettle sings
Laughter of children brings
To a boil all savory things.
 Higher than beam or rafter,
Laughter of children brings
 The kitchen down with laughter.

So ends an autumn day,
 Light ripples on the ceiling,
Dishes are stacked away;
So ends an autumn day,
The children jog and sway
 In comic dances wheeling.
So ends an autumn day,
 Light ripples on the ceiling.

They trail upstairs to bed,
 And night is a dark tower.
The kettle calls: instead
They trail upstairs to bed,
Leaving warmth, the coppery-red
 Mood of their carnival hour.
They trail upstairs to bed,
 And night is a dark tower.

[8] From Barbara Howes, *Light and Dark* (Middletown, Conn.: Wesleyan University Press, 1959). "Early Supper" is © 1956 by Barbara Howes.

7 SOME PHASES OF MY WORK

John Brinnin

The life of poetry, it seems to me, moves in a dynastic succession. Poets become the ancestors of other poets in a series that reflects a cast of mind and a disposition toward language as surely as facial features identify members of a family. Like most poets, I was first moved to write poetry as a way of recognizing and responding to poems I had discovered by myself and which struck me with as much wonder and excitement as I would have felt on finding buried treasure. In school I was interested only in geography and history and in the wild excesses of the story of religion. Literature, particularly poetry, was to me something as dull and established and necessary as the multiplication table.

But when I was about fourteen, my own investigations beyond the classroom led me into libraries and art museums and concert halls. I stood in front of a Rembrandt and realized, with a shock from which I have never quite recovered, that it was the original painting and that I could reach out and touch it. I heard a symphony orchestra play *Le Sacre du Printemps* and, for all I knew, Stravinsky had just written it for the occasion. I read, with a kind of bewildered joy, the poems of Hart Crane and Gerard Manley Hopkins and William Carlos Williams. All of a sudden I had entered a world within my world, a world whose language was poetry. My elation was indescribable and seemed inexpressible, as if it were locked away in some part of me that was private and entirely unrelated to what I did every day. Some kind of energy had charged my thoughts and fired me to action. The only way to live with this feeling was to put it to use, to try to write something that would prove, if only to myself, that I had grasped a new idiom and was somehow entitled to speak in its terms.

This is the familiar situation, I suppose, of young people who have seen more than they can comprehend. In the grip of it, I wrote poems with the same hopes that castaways, begging for rescue, launch bottles with notes in them. Inevitably, these first works of mine were fragmentary and inchoate—pastiches and echoes I had absorbed emotionally but which I could not pretend to understand. But in those years and to a degree ever since, I was less interested in understanding a poem than in feeling it. What moved me then, as now, was the language and the music of language, the perception of the sheer poetic thing, without reference to the ideas which it is meant to serve or to promote. When I began to attend Shakespearean plays, I had little interest in their plots, or in those famous speeches one learns by heart, or even in the pageantry. What I waited for were the little moments when, clear as a star, a sentence or a phrase would leap out of context. These were the moments when language does what only language can do, subsuming all the functions of painting and music and the cinema in its instantaneous re-creations of a scene, a sound, or a movement. In other words, poetry for me was, from the very beginning, not a vehicle, nor an agent, nor a means to salvation, but the liveliest art, the most gloriously useless and the most necessary.

When I was eighteen I published a few poems in some eva-nescent little magazines and, about that time, began with the bravado of ignorance to take myself seriously as a poet. The year was 1934, the nadir of the Great Depression. In the city of Detroit where I lived, breadlines were familiar things, and so were pan-handlers and the little stands where unemployed men sold apples for five cents. I saw women and children digging in garbage pails along the streets I took to school, and I saw mounted policemen, their clubs swinging, charging into groups of workers who had gathered in a public square to advertise their poverty and need for jobs. I began to read books and journals acquainting me with the phenomenon of fascism and with its quick accession to power in Germany. At first, fascism was something quite comfortably far away, something outside the scope of American experience. But before long I could recognize signs of fascism under my nose . . . in the brutal attempts to keep factory workers from forming themselves into a union, and in the voices of demagogues on the radio which, Sunday after Sunday, echoed the voice of Adolf Hitler.

As soon as fascism became an immediate reality for me, I quite naturally joined movements dedicated to opposing it. This led me to work as the editor of a strike bulletin in the headquarters of the newly organized United Automobile Workers, located in a few barren office rooms in a rickety building in the Polish section of the city. Here, during the period of the first famous sit-down strikes, I wrote much of the material that went into the strike bulletin, mimeographed it at night and, next morning, handed it through the factory windows to self-imprisoned strikers. In this experience, my impulses as a poet began to lose their heavily aesthetic character and to take on an urgency that directed me to think of poetry as public speech and even as a political instrument. Consequently, the first phase of my career as a poet had a high political content. Yet the word political is deceptive and narrowing. I did not think of politics in the sense of maneuvers for advantage on the part of special and equal power interests. Politics to me was a way of interpreting the time in which I lived as a contest between the forces of humane justice and the calculated brutalities of those who controlled money and property. My first book of poems was entitled *The Garden Is Political.* In choosing that title, I meant to suggest the breadth of my sense of politics and perhaps to confirm an idea put forth by Thomas Mann, who said: "In our time the destiny of man presents its meaning in political terms."

Two very early poems may illustrate this preoccupation. The first, "Cadillac Square," takes its title from a broad open area in downtown Detroit not far from the high school I attended. Here I first saw violence in the streets, and here, as a spectator, I attended the enormous rallies that signaled the swift and powerful rise of the UAW. I think the lyrical quality of the poem is somewhat at odds with its subject; and yet, as naïve as it must seem today, the lyrical sense of a new era, a new life, was as much a part of those troubled times as was the helpless sense of fear before a rising tide of reactionary power.

Cadillac Square[1]

Whoever know a city, know this square:
The loud and quaking air
That breaks on brick or scales the sun-choked glass,
The travelers who pass
One minute of one day and nevermore,
The neo-Grecian door
Poised like the needle's eye, open and shut
For the mythical feet
Of some squat nobleman of fields and mines,
Industrial scenes,
Or eggshell yachts afloat in summer water,
The pink expensive daughter
With a flair for shady friends and maybe Bach,
The colonnaded house and the Chinese cook.

In early spring this heartlike acre shines:
Canyoned streets, carlines
Flow with violence of union, men
Learn faith in fathers then;
The butcher from the suburb and the clerk
Hear the organizers speak
The echoing language of the pioneer,
And in that press they cheer
With such a swirling and reproachless voice
The city swims in noise;
Those sooty faces and grime-sculptured hands
Live where the river bends,
They own the rotted gardens made to green
Where but the fossils of machines have lain.

All interweaves among the changing years:
Progress is in arrears
Until some chanticleering message raids

[1] From *The Selected Poems of John Malcolm Brinnin* (New York: Little, Brown, 1963). "Cadillac Square" is copyright 1942 by John Malcolm Brinnin.

The disparate multitudes,
Or the bark of some command, made sharp with hate,
Sends Property's gunmen out.
Poised in that infinity of death
Or life, or barely both,
The human balance sways; away, away,
The bleak night and the day,
The bankers couched in limousines, the poor
Jackknifed against a door,
The bankers conscious of defeat, the poor
Jackknifed, oblivious, against a door.

In the next of these early poems, I wanted partly to record, partly to evoke, the ominous quality of intellectual life in the mid-1930's. While democratic governments still tended to regard fascism as a nuisance, as something that might just go away if no attention were paid to it, individuals recognized fascism for what it was and knew that it was preparing a confrontation that would decide the course of history. We had come to see that fascism was a real and present danger; we had come to feel that every aspect of our lives was shadowed and threatened. As one English poet said, we were "waiting for the gun butt on the door." Here is my attempt to catch that omnipresent sense of jeopardy.

The Garden Is Political[2]

The garden is political,
Nor may the moody eyes
Of larkspur, zinnia, phlox
Stare that manifest horror down.

Nor will percussive rain come down,
Exciting, quick to change
Flower to essence, essence to flower,
As though the planted headlines

---

2 From *The Selected Poems of John Malcolm Brinnin* (New York: Little, Brown, 1963). "The Garden Is Political" is copyright 1942 by John Malcolm Brinnin.

Were a row of four-o'clocks, not headlines,
As though the garden were
A progeny of earth
And not a mask for tragedy

O, no, garden is tragedy
Up to its generous eyes,
Its sensual order, its élan.
The whole beguiling summer burns

With guilty pleasure, gaily burns
Waltzes and rounds before
The glimmering imminence of guns.
People like headstones walk

Among the twilit hedges, walk
Slow-motioned, fearing the sudden
Scream, the mutilated body,
Headless, under the leaves.

The lisp and grinning of the leaves
Lasts all the dripping night;
Even the illiterate snake must know
The garden is political.

In both of these poems, the main literary influence is that of
W. H. Auden. He was the most articulate and persuasive voice in
a new generation of English poets who continually assessed the
conditions of modern society, and his impact on young poets both
in his own country and in America was incalculable. Some poets
who came under his influence lost all traces of their own individuality, and became merely Audenesque satellites; like other
young poets, I found that in order to save my poetic soul, I had
to break the spell of the idiom Auden had invented and to break
the domination of that clinical view of man and society which
was so variously useful as interpretation and as a source of
imagery.

While my political poems were the natural consequence of
political involvements and my political view of destiny, my first

successful lyric was political, I think, only in the most marginal sense. The poem is entitled "Rowing in Lincoln Park." It is an elegy for my father and a lament for the lost chances of childhood. Its appearance among my very earliest poems indicates an interest that would continue through my work until, finally, it would become the predominant one. Nostalgic reminiscence would probably be the right words to use in reference to these poems; the notion behind them is to find, to touch, to suggest those aspects of an intimately personal circumstance that may have a general relevance.

Rowing in Lincoln Park[3]

You are, in 1925, my father;
Straw-hatted, prim, I am your only son;
Through zebra-light fanwise on the lagoon
Our rented boat slides on the lucent calm.

And we are wistful, having come to this
First tableau of ourselves; your eyes that look
Astonished on my nine bravado years,
My conscious heart that hears the oarlocks click

And swells with facts particular to you—
How France is pink, how noon is shadowless,
How bad unruly angels tumbled from
That ivory eminence, and how they burned.

And you are vaguely undermined and plan
Surprise of pennies, some directed gesture,
Being proud and inarticulate, your mind
Dramatic and unpoised, surprised with love.

In silences hermetical as this
The lean ancestral hand returns, the voice
Of unfulfillment with its bladelike touch
Warning our scattered breath to be resolved.

[3] From *The Selected Poems of John Malcolm Brinnin* (New York: Little, Brown, 1963). "Rowing in Lincoln Park" is copyright 1942 by John Malcolm Brinnin.

And sons and fathers in their mutual eyes,
Exchange (a moment huge and volatile)
The glance of paralytics, or the news
Of master-builders on the trespassed earth.

Now I am twenty-two and you are dead,
And late in Lincoln Park the rowers cross
Unfavored in their odysseys, the lake
Not dazzling nor wide, but dark and commonplace.

My first two volumes of poetry were published in the early years of World War II and my third book in the last year of the war. I was kept from personal participation in any military service for reasons of health. At a time when my classmates were being shipped to all parts of the world, I found myself en-isled in a college for young women where the impact of the war was registered only in tremors, as if from a distant earthquake. Many of the poems I wrote during these years have been classified as war poems, but of course they are civilian poems—the experience of war at second hand and by report. The enormous breadth and scale of the war and its massive deploys of men and machinery were subjects for another Homer. But for the lyric poet the only possible way to come to terms with the war as usable experience was to translate its meanings into human terms. Consequently, all of my wartime poems have one theme: the persistence of human aspiration.

A Salient of War[4]

In time's unconscious shadow and return,
Turning its flames impartially through leaves,
Cathedrals and deep seas, our only sun
Contrives to shepherd us in days of love
And nights of music full as heart will bear.

[4] From *The Selected Poems of John Malcolm Brinnin* (New York: Little, Brown, 1963). "A Salient of War" is copyright 1945 by John Malcolm Brinnin; originally appeared in *No Arch, No Triumph* (Alfred A. Knopf).

Waking, walking through those early palaces
The frost erects among familiar branches,
We know by small traditions how the dark
Is spooling in its net the single spears
Of palms, the flashing tips and blue plateaus
Of ice, the soldier's memories of home.

This incident of war that sifts our will
And pulls apart the wide community
Of nakedness is war against itself.
Its purpose has no parallel on hillsides
Melting the sense with tangled arms of foam,
Nor on the adolescent greens where men
Quite naturally throw off their orchard wreaths
To learn the weather and the facts of love.
Because our memories are mutual,
The world is webbed with veins, and moves
Below its surface like a beating heart.

Not Plato in his universal jail,
Nor glum Napoleon, Emperor of Snow,
Escapes the fine equation so long joined.
The balance is much tried; our records tell
How the excellent corrupt Marquis, the Saint
With sparrows on his fingers, conquistadors
To margins of the mind that blaze, or clap
The senses in a cold paralysis,
Even the physicians with mechanical third eyes,
Have all come back. In such rich agony
Our skeletons and embryos embrace.

The sun survives, and many definitions
Meaning wonder, meaning more than words
May say. The sea is one, and when we sleep
We sleep upon those shores where darkness is
Discriminately wary of our need
To make, of what we know and wish, our dreams.
In the great equity of daylight and dark,
There will be space for many errors more,

And time to marry what we were and are;
The burning years, like letters overseas,
Make splendid our impossible desires.

By this time, as I continually attempted to develop greater technical skill, my natural inclination was toward set forms that I might adapt to my own particular use. I wrote in iambics as a rule, and I liked the various iambic patterns employed by the Metaphysical poets of the seventeenth century. I used rhyme consistently and the more intricate the rhyme-scheme, the more happily I worked to perfect it through the course of one long stanza after another.

While I had learned that the greatest freedom lies in the most rigorous discipline, I soon began to feel a need for a loosening up of my metrical patterns, a need to break the habits of thought that attend the orderly progression of metrics. I knew that meter was infinitely flexible and yet I felt that I had probably gone as far as I personally could go in handling it. I was still a long way from breaking the habit, but a new influence in my thought and in my way of seeing helped me toward that end. This new influence came from painting, specifically from that kind of painting that is now categorized as Abstract Expressionism.

Far more than music or any other art, painting has always been the thing to which my responses are immediate, unthinking, intuitive. Among poets, there is usually a very strong predominance of either the aural faculty or the visual. In my case, it is visual— to the extent that I "see" music as soon as I hear it and even before I can feel it. Abstract Expressionism, historically speaking, is one of the few indigenous movements in American art. I was personally acquainted with some of the painters who were defining this new mode and, to me, their work was more exciting than any painting since the early "analytical" period of Cubism. These painters had their roots in American soil, in the rough romanticism of Albert Pinkham Ryder and Arthur G. Dove and Marsden Hartley. The subjects of these men were not topical or programmatic but, one might say, primordial. They dealt with the basic designs and the brute force of natural things. It seems to me that the new painters whom they influenced were recapturing for painting a mythical quality that had been lost, or had been superseded by the intellectual constructions of the later phases of Cubism and the vulgar sensationalism that marks so much of Surrealism. I used to discuss their work with these painters, and the conceptions that lay behind it; sometimes I would be called in to provide titles for their paintings for exhibition.

Sooner or later, I felt, I would have to find a way to bring their visual and evocative qualities into a kind of poetry that also reduced occasion and event to a basic gesture and a basic image. I knew this could not happen by an act of will, so I devised a way in which the programmatic content of a poem would not depend on deliberate choice but on a sort of contrived accident. I decided to write a series of acrostics—that is, poems in which the first letter of every line, when read vertically down the page, spells out a name or makes a statement. These acrostics, I decided, would spell out the names of my friends. I did not plan to have poems shape up as portraits of these friends, or to make any overt comment on their personalities. But it was inevitable that, in the course of composition, certain personal references would creep into the poem. In any case, this was my way of opening up subconscious sources of poetry, my way of using that store of natural forms and images which are part of the subliminal language that precedes words and which is spoken by all living things. Here are two acrostics from a long series published under the general title, *The Sorrows of Cold Stone*. In the first poem, the name spelled out acrostically is Theodoros Stamos, a painter whose name is prominently associated with the Abstract Expressionist movement. The name spelled in the second poem is Truman Capote, the American novelist whose literary imagery sometimes perfectly catches the hypnagogic state rendered by the painters.

Think of that place among all buried places,
Hideout of dog and angel: there children stand
Eternal, mindless, in the bandaged dress
Old scarecrows hurl, all sleeves, against the wind;
Dead-white, with sad top-heavy heads entwined,
Of love the monuments, love-locked they fall,
Root, rib and swaddling cerement one grave,
One tidal wave the fishing moon's long pull
Shores like a cockleshell but cannot save.

Sun of their sleep, the good year's native light
Tunes the young engines of earth's changelessness,
And through the world's veined head, all moss and eyes,
Mortality unwinds—night after night
On mandrake roots to scream, half man, half tree,
Saying to scarecrow children, Wait for me.[5]

The blue swan from Wyoming to Peru
Resumes, one feather lost, his cold patrol;
Upset at times, at times volplaning low,
My soaring sailor on his snow-white sail
Arrives nowhere; his sorry shadow hangs
Nightlong on rock, and daylong lines his wings.

Captivity of self, like the guitar's
Abundant silences, attracts the wind
Put forth for sorrow, the grief that wears
Only the landscape proper to his kind.
This folded bird, for all he bear another,
Endures a blizzard in one falling feather.[6]

In both of these instances, the matter of the poem is mainly a mood and only incidentally an idea relevant to other ideas. The poems are explorations rather than statements, and yet I am hopeful that each is held together by a logic and an order that keeps it from being an indulgent piece of automatic writing. If either of the poems refers back to the person whose name provides the acrostic sequence, the reference is unconscious. This does not mean that, in poems of this nature, such references are not often precise and revealing.

[5] From *The Selected Poems of John Malcolm Brinnin* (New York: Little, Brown, 1963). "Think of That Place" is copyright 1951 by John Malcolm Brinnin.
[6] From *The Selected Poems of John Malcolm Brinnin* (New York: Little, Brown, 1963). "The Blue Swan from Wyoming to Peru" is copyright 1951 by John Malcolm Brinnin.

For about two years I worked in this phase of Abstract Expressionism, but I soon found that it was not in my nature—and perhaps not in the nature of poetry—to strive for the abstract. A strong influence that now began to show itself in my work was that of Dylan Thomas. He was already making use of the primordial sort of imagery I had hoped for and his vision seemed to encompass without strain the whole history of the race of man. For a time, some of my poems sounded vaguely like his, but they lacked his sustained energy and tended to be more ingenious and graceful than powerful.

To conclude this phase, I wrote my longest and most ambitious poem, "The Worm in the Whirling Cross." This was an attempt to describe, or to recreate, a huge moment in which consciousness is awakened—to show a nameless individual, Adam and Everyman, dreaming his organic history and his cultural history and finally waking up in a world where he is what he has experienced, where everything he sees is newly urgent and potential. The shape and meter of the poem were taken from Milton's "Lycidas." The method of the poem is derived, in part, from James Joyce, and in part from T. S. Eliot. From Joyce I took the notion of portmanteau words and the sort of pun that doubles or triples a particular meaning, as distinct from the usual sort of pun that cuts a meaning in half or satirizes it or makes it farcical. From Eliot I took the idea of cultural history as a series of notations in which a word or a phrase serves to illuminate whole corridors of experience. Unlike Eliot's practice in *The Waste Land*, however, notes are not appended to the poem but, in an elaborate reticulum of cross-reference, are made to serve as part of the text of the poem. Here is a sample passage from "The Worm in the Whirling Cross":

Good-bye, god-father; sons go on their own
In the long run; farewell, old potentate,
Old lion-heart; though I know woebegone
And prophetless travail avail me nought.
Cast-off of dust, I bolt your five-barred gate
Once more, and clapped anew, through avenues
Of sand-stormed hours spilled time-counterwise,

Fall backward back to the embalming lake
Where cold, infertile, the moon's eye keeps one
Twin cradle with the whole soft seed of man.
O bridegroom floating in the white bride's wake,
O mirror-peeling, moon-appalling face,
Your fire falls, locked antlers in the bough,
As over cowls of snow,
Arising, haloed with hot sapphire and ice,
First born offspring of metamorphosis,
I ride my beast-king Christ through Paradise;
Yet will taboos their cutthroat totems raise,
And soon in blood-soaked sorrow Sophocles
Will publish my dead issue and its name.
O fatal apple of your father's eye,
At this core of the matter lies your dream.
Ah well, ill-webbed or well this net plots my
Hell-bent heyday—coiled from the eggshell skull,
Foundering truth of that profound doom's day
Dumbfounding all, boomeranged bone again,
Whistling fissions howl through God's cracked bowl;
Who loves his life leaves well enough alone,
Holding his tongue at Pentecost of death,
While somewhere shuttling slowly something weaves
For saw-toothed worms his ragbag mummy cloth,
—Sleep soundly, doom's man, sleep, and be dream's child:
—For, when all's twice told, all told we lie cold.[7]

This poem gained considerable attention when it was first published, but it was noticed largely by critics intrigued by the sense
of the poem as an elaborate puzzle to be solved. Though I had
hoped to produce a poem of epical range within the compass of a
lyric, I had produced something that appealed mainly to people
who approach poetry as mechanics approach machinery. A few
people clearly admired the poem, but I don't think anyone really
liked it. It was the most exhausting single work I had ever com-

[7] From *The Selected Poems of John Malcolm Brinnin* (New York: Little,
Brown, 1963). "The Worm in the Whirling Cross" is copyright 1951 by John
Malcolm Brinnin.

pleted; when I arrived at the final version I found that my work sheets for the poem's less than two hundred lines added up to nearly five hundred. I was disappointed to find that its hermetic aspects were so forbidding as to frighten readers away, yet the poem served to bring the Abstract Expressionist phase of my work to an irrevocable ending and it released me, or perhaps forced me, to turn to other devices.

We are, after all, what we remember. Identity, connection, a sense of a personal past, are apt to be problems for most Americans, and sometimes these problems assume the nature of profound dilemma. My own case is not untypical. I was born in Canada of American parents whose heritage was Scottish on my mother's side and Irish on my father's. My childhood was spent, year by year, partly in Nova Scotia and partly in Michigan, and the contrast between these places could hardly have been greater. Nova Scotia was provincial and Victorian, polite and reserved; Michigan was booming and modern, the rough and prosperous cradle of the automobile age. By the time I was twenty-one, I had lost the religion into which I was christened and under whose auspices I had been educated. I had little faith in the ability of capitalism to create a just and equitable world; and by the early death of my father I had lost the one connection with my inherited scheme of things that might have supported and sustained me.

In my early adult years, I knew who I was by what I believed. I considered myself part of that international society of men of good will who were ready to make any sacrifice to defeat fascism and to promote the hopes of the democratic revolutions of the eighteenth and nineteenth centuries. But when in the disillusion and *real-politik* of the times, I was no longer able to find identity in what I believed, I sought identity in what I remembered. This led me to recreate my past, so to speak, sometimes in psychological terms, sometimes by attempting to find those Proustian touchstones and emblems by which a buried life is resurrected. Consequently, many of my poems are documents in a crisis of identity or, one might say, inquiries into the nature of identity. The most representative of these, one that attempts to perceive the true psychological dimensions of a personal situation, is a poem entitled "Oedipus: His Cradle Song." To read this poem in the terms in which it was conceived, it is necessary to assume that the infant Oedipus, as he lies abandoned on a mountainside, already knows his tragic destiny and the steps by which it will be fulfilled.

Oedipus: His Cradle Song[8]

Who is my shepherd, that I shall not want?
Who with earth-roughened hands
Will loose the spike that joins my anklebones,
And bear me home, and have me in his house?

I seek a father who most need a son,
Yet have no voice to call
One or the other, nor wind nor oracle
To publish me, where I am meant to die.

Who is my uncle, that shall intervene,
Assist the turning wheel
That like the running towers of the sun
Will smash my king's house and my cockleshell?

Who is my mother, that shall make my bed?
Who with gold-beaten rings
Shall quicken me, that I beget my son
Where my cold father with his lust lay down?

Who is one blind, that has already seen
Blood where it shall fall soon?
He knows my ways and how I rule this ground.
In his perpetual light I would be found.

The day is in the sea, the night grows cold.
Is the event long past?
The suckling beast knows where I lie alone.
I seek a father who most need a son.

[8] From *The Selected Poems of John Malcolm Brinnin* (New York: Little, Brown, 1963). "Oedipus: His Cradle Song" is copyright 1951 by John Malcolm Brinnin.

I am never quite sure just what philosophical and aesthetic sources most clearly nourish my poetry and I think this may be a good thing. By its nature, poetry is a groping toward clarity and definition rather than a statement of something arrived at and comfortably accepted. Poetically speaking, I prefer to dwell in a flux of impressions and ideas and to await those moments when a thought or an emotion calls out to be delineated and objectified. In recent years, along with poems that make particular inquiries into my personal history, I have found myself writing poems that could only have been possible as a result of my experience of Europe. While I have never lived in Europe for any period longer than a few months, I have come to feel that Europe is an essential and continuing aspect of my life. For a part of every one of the past fifteen years I have been in Europe on travels and sojourns that have taken me almost everywhere on the Continent, including the Soviet Union, which I have visited on two occasions. I have never thought of Europe or any place in Europe as subject matter per se, but quite naturally certain ideas and feelings lend themselves to European settings.

Perhaps the most deliberate of these is concerned with a visit to Ireland, a personal pilgrimage to the countryside from which my paternal ancestors came, in the middle of the nineteenth century, to the city of Boston. Most of what I knew and felt about Ireland I had gained from reading James Joyce, with whom my affinities are strong. His father and my great grandfather came from the same district—County Cork; I had been subject in my early years to the same Jesuitical disciplines as he had; we shared a rebellious attitude toward the middle-class conservatism and Roman Catholic puritanism by which we were governed as children; and, for me, Joyce was always the greatest of modern literary artists who used the English language. But when I actually went to Ireland, I wanted to forget all of these things and simply, by myself and for myself, recapture if I could a sense of the land and the people from whom I am descended.

The following poem is a record of that pilgrimage. The title is "Ich Am of Irlaunde," or "I am of Ireland," and it comes from any anonymous little ballad of early Irish history.

Ich Am of Irlaunde[9]

Where sea gulls, holy-ghosting rainbows, ran
With the weather on the piebald landfall lea,
I came to Ireland, an Irishman,
To dress a grave for *saynte charite;*
Since I could bare no emblem, stag or swan,
And stood three generations out of fee,
I held my tongue, and crossed my knife and fork
In the black kitchens of the County Cork.

Morning that breaks a prodigal to sight
Brought squires, bitch-hard ladies, fat priests who,
Gifted with gab, grace, and good appetite,
Bellwethered ignorance into its pew;
While under high heaven and the low birth rate
Potato pickers fed the status quo,
Barbaric stallions, hitched to brass-hung drays,
Rolled thunder from imperial breweries.

On the cross of the Celt I laid my wreath.
My father's hand in mine kept my heart still:
Once more, under a Yankee shibboleth,
We walked the slattern side of Beacon Hill
On the seventeenth of March. To prove our faith,
A crosier pointed and the State House fell;
The lace-curtain banners of the Boston poor
Hoisted the tribe of Brennan-on-the-Moor.

Full summer in their suit, sheep-soft with corn,
The lowing meadows of my race and creed
Beguiled my rite, as if a far-off horn,
Lifting to summons neither quick nor dead,
Sang the long daydreams of cromlech and cairn
And would with bees and heather fill my head.
To the invitations of that afternoon
I had come late; blood would not flow from stone.

[9] From *The Selected Poems of John Malcolm Brinnin* (New York: Little, Brown, 1963). "Ich Am of Irlaunde" is © 1960 by John Malcolm Brinnin; originally appeared in *The New Yorker*.

Twilight on castle keep and highland throne
Brought Sean from his alehouse, Deirdre from her shop.
Their sorrows had a name; their day was done.
If from a blazing vault some druid shape
Keened on cold cottage and pinchpenny town,
Who was my witness? All night, fast asleep,
Toward Dublin in the rocking Night Mail curled,
I wept for visions, nothing in the world.

In the current phase of my work, the conscious impulses that move me are several. Technically, whether working in meter or in free cadences, I am still searching for the rigorously spare sort of language that gives the illusion of spoken language without falling into the carelessness and redundancy of actual speech. I am trying to articulate states of mind by juxtaposition and innuendo rather than by statement, and I am hoping to develop an idiom sufficiently inclusive to accommodate all aspects of my thought and feeling rather than to settle for an idiom that serves only the obvious, elevated, poetic thing.

This latter attempt is perhaps too familiarly a part of every poet's ambition to seem worthy of mention. However, in my case, I find that I am drawn, on the one hand, to any means I can find to evoke primitive states of feeling and, on the other, to write a kind of poetry that examines certain of the ideas I share with other disengaged intellectuals, a kind of poetry based on ironic observation, one that often turns out to be lighthearted and purely comic. The challenge for me, once more, is of a nature that cannot be met by an act of will. My poetry, no matter how extremely various its methods and subject matter may be, will be my poetry insofar as it maintains a tone dependent upon a cast of mind which, in turn, is the expression of a whole personality. In the long run, poems are an autobiographical record; to write a false poem is, in this sense, to be untrue to oneself.

While I have not been consciously aware of the fact when I wrote them, a number of my recent poems are, finally, about aesthetics—about aesthetic order as it is related to moral order. The typical situation in any one of these poems is that in which the speaker is confronted with a new setting and a number of things which, at first, he merely observes and describes. As the poem proceeds, however, he attempts to relate one thing to another and to arrive, in that process, at a meaning. This meaning is not stated in any one thematic line but is implicit in the process of the poem itself. In other words, the point of the poem and the method of the poem have everything in common. There is no point, so to speak, beyond the method; the method itself articulates the point. Perhaps the following poem will illustrate what I have in mind.

Hotel Paradiso e Commerciale[10]

Another hill town:
another dry Cinzano in the sun.
I couldn't sleep in that enormous echo—
silence and water music, sickly street lamps
neither on nor off—a night
of islands and forgotten languages.

Yet morning, marvelously frank, comes up
with bells, with loaves, with letters
distributed like gifts. I watch a fat priest
spouting grape seeds, a family weeping
in the fumes of a departing bus.

This place is nowhere
except on the map. Wheels spin the sun,
with a white clatter shutters are shut to,
umbrellas bloom in striped and sudden groves.

The day's away, impossibly the same,
and only minutes are at all important—
if women by a wall,
a lean dog, and a cheerful humpback
selling gum and ball-points
are important. My glass is empty.
It is Wednesday. It is not going to rain.

[10] From *The Selected Poems of John Malcolm Brinnin* (New York: Little, Brown, 1963). "Hotel Paradiso e Commerciale" is © 1960 by John Malcolm Brinnin; originally appeared in *The New Yorker*.

Observation
without speculation. How soon
the eye craves what it cannot see,
goes limpid, glazed, unanswerable,
lights on a pigeon walking in a circle,
hangs on a random shadow,
would rather sleep.

How old am I?
What's missing here? What do these people
feed on, that won't feed on them? This town
needs scrolls, celestial delegations,
a swoon of virgins, apostles in apple green,
a landscape riding on a holy shoulder.

The morning stays.
As though I kept an old appointment,
I start by the cats' corridors (Banco di Roma,
wineshops, gorgeous butcheries)
toward some mild angel of annunciation—
upstairs, most likely, badly lit,
speaking in rivets on a band of gold.

Praise God, this town keeps one
unheard-of masterpiece to justify
a million ordinary mornings
and pardon this one.

As I review these several phases of my work, represented in
less than a hundred poems written over a period of nearly twenty-
five years, I think it is clear that my progress has involved a less-
ening of public and political concerns as subjects for poetry, and
an increase of personal concerns, to the degree that all of my
poems seem related to occasions in my personal life. Poetry remains for me an autonomous form of art and not a form of discussion or polemics—primarily an act of creation and only secondarily a mode of expression.

I can read with interest many of the new poets, from San

Francisco to Moscow, who write urgent, open, and hortatory poems which they read to huge assembled audiences. I share their discontent and impatience, and their hunger for a realization, in our lifetime, of those potentialities for man that the twentieth century tends inexcusably to curb and to corrode. I meet these poets on common ground in the realm of ideas, but I cannot believe that their deliberate impoverishment of poetry as an art, their deliberate turning away from the marvelous poetic inventions of the late-nineteenth and early-twentieth century does anything, finally, but muffle the voice of poetry at a time when its resonance is most urgently needed. When a poet leaves his study to mount a platform he makes a noise that will soon be spent. When he must deny the infinite richness and complexity of his art to make what he thinks is a necessary communication, he dishonors his calling and betrays the inadequacy of his gifts. Poets cannot save the world, but they can contribute to the civilizing process that might make the world more worthy of salvation. Assertion in poetry, whether it is the act of the idealist or the self-appointed court jester, serves ends that have little to do with the meaning or spirit of poetry; and self-expression is a form of aesthetic aberration that has less to do with poetry than with psychopathology. The greatest need we all have, I think, is to keep alive the sense of wonder that will enable us to overcome the brutalizing forces of expediency and conformity in the mass societies of which we are a part. Only man wonders; only man imagines. When the sense of wonder is allowed to diminish, poetry becomes, inevitably, a matter of assertion and thus loses all of its Orphic power to enchant, beguile, and otherwise extend the range of our attention. Assertion is an impulse of the ego; wonder is a faculty of the soul.

8 CHANGES

John Berryman

This slight exploration of some of my opinions about my work as a poet, you may wish to bear in mind, is the statement of a man nearing fifty, and I am less impressed than I used to be by the universal notion of a continuity of individual personality—which will bring me in a moment to the first and most interesting of the four questions proposed by Mr. Howard Nemerov. It is a queer assignment. Sometimes I've complied with similar requests before, but never without fundamental misgivings. For one thing, one forgets, one even deliberately forgets in order to get on with new work, and so may seriously misrepresent the artist-that-was twenty years ago. For another, there are trade secrets. At the same time that one works partly to open fresh avenues for other writers (though one would not dream of admitting it), one has secrets, like any craftsman, and I figure that anyone who deserves to know them deserves to find them out for himself. So I do not plan to give anything away.

The question was this: "Do you see your work as having essentially changed in character or style since you began?"

I would reply: *of course*. I began work in verse-making as a burning, trivial disciple of the great Irish poet William Butler Yeats, and I hope I have moved off from there. One is obsessed at different times by different things and by different ways of putting them. Naturally there are catches in the question. What does "essentially" mean? What is "character"? What is "style"? Still the question, if semantically murky, is practically clear, and I respond to it with some personal history.

94

When I said just now "work in verse-making" I was leaving out some months of protoapprenticeship during which I was so inexperienced that I didn't imitate *anybody*. Then came Yeats, whom I didn't so much wish to resemble as to *be*, and for several fumbling years I wrote in what it is convenient to call "period style," the Anglo-American style of the 1930's, with no voice of my own, learning chiefly from middle and later Yeats and from the brilliant young Englishman W. H. Auden. Yeats somehow saved me from the then crushing influences of Ezra Pound and T. S. Eliot—luckily, as I now feel—but he could not teach me to sound like myself (whatever that was) or tell me what to write about. The first poem, perhaps, where those dramatic-to-me things happened was (is) called "Winter Landscape." It is mounted in five five-line stanzas, unrhymed, all one sentence. (I admit there is a colon near the middle of the third stanza.)

Winter Landscape[1]

The three men coming down the winter hill
In brown, with tall poles and a pack of hounds
At heel, through the arrangement of the trees
Past the five figures at the burning straw,
Returning cold and silent to their town,

Returning to the drifted snow, the rink
Lively with children, to the older men,
The long companions they can never reach,
The blue light, men with ladders, by the church
The sledge and shadow in the twilit street,

Are not aware that in the sandy time
To come, the evil waste of history
Outstretched, they will be seen upon the brow
Of that same hill: when all their company
Will have been irrecoverably lost,

---

1 From *The Dispossessed* (New York: Farrar, Straus & Giroux, 1948). "Winter Landscape" is copyright 1948 by John Berryman; reprinted by permission of Farrar, Straus & Giroux, Inc.

These men, this particular three in brown
Witnessed by birds will keep the scene and say
By their configuration with the trees,
The small bridge, the red houses and the fire,
What place, what time, what morning occasion

Sent them into the wood, a pack of hounds
At heel and the tall poles upon their shoulders,
Thence to return as now we see them and
Ankle-deep in snow down the winter hill
Descend, while three birds watch and the fourth flies.

This does not sound, I would say, like either Yeats or Auden—or
Rilke or Lorca or Corbière or any of my other passions of those
remote days. It derives its individuality, if I am right, from a
peculiar steadiness of somber tone (of which I'll say more presently) and from its peculiar relation to its materials—drawn, of
course, from Brueghel's famous painting. The poem is sometimes
quoted and readers seem to take it for either a verbal *equivalent*
to the picture or (like Auden's fine Brueghel poem, "Musée des
Beaux Arts," written later) an *interpretation* of it. Both views I
would call wrong, though the first is that adopted in a compara-
tive essay on picture and poem recently published by two aestheticians at the University of Notre Dame.[2] After a competent study,
buttressed by the relevant scholarship, of Brueghel's painting,
they proceed to the poem—where, there being no relevant scholarship, they seem less at ease—and so to the relation between the
two. Some of the points made are real, I believe. To quote the
two with which they begin: they say the poem's "elaborative sequence urged on by the sweeping carry-over lines"—they mean
run-on—"within the stanza or between stanzas—preserves the
same order of presentation and the same grouping of elements as
the Brueghel composition. . . . Purposively restricting himself to
a diction as sober, direct, and matter-of-fact as the painter's treatment of scene and objects, Berryman so composes with it that he
achieves an insistent and animated pattern of strong poetic

[2] If anyone is *truly* curious this can be found in the University of Texas
Studies in Literature and Language, V. 3, Autumn 1963.

effect." And so on, to the end of the article where the "disclosed affinities" of the two works are found testifying to the "secret friendship" of the arts. Nowhere is anything said as to what the poem is *about,* nor is any interest expressed in that little topic; the relation between the works is left obscure except for the investigation of affinities. An investigation of *differences* would have taken them farther.

Very briefly, the poem's extreme sobriety would seem to represent a reaction, first, against Yeats's gorgeous and seductive rhetoric and, second, against the hysterical political atmosphere of the period. It dates from 1938–1939 and was written in New York following two years' residence in England, during recurrent crises, with extended visits to France and Germany, especially one of the Nazi strongholds, Heidelberg. So far as I can make out, it is a war poem, of an unusual negative kind. The common title of the picture is *Hunters in the Snow* and of course the poet knows this. But he pretends not to, and calls their spears (twice) "poles," the resultant governing emotion being a certain stubborn incredulity—as the hunters are loosed while the peaceful nations plunge again into war. This is not the subject of Brueghel's painting at all, and the interpretation of *the event of the poem* proves that the picture has merely provided necessary material from a tranquil world for what is necessary to be said— but which the poet refuses to say—about a violent world.

You may wonder whether I dislike aestheticians. I do.

Very different from the discovery made in "Winter Landscape," if the foregoing account seems acceptable—namely, that a poem's force may be pivoted on a missing or misrepresented element in an agreed-on or imposed design—was a discovery made in another short piece several years later. (It also is twenty-five lines long, unrhymed, but, I think, much more fluid.)

The Ball Poem[3]

What is the boy now, who has lost his ball,
What, what is he to do? I saw it go
Merrily bouncing, down the street, and then

[3] From *The Dispossessed* (New York: Farrar, Straus & Giroux, 1948). "The Ball Poem" is copyright 1948 by John Berryman; reprinted by permission of Farrar, Straus & Giroux, Inc.

Merrily over—there it is in the water!
No use to say 'O there are other balls':
An ultimate shaking grief fixes the boy
As he stands rigid, trembling, staring down
All his young days into the harbour where
His ball went. I would not intrude on him,
A dime, another ball, is worthless. Now
He senses first responsibility
In a world of possessions. People will take balls,
Balls will be lost always, little boy,
And no one buys a ball back. Money is external.
He is learning, well behind his desperate eyes,
The epistemology of loss, how to stand up
Knowing what every man must one day know
And most know many days, how to stand up.
And gradually light returns to the street,
A whistle blows, the ball is out of sight,
Soon part of me will explore the deep and dark
Floor of the harbour . . . I am everywhere,
I suffer and move, my mind and my heart move
With all that move me, under the water
Or whistling, I am not a little boy.

The discovery here was that a commitment of identity can be "reserved," so to speak, with an ambiguous pronoun. The poet himself is both left out and put in; the boy does and does not become him and we are confronted with a process which is at once a process of life and a process of art. A pronoun may seem a small matter, but she matters, he matters, it matters, they matter. Without this invention (if it is one—Rimbaud's "*Je est un autre*" may have pointed my way, I have no idea now) I could not have written either of the two long poems that constitute the bulk of my work so far. If I were making a grandiose claim, I might pretend to know more about the administration of pronouns than any other living poet writing in English or American. You will have noticed that I have said nothing about my agonies and joys, my wives and children, my liking for my country, my dislike of communist theory and practice, etc., but have been technical. Art is technical, too.

So far I have been speaking of short poems and youth, when enthusiasms and hostilities, of an artistic kind I mean, play a bigger role in inspiration than perhaps they do later. I do not know, because I see neither enthusiasm nor hostility behind "The Ball Poem." But I was nearly thirty then. I do know that much later, when I finally woke up to the fact that I was involved in a long poem, one of my first thoughts was: Narrative! let's have narrative, and at least one dominant personality, and no fragmentation! In short, let us have something spectacularly NOT *The Waste Land,* the best long poem of the age. So maybe hostility keeps on going.

What had happened was that I had made up the first stanza of a poem to be called *Homage to Mistress Bradstreet* and the first three lines of the second stanza, and there, for almost five years, I stuck. Here is the passage:

> The Governor your husband lived so long
> moved you not, restless, waiting for him? Still,
> you were a patient woman—
> I seem to see you pause here still:
> Sylvester, Quarles, in moments odd you pored
> before a fire at, bright eyes on the Lord,
> all the children still.
> 'Simon . . .': Simon will listen while you read a Song.
>
> Outside the New World winters in grand dark
> white air lashing high thro' the virgin stands
> foxes down foxholes sigh . . .[4]

The dramatic mode, hovering behind the two meditative lyrics I've quoted, has here surely come more into the open; and also here I had overcome at once two of the paralyzing obstacles that haunt the path of the very few modern poets in English who have attempted ambitious sizable poems: what form to use and what to write about. The eight-line stanza I invented here after a lifetime's study, especially of Yeats's, and in particular the one he adopted from Abraham Cowley for his elegy "In Memory of

[4] Reprinted from *Homage to Mistress Bradstreet* by John Berryman by Farrar, Straus, & Giroux, Inc. © 1956 by John Berryman.

Major Robert Gregory." Mine breaks not at midpoint but after the short third line; a strange four-beat line leads to the balancing heroic couplet of lines five and six, after which seven is again short (three feet, like line three) and then the stanza widens into an alexandrine rhyming all the way back to one. I wanted something at once flexible and grave, intense and quiet, able to deal with matter both high and low.

As for the subject: the question most put to me about the poem is why I chose to write about this boring high-minded Puritan woman who may have been our first American poet but is not a good one. I agree, naturally, and say that I did not choose her—somehow she chose me—one point of connection, at any rate, being the almost insuperable difficulty of writing high verse at all in a land that cared and cares so little for it. I was concerned with her though, almost from the beginning, as a woman, not much as a poetess. For four-and-a-half years then I accumulated materials and sketched, fleshing out the target or vehicle, still under the impression that seven or eight stanzas would see it done. There are fifty-seven. My stupidity is traceable partly to an astuteness that made me as afraid as the next man of the ferocious commitment involved in a long poem and partly to the fact that although I had my form and subject, I did not have my theme yet. This emerged, and under the triple impetus of events I won't identify, I got the poem off the ground and nearly died following it. The theme is hard to put shortly but I will try.

An American historian somewhere observes that all colonial settlements are intensely conservative, *except* in the initial break-off point (whether religious, political, legal, or whatever). Trying to do justice to both parts of this obvious truth—which I came upon only after the poem was finished—I concentrated upon the second and the poem laid itself out in a series of rebellions. I had her rebel first against the new environment and above all against her barrenness (which in fact lasted for years), then against her marriage (which in fact seems to have been brilliantly happy), and finally against her continuing life of illness, loss, and age. These are the three large sections of the poem; they are preceded and followed by an exordium and coda, of four stanzas each, spoken by the "I" of the twentieth-century poet, which modulates into her voice, who speaks most of the poem. Such is the plan.

Each rebellion, of course, is succeeded by submission, although even in the moment of the poem's supreme triumph—the presentment, too long to quote now, of the birth of her first child—rebellion survives. I don't remember how conceptual all this was with me during the months of composition, but I think it was to a high degree. Turbulence may take you far toward a good short poem but, it is only the first quarter-mile in a long one.

Not that the going is ever exactly tranquil. I recall three occasions of special heat, the first being when I realized that the middle of the poem was going to have to be in *dialogue,* a dialogue between the seventeenth-century woman and the twentieth-century poet—a sort of extended witch-seductress and demon-lover bit. The second was a tactical solution of a problem arising out of this: how to make them in some measure physically present to each other. I gave myself one line, when she says:

A fading world I dust, with fingers new.

Later on it appears that they kiss, once, and then she says—as women will—"Talk to me." So he does. in an only half-subdued aria-stanza:

It is Spring's New England. Pussy willows wedge
up in the wet. Milky crestings, fringed
yellow, in heaven, eyed
by the melting hand-in-hand, or mere
desirers, single, heavy-footed, rapt,
make surge poor human hearts. Venus is trapt—
the hefty pike shifts, sheer—
in Orion blazing. Warblings, odours, nudge to an edge—

Noting and over-considering such matters, few critics have seen that it *is* an historical poem, and it was with interest that I found Mr. Robert Lowell pronouncing it lately, in *The New York Review,* "the most resourceful historical poem in our literature." The third pleasant moment I remember is when one night, hugging myself, I decided that her fierce dogmatic old father was going to die blaspheming, in delirium.

The Bradstreet poem was printed in 1953 (as a book here in

America in 1956 and in London in 1959) and a year or so later, having again taken leave of my wits, or collected them, I began a second long poem. The first installment, called 77 *Dream Songs* (recently published in New York) concerns the turbulence of the modern world, and memory, and wants. Its form comprises eighteen-line sections, three six-line stanzas, each normally (for feet) 5-5-3-5-5-3, variously rhymed and not but mostly rhymed with great strictness. The subject is a character named Henry, who also has a Friend who calls him "Mr. Bones." Here is the first section, or Song, where the "I," perhaps of the poet, disappears into Henry's first and third persons (he talks to himself in the second person too about himself).

Huffy Henry hid the day,
unappeasable Henry sulked.
I see his point,—a trying to put things over
It was the thought that they thought
they could do it made Henry wicked & away.
But he should have come out and talked.

All the world like a woolen lover
once did seem on Henry's side.
Then came a departure.
Thereafter nothing fell out as it might or ought.
I don't see how Henry, pried
open for all the world to see, survived.

What he has now to say is a long
wonder the world can bear & be.
Once in a sycamore I was glad
all at the top, and I sang.
Hard on the land wears the strong sea
and empty grows every bed.

This is Number One of Book One (the first volume consists of the first three books) and editors and critics for years have been characterizing them as poems but I do not quite see them as that; I see them as parts—admittedly more independent than parts usually are. Once one has succeeded in any degree with a long poem (votes have been cast in favor of, as well as against, *Homage to Mistress Bradstreet*) dread and fascination fight it out to exclude, on the whole, short poems thereafter or so I have found it. I won't try to explain what I mean by a long poem, but let us suppose (1) a high and prolonged riskiness, (2) the construction of a world rather than the reliance upon one already existent which is available to a small poem, (3) problems of decorum most poets happily do not have to face. I cannot discuss "decorum" here either, but here is a case:

> There sat down, once, a thing on Henry's heart
> so heavy, if he had a hundred years
> & more, & weeping, sleepless, in all them time
> Henry could not make good.
> Starts again always in Henry's ears
> the little cough somewhere, an odour, a chime.
>
> And there is another thing he has in mind
> like a grave Sienese face a thousand years
> would fail to blur the still profiled reproach of. Ghastly,
> with open eyes, he attends, blind.
> All the bells say: too late. This is not for tears;
> thinking.
>
> But never did Henry, as he thought he did,
> end anyone and hacks her body up
> and hide the pieces, where they may be found.
> He knows: he went over everyone, & nobody's missing.
> Often he reckons, in the dawn, them up.
> Nobody is ever missing.[5]

Whether the diction of that is consistent with blackface talk, hell-spinning puns, coarse jokes, whether the end of it is funny or frightening, or both, I put up to the listener. Neither of the American poets who as reviewers have quoted it admiringly has committed himself; so I won't.

[5] Reprinted from *77 Dream Songs* by John Berryman by permission of Farrar, Straus & Giroux, Inc. © 1959, 1962, 1963, 1964 by John Berryman.

9 THE LANDSCAPE OF AMERICAN POETRY IN 1964

Jack Gilbert

Poetry, for me, is a witnessing to magnitude. It is the art of making urgent values manifest and of imposing them on the reader. It is the housing of these values in poems, so they will exist with maximum pressure and for the longest time. It is the craft of doing so in structures that are a delight in themselves. And it is the mystery of fashioning poems in such a way that the form and the content are one.

What poetry chiefly is *not* for me is an entertainment. I recognize that there are other ways than mine to approach poetry: that for many it is an aesthetic recreation, the making of beautiful objects; or it is the congenial play of imagination over a subject; or it is an exercise in expertise. It is not so for me. There is a voice in me that stubbornly sings of a largeness beyond formal considerations; sings of love and death, god and evil, lust, honor, and the other major business of life. I believe these can be considered with profit. I am convinced that poetry is the best way to do so. I believe that poetry does make things happen—finally. I believe poetry deals with life—with my life. That it gives me my life more fully, and that it helps me in that direction in which I must proceed. Poetry is not, for me, a beautiful alternative to living.

This position is not fashionable in America today. The prevailing mood, set by the critics and a consensus of the respectable poets, is one of modesty. Most poets aspire to the adequate poem, not the important one. A masterpiece is thought of as something people used to write. And the critics, being nearly all scholarly, sedentary men, have imposed an aesthetic which insists that the primary values in poetry are those most available to a sedentary, scholarly life. For these critics, a poem is (as Robert Creeley says) "a machine of manner": a formal construct in which the content is ancillary. Most poets and critics are like well-behaved and highly educated visitors to a cathedral who are tactful, graceful, conscientious, and admiring. They are impressively respectful of the liturgy and informed about the true pendentive. But, to use a figure of Robert Penn Warren's, they do not come to pray.

This is not true of all poets nor of all critics, of course. It is not true of the best. I do not mean to disparage either twentieth-century American poetry or criticism. On the contrary, I feel the last fifty years have been the first golden age in our poetry. In the previous three centuries, this country produced only two major figures: Walt Whitman and Emily Dickinson; and they were individuals, not an age. Since 1914, however, we have had Ezra Pound, T. S. Eliot, Wallace Stevens, William Carlos Williams, Robert Frost, and Hart Crane; plus an abundance of the fine minor poets who are always the ground of an important epoch.

Certainly, it was a great time. But now we are entering upon a new one. In 1963, William Carlos Williams and Robert Frost died, as well as E. E. Cummings, Theodore Roethke, and Sylvia Plath. Suddenly it is apparent that we are at one of those invisible dividing points that historians deny and locate. Wallace Stevens and Hart Crane have been dead some time and T. S. Eliot has just died. Ezra Pound is almost eighty. All at once, one can feel an era ending.

At the same time, it persists—most importantly in the influence of Pound and Williams. Eliot, who reigned for so long, seems to have come to an end. He is rarely mentioned by young poets. Recently when I attended a symposium at Princeton University that included a representative cross section of the leading writers in America today, I did not hear Eliot mentioned once during the three days of conversation. He is a dominant force now only for those poets who believe they can will poems into being out of intelligence, scholarship, and indefatigable labor. These have made of him (with Eliot's help) a technology for old men. In contrast, Pound and Williams speak to the poets who are most alive in the world outside universities.

But despite this continuance, it is nevertheless clear to anyone wandering the poetry community of the United States now that the time of the elders is finished. There is a feeling that they were of that time, and that this time is ours. My quarrel is with the poetry that presents itself as a successor. It is exactly because the previous poetry was so great that I refuse to be tolerant of poetry that expects to prevail by default.

There is no scarcity of new poets, god knows; but they generally seem to be working at the top of their inconsiderable talent to produce a high level of mediocrity. And even the poets who are interesting seldom seem important—even potentially. Poets of the previous half-century had an appetite for something paramount. The ambition of most current ones seems to be either the satisfactory or the novel. Last year I was poetry editor (though briefly) of the literary magazine *Genesis West*. In my first three weeks, I rejected over five hundred poems. And I rejected them sadly, because the deadline for a new issue was near and I needed poems. But there was hardly anything usable. At least, not usable if one was looking for more than a minimum of distinction. Yet many of the manuscripts were from the poets who are published most often these days. When I tried to explain to them that I wanted significant poetry, not just something sufficient, they were shocked and resentful. It is evidently a demand not much heard now.

Instead, most poets in America today are concerned with their careers as poets far more than with their poetry. They devote their main energy to achieving a kind of journeymanship in one of the two factions that dominate our poetry now. This is attained usually not through the quality of the verse, but more by publishing poems of minimum merit often enough to establish gradually a membership in the guild. The nature of the guild automatically assures benefits to all active members; there are spoils to be distributed, and over a period of time, some will go to the lowest loyal, hardworking member—no matter how pedestrian.

One of these factions might be called the Establishment. Often it is termed academic poetry. The other has no name. It is usually referred to as Beat poetry, which it is not—except in part. It is sometimes called the American Underground. They might be thought of as the Left and Right in American poetry; the Conservative and the Radical. The divisions are Procrustean, but they approximate the components of what current serious poetry there is in this country.

The work of the Establishment is called academic poetry because the poets all teach in universities; but more because they are committed to a poetry concerned with traditional concepts of competence rather than to radical values in either content or form. In a broad sense they are committed to the status quo—or to a reasonable modification and improvement of it. Their poems are often critical of our society and its values, but they are clearly by men who are members in good standing whose minds are conditioned, even in the demurrer, by an affinity with it. It is like someone who is fluent only in English trying to judge objectively the merits of English poetry against the claims to beauty of poetry in another language.

The world of these poets is usually limited to a university environment, except for frantic sabbatical leaves which are spent in even greater seclusion from the world (either in an isolated spot or in the isolation of constant travel). They are usually gentlemen (or ladies), moderately prosperous, of good character, and hard workers. They publish regularly in solid literary quarterlies and periodically receive prizes. They know literature thoroughly, are well trained, highly skilled, and except for five or six have nothing to say.

They have nothing to say because they have no life in them pressing toward speech. Most have been in school all their lives as students and teachers. They have lived almost entirely in the artifice of that world, swathed against encounter in graciousness, nourished by association with bland people in hiding from the outside (and by association with immature minds—both leading to intellectual malnutrition), given words for experience, and trained to accommodate themselves always to the need for decorum. How can a man who has always depended on such an environment know anything of the earth? Of what can he speak as a veteran to me? Of course, the academics protest that they *have* had experience; but when you inquire further, it always proves to have been a quarter of a century earlier. But, they then protest, the academy is as much a real world as any other; there is conflict, jealousy, disappointment, ambition, venery, deceit, weakness, corruption, and all the other harsh realities. I would reply that one can find these also in a nunnery.

I insist that there is a vital difference between a locale and the world. There is a difference between mere existence and a life sufficient to the fact that we are all dying. Well, they persist, isn't family life one of the truly basic aspects of existence? Isn't it an important courage (as one professor asked me recently) to force oneself to take the garbage out each night year after year? I say that it is not courage; it is assiduity. I know that there is a difference between reality conceived of as suburban life and that which confronts things in their essence and huge importance: hunger, death, the beast we are, suffering, morality, loneliness, love, and the other great matters.

But love in marriage is love also, they cry. And so it is in a way; but usually it is something closer to tender friendship or patient disappointment. I am startled by how many men take it for granted they understand love just because they are married. I have little confidence in the opinion of a man whose total background in the subject has been some brief experiences in colleges followed by decades of proper marriage to one woman. It may be admirable, but it is unlikely to produce an expert. The truth is, I have found these long-married men bewilderingly innocent about women, love, or even lust. They equate love with loyal affectionateness, speaking as though the astounding magnitude love can be in its miraculousness is infatuation, and proper only to adolescents. As to understanding women, each is convinced that because he can recognize some of his wife's foibles, moods, and strategies he is an authority.

Similarly, I have found it impossible to rely on the judgment of such men about what to do in the face of danger, or significant temptation; how to act with fairness (as distinct from justice); what the good life is; or in fact any of the serious problems of life. Some wisdom can certainly be learned from books, but it must be joined to experience. Otherwise, it is like the Chinese crew who put into the kingdom of Prester John asking about unicorns. (After listening to the recitation of characteristics, the natives said "oh yes" and everyone set out on the great hunt. They caught the animal and carefully transported it home—

where, I have read, the word for "unicorn" in Chinese is still the same as the word for "giraffe.")

I find it difficult to trust these sequestered men about the things that matter to me; just as I would not ask the customers in a healthfood store for the best restaurant in town, nor ask a gardener about the forest. And I am deeply convinced that it is legitimate to question the competence of poets in such matters. If poetry is truly about man's life in any important way, then it is essential to know whether the poet is qualified to tell us significantly about it. And if it is objected that the poet is reporting someone else's understanding, then I would reply that I prefer the primary source. There can be true comprehension of these basic understandings only when the poet participates in the knowledge. The insight must be earned as much as the poem.

To be fair, one must admit that these academic poets are not concerned with speaking of the world. They want, instead, to make—to make a thing of beauty. Form is their content. And undeniably there is joy in a poem accomplishing its being. It is a fine, pure thing. But for me, if poetry is only that, it would not be enough to justify the investment of my life. If poetry were merely a felicity of form, I would enjoy it like chess or food; but I would not forego any large part of my life for it. If it is not about something that matters, it will never hold me beyond pleasure—however well made. The Greeks divided poets into craftsmen and perceivers. Both are equal, but one is always more equal than the other. If the content establishes its primacy too much at the expense of form, the result is prose. But if form becomes an Orpheus so concerned with the perfection of the song he is making about his journey, Eurydice will always be lost. The amount of important life that is communicated grows smaller and smaller. It is like Louis XIV asking for a hot cup of coffee: by the time it has passed through the marvelous hierarchies of who can pass it to whom, it is always tepid.

The content must be important if any large body of poetry is to be great. When one thinks of our really large poets, they are always men confused with the world: Chaucer, Shakespeare, Milton, Donne, Blake, Hopkins, Whitman, Byron, Hardy, Yeats. The content of *King Lear* or the *Bacchae* matters to me as much as their well-madeness. Content, that is, in terms of the important vision to be shared. I am not talking of the plot, nor of the simple presence of an idea. The knowledge in the poem must be *felt* knowledge, and preferably knowledge known directly. Love, for example, is not to be understood by dialectic alone. It must be experienced: not only, but also. Of course, the poem must always have sufficient form as well. My point is that it cannot be only one. Everyone seems to agree to this when it is proposed, but then they go right on talking in the universities about the poem being the best words in their best order as though the subject were merely an occasion for the poem. An old German once said to me about our marches: "This Sousa's music is always going *BOOTS, BOOTS, BOOTS, BOOTS.* The German marches also go *BOOTS, BOOTS, BOOTS;* but above the music is calling, 'Good-bye, my love. Good-bye, my love.' " There must be a voice above the craft singing meaningfully of the life of man.

I am perhaps too severe with academic poetry, but severity is necessary now—both because mediocrity grows like crab grass in a climate of politeness until it chokes out everything else and because it has already established such control of the power that conditions poetry: money, publication, publicity, anthologies, awards, and the like. Also because tolerance will allow people to evade the seriousness of poetry by praising harmless verses of domesticity. It encourages critics who say: We are genuinely anxious to hear more of your whale, Mr. Ahab, and we understand that a sailor learns to speak large so as to fill the sea's emptiness; but could you talk just a little softer? The room is so small and the children are asleep upstairs. . . . (A voice from the back will always add: And for god's sake stop those easy generalizations!)

Propriety is exactly what we should *not* ask of poetry. If it is important poetry, it is necessarily a disturbance of the peace. The best poets are never Good Joes, never housebroken. They threaten the shape and assumptions of our lives, stretching us toward what we are to be rather than easing us in what we are. Important poetry is likely to leave us in disarray. The poetry that is only a mild order is a wilderness.

The alternative to polite, academic poetry is what I have earlier called the American Underground. Most of these poets might justly be called bohemian. They live marginal existences, own few things, win no awards, and publish prolifically in a wide range of fugitive amateur magazines. Their work is always experimental, and much of it is avant-garde. The better part is redolent of the world. Despite its many shortcomings, this community has produced the bulk of what original poetry has been written in the last twenty-five years. Certainly, it has been the most significant *movement*.

The best known of these poets can be found in Donald Allen's anthology, *The New American Poetry: 1945–1960*. The forty-four names can be divided roughly into three elements: the Beat, the Black Mountain, and the New York group. The best known is the Beat movement. It developed around Allen Ginsberg in 1954 during what has been called the San Francisco Renaissance. It ended about 1957 when it was discovered by *Time* magazine and turned into a fad. The writers associated with Ginsberg in San Francisco were primarily Gary Snyder, Phil Whalen, Michael McClure, Gregory Corso, and novelist Jack Kerouac; but while all of these contributed to a Beat style of life, only Ginsberg and Corso really subscribed to the style of poetry which came to wear that name. This was the product of Ginsberg's belief that art falsifies communication and that we should therefore simply say directly what we feel. If the thing was felt strongly and truly enough, it was supposed to come out a poem. This Orphic Fallacy (as Dudley Fitts called it) is now popular among only very young or very innocent poets. Ginsberg's own work, however, is sometimes of a very high quality.

The Black Mountain element developed a little earlier at Black Mountain College in North Carolina. Its mentor and chief theoretician is Charles Olson. Its best poets are Robert Creeley and Robert Duncan. The major concern is for exploring the technical aspects of poetic theory. In practice this means approaching the poem as a field of energy, insisting on speech rhythms and demotic vocabulary, relying on "open" forms instead of the traditional fixed forms, and trying for objective rather than subjective content. (The theories can best be found in Olson's essay, "Projective Verse.") The poetry of this group is the most vital and influential in America today.

Finally, the New York group is a younger generation that came to the fore in New York about five years ago. It derives mostly from the Black Mountain tradition, but with an uneasy incorporation of the Beat mystique. Its most important poets are Denise Levertov, LeRoi Jones, and Frank O'Hara. Unfortunately, for all their talent, a prohibitive part of the energy of this group (with the exception of Levertov) is wasted on shock poems and joke poems.

Such frivolousness is a frequent fault in this Underground poetry. The Beat poets, the Black Mountain people, and the New York group are generally self-indulgent. All but the very best are content with the approximate poem. They produce a flood of trivial poems that don't have even the excuse of technical finish. If the academic poets often seem to be doing something very well that isn't worth doing at all, these others tend to deal with matters of real importance with slovenliness. Moreover, they usually treat fairly rudimentary ideas as great profundity. The academics spend their art on fashioning a mechanical lily; the alternate faction usually is busy discovering that a rose is a rose is a rose. (This last is a true insight, but it does not sustain a reader's interest very long.)

It is obvious that bad writing and simplistic thinking cannot make good poetry, no matter how strange the format. As Howard Nemerov has said: "Civilization, mirrored in language, is the garden where relations grow; outside the garden is the wild abyss." If the mind is content with only the first giant step of exploration, the abyss is soon a poverty—and boring. Too often these poets reveal a coarseness of sensibility and an impatience of temperament that closes them away from all but the obvious. Frequently the passion for reality declines to a fondness for remembering with great precision details from the comic books we read as children. It becomes an obsession with the insufficiently important shock of recognition. The product is poetry that is strange but unimportant.

Thus, we are often asked today to choose between these two factions: between the vacant academic exercise and the petty novelty. It is like one of those debates in which you are supposed to defend either legal murder or sentimental permissiveness. It is a choice between Versailles and Stanleyville. Neither is acceptable.

I do not speak so exigently of the present poetry in America from an easy impulse to find fault. Rather, I do so out of love for and loyalty to the quality of the poetry which was produced in the United States in the first half of this century; and in the belief that such an insistence on excellence is the best way to produce equally great poetry in the next fifty years. Finally, I so insist out of admiration for those poets who are already at work on such poetry; poets like Robert Lowell, Robert Creeley, Stanley Kunitz, Robert Duncan, Allen Ginsberg, and Richard Wilbur. Praise to them.

I would like to conclude with one of my own poems—one that tries to say in poetry what I have here been saying in prose.

For Example[1]

For example, that fragment of entablature
In the Museo della Terme. It continues,
Giant so, forever. Without seasons.
Ambergris of the Latin whale.
For three years I have carried it
In me, with the sad other love.
Dealt with it month by month
In my white room above Perugia,
While thousands of swifts turned
In the structures of sun with a sound
Like glass. Every week the professors
Went home, unconfused. Back
To America. While I endlessly followed
The empty streets of Rome.
Working to accommodate it. Singing
According to whether its bells
Pre-empted the dark, or whether
Rain ordered the earth.
And later still, in summer
On the lower East Side even,
I tried to acknowledge that merit.

It is impossible that tigers mate.

[1] Reprinted from *Genesis West* (Fall 1962). Copyright 1962 by The Chrysalis West Foundation.

10 WHAT IS A POET?

Vassar Miller

I have always felt in writing about poetry (my own or anybody else's) that it was rather like theology—a little goes a long way. Not that I wish to be a literary idiot any more than a theological one. But just as for a person who has the art, it must be more wonderful to serve God than to discuss Him, so it is more engaging to write a poem than to describe the process of writing it.

However, Mr. Nemerov's questions intrigued me by recalling me to an order long lost since college days. They summoned me to explain exactly how a poem stands on its own feet. They reminded me of just what a poem does. So, I shall stick my neck out without further explanation. For why not? As I point out in a poem called "Or as Gertrude Stein Says":

> a poem is only
> taking a child's down skull
> gently between your hands
> and, with not so much breath as might
> startle a gnat's wing,
> whispering,
> "Look!"[1]

But, after all, like a reluctant student, I put off taking my examination.

I

Has your poetry changed in character or style?

[1] From Vassar Miller, *My Bones Being Wiser* (Middletown, Conn.: Wesleyan University Press, 1963), p. 43. "Or as Gertrude Stein Says" is © 1962 by Vassar Miller.

In character, no. In style, yes. In character, I find myself essentially the same human being that I was when a child. But in appearance I have changed. The character of a poem reflects the character of the poet. And what appearance is to a person, style is to a poem.

The character of my poetry is no different from that of other poetry. To make my point more precise, my character as a poet differs not a bit from that of other poets. Two years ago a small religious press asked me to edit an anthology of religious poetry with appropriate comments. Although the anthology never saw light, I did manage to write the introduction entitled, as this essay is, "What Is a Poet?"

My definition must have shocked that small religious press out of fifty-two Sundays' growth, because what I said was this: a poet is someone who falls in love with whatever and whomever he likes and no one, not even all the Mrs. Grundys of the world, has cause for a single complaint. This is another way of saying that the poet is a child. For a child is frequently charged with "going crazy" or "going off the deep end" over something or other. If he is wise, he ignores the accusation. If not, he may grow up, if society is lucky, to be a poet instead of a criminal. I said that all the Mrs. Grundys of the world have no cause for complaint, but they often find cause just the same.

With what, then, am I (as a poet, of course) in love? For poets have been in love with any number of things. Shelley, for instance, had a brief but ardent encounter with a skylark, much to the despair of every hapless student who must recite, at one time or another, "Hail to thee, blithe spirit,/Bird thou never wert," wishing devoutly that the latter phrase were not so. But, alas, for Shelley the mythical bird was all too real. Yeats fell in love with the Never-never land of Byzantium. T. S. Eliot had a long-standing affair with Anglo-Catholicism, monarchy, and aristocracy. No wonder most of his *Four Quartets* are so abstract! A child cannot get his arms around abstractions. Eliot recovers his poetry in the aforementioned poem with such lyrics as "The wounded surgeon plies the steel." Here he is expressing what he has experienced. And in so doing he also comes closer to the Christianity he embraced. For Christianity is the religion of the Word-made-flesh and poetry is its most natural voice.

To continue: Hart Crane fell in love with a bridge; Dylan Thomas with "the force that through the green fuse drives"; and Hopkins fell in love with a windhover, a blacksmith, dawn, speckled things, the whole of creation, and God Himself. So does every poet, secretly, even though he may with fury deny it. That is why every poet is, as Rupert Brooke called himself avowedly, "the Great Lover." So is Everyman. The poet is simply more keenly aware of it and goes around wearing his heart on his sleeve and its unfortunate counterpart, a chip on his shoulder. No poet worth his salt was ever all sweetness and light. He has too often been ridiculed for being indiscriminate with his affections.

And I? For in the end I am all I shall ever know of "every poet." One example may suffice, although, of course, it will not cover everything:

Trimming the Sails[2]

I move among my pots and pans
That have no life except my own,
Nor warmth save from my flesh and bone,
That serve my tastes and not a man's.

I'm jealous of each plate and cup,
Frail symbol of my womanhood.
Creator-like, I call it good
and vow I will not give it up.

I move among my things and think
Of Woolman, who, for loving care
He had for slaves, used wooden ware,
And wash my silver in the sink.

Wishing my knives and forks were finer.
Though Lady Poverty won heart

2 From Vassar Miller, *My Bones Being Wiser* (Middletown, Conn.: Wesleyan University Press, 1963), p. 56. "Trimming the Sails" is © 1963 by Vassar Miller.

Of Francis, her male counterpart
Would find in me a sad decliner.

Sometimes regret's old dogs will hound me
With feeble barks, yet my true love
Is Brother Fire and Sister Stove
And walls and friends and books around me.

Yet to renounce your high romances
Being part pain—may so to do
Prove half humility that you
May bless, good Woolman and sweet Francis!

Some of this poem implies that I am in love with God myself, at
least a little. For the poet, says the Abbé Bremond, is a *mystique
manqué,* an aborted or frustrated mystic. The mystic, Bremond
explains, beholds the Ineffable Vision and it lures him over the
threshold of silence. Whereas the poet takes a quick peek and
scurries back while there is still time to tell what he has glimpsed.
However, one could quarrel with the Abbé because, in the first
place, mystics have been rather wordy in trying to describe the
indescribable. In the second place, mystics, especially those who
are Christians, are evangelists at heart. Some, like St. John of the
Cross, have been poets. But let us be fair to the non-Christians,
for what else is a Zen riddle like "to clap with one hand," except
a poem?

Yet, assuming that Bremond is correct, the poet cannot be a
pure mystic. Otherwise he would take the advice of the ancient
Chinese, "He who knows does not speak; he who speaks does not
know," and put himself out of a job. The poet has good news to
tell, in Richard Wilbur's phrase, of "the things of this world"—
even if it is only bad news, because in poetry, as indeed in all art,
the ugly, the painful, even the obscene, become transmuted. A
transubstantiation takes place as in the Holy Eucharist when we
give thanks for the Bread and the Wine, the symbols and the
sacraments of what were once agony and death. I did not think
about it at the time I wrote it, but this very idea is implicit in
the poem "For a Christening."

For a Christening[3]

Like the first man to glance
Into a face and fathom
The word as welcome, dance
The common human rhythm;
Like all fish or fawn that came
At Adam's cry, or dove—
So you are what we name,
And what we name we love.

Or like the stars recorded
By shepherds who had striven
With wonder and thus worded
The wilderness of heaven,
Shy creature growing tame,
Taken from womb's dense grove—
You now are what we name
When what we name we love.

One with all precious things
Called from the dusk of death,
Rose-texture, whir of wings,
Garrisoned with our breath—
You wear its sheath of flame
Around, beneath, above
You, being what we name
For you are what we love.

One with the sacred powers
Man cradles on his tongue
During time's timeless hours
Whereon his heart is hung—
In the adoring frame
Made by our arms, you move;
For you are what we name,
And what we name we love.

---

3 From Vassar Miller, *Wage War on Silence* (Middletown, Conn.: Wesleyan University Press, 1963), p. 38. "For a Christening" is © 1963 by Vassar Miller.

In the Name of the Three in One,
More awesome still than ours,
From whence your mystery spun,
Wherein it yet endures,
Speaking, though holy shame
Would silence us, we prove
How what we love we name
How what we name we love!

The refrain expresses what a mother feels for her child, and the child, when angry and stubborn, is not good news to its mother. But she, like Adam and the good shepherd, calls it by name and the child knows her voice. Likewise, "you are what we name/ When what we name we love," the poet says impartially to his troubles and his joys. For sometimes the poet has no other children.

I was still thinking of the poet as *mystique manqué*, when I described in my poem entitled "Contemplative," a nun

washing with words
from her clear springs of singing
a dark world white.[4]

If a poet cannot afford to be a pure mystic, he cannot always afford to be pious. Blake did not always sound pious, nor did Burns. Baudelaire was a scandal to the faithful; Rimbaud's blasphemies resulted from a piety gone mad. Even good Jesuit Hopkins wrote his "Terrible Sonnets." I am not Hopkins' equal, but maybe a small church press would consider my poem "Reverent Impiety" terrible in a different sense.

Reverent Impiety[5]

I will not fast, for I have fasted longer
Than forty days and known a leaner Lent

[4] From Vassar Miller, *My Bones Being Wiser* (Middletown, Conn.: Wesleyan University Press, 1963), p. 71. "Contemplative" is © 1963 by Vassar Miller.

[5] From Vassar Miller, *My Bones Being Wiser* (Middletown, Conn.: Wesleyan University Press, 1963), p. 14. "Reverent Impiety" is © 1963 by Vassar Miller.

Than can be kept with ceremonial hunger.
Since life's a lengthier season to repent
Than the brief time when spring's first winds may tease
The misereres chanted on our knees,
And ritual tears that I such hours have wept
Mirror a double and a muddy vision
That would not win a blessing from a priest.
Hence, purity born from my pain's precision
Refuses here to fast upon a feast,
Glutted till now on sacraments of air,
Memorials to loves that never were.

I say "maybe." For I have found charity in the most hidebound churchgoer as well as smugness in self-styled nonconformists. There are nominal pagans as well as nominal Christians. The poet has a better chance of converting the first group. The nominal pagan does not know what he disbelieves. Frequently the poet does not either. But as Amos Wilder remarked, A poet like Wallace Stevens, who writes about oranges and sex and Sunday mornings, is often more incarnational than many a preacher of the Gospel, who bids his congregation to go home and pray about the matter. Jesus said, "Man shall not live by bread alone," but he said it to the devil, not to the hungry multitudes whom He fed.

Yet the poet is suspect in any group. I shall never forget a musical comedy in which a well-known fan-dancer had a small part. She was late. So, what happened? A police escort, sirens screaming, rushed her from the airport so that she could wiggle her hips for a few minutes. I turned to my friend and said bitterly, "A famous poet could come to town walking barefoot and ragged, and nobody would notice." "But a poet wouldn't care," he replied. I'm not sure that I agree. I must have cared a good deal when I wrote "Note to the Reader."

Note to the Reader[6]

This book, these sheets of paper you pick up

And toss aside for being only ink—

[6] From Vassar Miller, *My Bones Being Wiser* (Middletown, Conn.: Wesleyan University Press, 1963), p. 83. "Note to the Reader" is © 1963 by Vassar Miller.

This is soul's sweat and bile, black slag, outcrop
Of heart's New England, apples of its stone.
I loafed to write it, but, how toilingly
Prone on the earth and felt it knock
Hard on my breasts and belly, needling me
With grass for fingers, muttering, "Unlock!"
It may be luxury that wind has mussed
My skirt and blouse, to coax my body bare,
Or that my maid's the wind, my suitor's dust,
My bed and boudoir everywhere nowhere,
Yes, call it ease—but name my book's each word
What angels flask to pour before their Lord!

But, lest I belabor an already belabored point, I hasten to add
that poets, as everyone who has interested himself in the subject
knows, are the greatest conformists of them all. Witness not only
the Beats, but also the ladies' poetry circle as well. Often, too, a
poet is rejected by his own circle if he starts being "different" or
is different to begin with. His fellow poets didn't exactly like it
when Eliot got religion and viewed his conversion as detrimental
to his poetry. If he had ever recanted, the good Christian brethren
who regard him as a trophy for the Lord would not have liked it
any better. Enough said. All of us would enjoy being at ease in
Zion, and, if we are not, we cry, "Woe!"

I come to the next question which seems to me only a restate-
ment of the first in broader terms.

II

*Is there, has there been, was there ever, a "revolution" in
poetry, or is it all only a matter of a few sleazy tricks? What is
the relation of your work to this question, if there is a relation?*

If by revolution one means change, of course there has been
one. Nothing remains static, whether it be styles in locomotion,
women's dresses, or literature. The Elizabethans wrote as they did
—in round, rhetorical style—probably because men had just discovered that the earth was round, were busy making voyages of
discovery, and felt for one golden moment that they had the

world by the tail. The poets of the 1920's wrote as they did—
E. E. Cummings' poems, for example, appearing as if the words
were about to take off from the page—because World War I had
irrevocably shattered the peace of Victoria. People were living it
up and poets were making their small contribution.

During the 1950's after World War II, people apparently did
not relish a reaction similar to that of the "mad" 1920's. Perhaps
there was too much chance of an atomic hangover. So here came
the New Traditionalists, embracing urbaneness and respecta-
bility. But the Space Age dawned simultaneously when the
heavens no longer declared for the majority the glory of God but
the terror of man lest he destroy himself, not to mention the
petty fright of some men lest America or Russia reach the moon
first. These facts may account for the Beats who produce opuses
like "Howl" and thumb their noses at the whole mess.

But there am I, attempting to sound like a college textbook or
literary journal, when the main point is how poetic revolutions
affect me. Well, I suppose any change in the air affects the most
secluded person. Emily Dickinson, who rarely left the house,
poked sly, outrageous fun at her stuffy Victorian heritage, as if
she felt the oncoming turn of the poetic climate in her bones.
I, too, led a sheltered life, although far less sheltered than hers,
and my personal literary history is this.

My earliest poem was to my mother. Even at the tender age of
eight, I had some sense of poetry as something apart from mere
sentiment. I remember her remonstrating with me for referring
to her hair as "gray," whereas it was really brown. "I couldn't
find a rhyme for 'brown,'" I explained. I hate to admit that I
took the easy way out! Yet I was dimly aware that poetry has a
life of its own that the shade of my mother's hair did not influence.

After that, as well as I can remember, my poetic activity lay
dormant until adolescence. I cannot say much for my poetry except that it was dreadfully pious and sounded like bad hymns.
My childhood and youth were lonely and religion—a rather
private affair—was an attempt at compensation. However, in high
school I won a prize and one or two of my poems appeared in a
high school anthology. I doubt whether the fact that I wrote the

class poem belongs in any literary history, even my own, still less that I wrote a parody of it twenty years later!

At any rate, I became aware of the sonnet and through college worked on that form. It had a neatness and an order that appealed to me, and I still like it. Its symmetrical fourteen lines formed a whole which my mind could grasp and harnessed an inner chaos. E. A. Robinson and Gerard Manley Hopkins were my first conscious influences. I liked Robinson for his lonely, spartan spirit, and was fascinated by Hopkins' taut metrics. I still feel better than I understand sprung rhythm. My first poem published in a magazine of any worth was "The Final Hunger," written under the influence of Hopkins.

The Final Hunger[7]

Hurl down the nerve-gnarled body hurtling head-
long into sworls of shade-hush. Plummeting, keep
The latch of eyelids shut to so outleap
Care's claws. Arms, legs, abandon grace and spread
Your spent sprawl—glutton ravening to be fed
With fats, creams, fruits, meats, spice that heavy-heap
The hands, that golden-gloss the flesh, of sleep,
Sleep, the sole lover that I take to bed.

But they couch crouching in the darkness, city
Of awakefulness uncaptured by assaulting—
Senses by sleep unravished and unwon.
Sun-sword night-sheathed, lie never between (have pity!)
Between me and my love, between me and the vaulting
Down the dense sweetness of oblivion.

During the past four years my style has loosened up considerably. I am no longer devoted so single-mindedly to the traditional strict verse forms. I say "traditional," because I have found what many another poet has before me, that so-called free verse has its disciplines. Robert Frost compared writing free verse to playing

---

[7] From Vassar Miller, *Wage War on Silence* (Middletown, Conn.: Wesleyan University Press, 1963), p. 21. "The Final Hunger" is © 1956 by Vassar Miller.

tennis without a net. I prefer the analogy of a spider weaving its web. A web does not grow any old way and neither does a free-verse poem. Nothing in this wide, weary world just grows like Topsy. Any real creation is forged from the agony of joy and sorrow. Nothing comes free, not even freedom, which according to classical Christian theology, is God's most precious gift to man. It is also His most perilous, because through it man has (as I complain in my poem "Complaint") "The full liberty to go to Hell."

In short, I've finally caught up with the "revolution" in my own small way, or maybe the revolution has caught up with me and won't let me go. I still like the older forms and of late have been using more of them—more rhyme, more rhetoric. In any case, each poet must ultimately make the current revolution his own.

I have also fought a battle against abstraction, which, to my mind, is death to poetry. I have won it insofar as I have dared to let my poems grow out of me, out of my flesh and bones, and not merely out of my ideas about something. For although a poem may have meanings hidden from its author, no artistic creation has any life that has not come from its creator.

Every revolution gives way to and is borne away by some other revolution and becomes old. Then a still newer revolution occurs and perhaps repeats an old revolution in some ways, but only in some ways. For "the trees bloom on forever,/But with the same leaves never." I was not thinking of poetry when I wrote these melancholy lines, but I might well have. For sometimes when the room falls quiet and my friends' voices die away, I, who have never wanted to be left alone to do nothing but write, share the secret fear of all artists that history will judge their works as bad, or worse, as merely indifferent. Immediately I shrug my shoulders and tell myself that history's future verdict is none of my business; my business is to write and let the devil take the hindmost.

I say that I have never wanted to do nothing except write, but I doubt that any other writer does either. For any writer, any poet, feeds on the world he writes about. The fame that may be achieved from his writing may be his only conscious goal; nevertheless, that goal is something apart from his writing.

I see that I have already answered the third question.

III

Does the question whether the world has changed during this century preoccupy you in poetry? Does your work appear to you to envision the appearance of a new human nature, for better or worse, or does it view the many and obvious changes as essentially technological?

All poets mirror the ever-altering world, each in his own way, and I in mine. The change in this present century need not preoccupy my poetry; for it *is* my poetry, just as it is every poet's. I wrote "Columbus Dying" before the onset of the Space Age. Yet in this poem Columbus becomes a myth representing the dread of the "Old order giving way before the new":

Columbus Dying[8]

His men in fever, scabs, and hunger pains—
He found a world and put to scorn his scorners.
Yet having learned the living sea contains
No dragons gnawing on drowned sailors' brains,
He missed the angels guarding the four corners,
And begged that he be buried with his chains

In token that he'd sworn to serve as thrall
His vision of men creeping to and fro,
Gum-footed flies glued to a spinning ball,
Whether they tumble off earth's edge or crawl
Till dropped dead in their tracks from vertigo,
He deemed would make no difference at all.

But I am glad to see more than the fear of change in the poems of my new book *My Bones Being Wiser*. Fear of change there is in them, yes, but also a knowledge that the change must occur. As a Christian, I do envision the appearance of a new humanity, which is certainly not the result of technological changes. Space ships and rockets do not affect the facts of sin and redemption.

8 From Vassar Miller, *Wage War on Silence* (Middletown, Conn.: Wesleyan University Press, 1963), p. 16. "Columbus Dying" is © 1956 by Vassar Miller.

The concept of the new humanity, the new Adam, as represented in Christ, is implicit in the title of my first book, *Adam's Footprint* and its title poem:

Adam's Footprint[9]

Once as a child I loved to hop
On round plump bugs and make them stop
Before they crossed a certain crack.
My bantam brawn could turn them back,
My crooked step wrenched straight to kill
Live pods that then screwed tight and still.

Small sinner, stripping boughs of pears,
Shinnied past sweet and wholesome airs,
How could a tree be so unclean?
Nobody knows but Augustine.
He nuzzled pears for dam-sin's dugs—
And I scrunched roly-poly bugs.

No wolf's imprint or tiger's trace
Does Christ hunt down to catch with grace
In nets of love the devious preys
Whose feet go softly all their days;
The foot of Adam leaves the mark
Of some child scrabbling in the dark.

True, this poem is about the old Adam, but the old Adam as redeemed by the new. In a sonnet I call the new Adam, the new Icarus, the One who outsoars pain by transforming that pain into the wings of a cross. The same idea is expressed negatively in "Paradox," in which a human being is described as literally choking to death on the realization that he must surrender to God, "Sweet bread and wine, bitter to me not sharing,/You scar and scorch the throat that will not take you."

The new Adam, or the new as implicit in the old, is less cramped in my second book. "Adam's Footprint" describes him

9 From Vassar Miller, *Wage War on Silence* (Middletown, Conn.: Wesleyan University Press, 1963), p. 9. "Adam's Footprint" is © 1956 by Vassar Miller.

as "some child scrabbling in the dark." This poem came as a result of my brooding over a crime committed by a deranged mother, who seemed no more responsible than her two children whom she had murdered. In "Joyful Prophecy," on the other hand, Adam is no more terrible than my little nephew, but that is all right. Here I have caught him laughing and in his native habitat, one foot out of Eden or just about to step into the New Jerusalem.

Joyful Prophecy[10]

If he is held in love,
the thin reeds of my baby's bones
are pipes for it, it hums
and chuckles from the hollows
as a flower whispers,
it ripples off him, suave
honey of the sunlight
stored for his kin, his kind, such lovely
mirrors of it, he
is tempted to hoard it in
his well where he may gaze at it,
yet held in love and gracious
he shares it with his sister;
but, lest death waste it on the wind,
love measures him for the man
who can hold its heartiness
fermented to a man's delight,
if he is held in love.

Poetry, whether consciously or not, tends to see life under a Christian aspect. For poetry, I have long believed, has a trinitarian function. For instance, in the lines just quoted, I have made a poem out of the nonpoetic material of my thoughts and emotions. Thus, a poem is, in a sense, a making out of nothings, which in Christianity defines the work of God the Father. "A poem should not mean, but be," says Archibald MacLeish. Its meaning

10 From Vassar Miller, *Wage War on Silence* (Middletown, Conn.: Wesleyan University Press, 1963), p. 40. "Joyful Prophecy" is © 1960 by Vassar Miller.

lies in its being. No amount of words can explain it. A poet can only point to his work, once he has done the best he can with it, and say with the God of Genesis, "Behold, it is very good." Of course, he can say it only in a very relative way, because no poet can know when he has done his best, and no human creation is ever finished. If no poem, as I have already said, just grows like Topsy, any poem has a growth, almost a will, of its own. To be specific, a poem usually comes to me in its own meter. Sometimes, however, it will fool me, and what I intended as a sonnet may end as a free-verse lyric or vice versa. More important, I most frequently know what I want to say only in the saying. Experience has taught me that although a poet is a god, he is a finite one indeed.

Some poets do not write their poems down until fully conceived, like Minerva from the brow of Zeus—not so with me. I have to learn by doing and to write by writing. I must struggle to pull a single line from the chaos of thought and feeling. Sometimes I write a poem quickly; at other times a phrase or a metaphor will lie at the bottom of my mind for years. So it was with the crucial metaphor of "Though He Slay Me," the metaphor of God's yes being distorted into a no by our ears.

"Though He Slay Me"[11]

Still tell me no, my God, and tell me no
Till I repeat the syllable for a song,
Or hold it when my mouth is cracked like clay
Cold for a pebble underneath my tongue;
Or to my comfort as my father's stir
In sleep once solaced my child's heart that knew
Although he did not waken he was near,
Still tell me no, my God, still tell me no
And opening thus the wound that will never heal
Save torn once more, as Jacob's in his thigh,
Chafed by the hand that dealt it, was made whole,
Still tell me no, my God, still tell me no
Until I hear in it only the hush

11 From Vassar Miller, *Wage War on Silence* (Middletown, Conn.: Wesleyan University Press, 1963), p. 60. "Though He Slay Me" is © 1960 by Vassar Miller.

Between Good Friday's dusk and Easter Day,
The lullaby that locked his folded lash—
I lulled to a like darkness with Your no,
No, no, still no, the echo of Your Yes
Distorted among the crevices and caves
Of the coiled ear which deep in its abyss
Resolves to music all Your negatives.

So it was with the title poem of "Wage War on Silence." I fear that I wrote it determined that the phrase "wage war on silence" should appear in it, a bad thing to do in general because any setting of the stage in poetry suggests artificiality, which is death to the poetic genius. But the phrase suggests the very nature of poetry, which is a war waged with the silence of misunderstanding between men, with the silence of God that Christ endured on the Cross, summing up in Himself our individual endurances. One critic protested that "Wage War on Silence" is an awkward title, but waging war on silence is an awkward thing to do. Indeed, I consider my sonnet "Without Ceremony," which incorporates the phrase, an awkward poem.

Without Ceremony[12]

Except ourselves, we have no other prayer;
Our needs are sores upon our nakedness.
We do not have to name them, we are here.
And You who can make eyes can see no less.
We fall, not on our knees, but on our hearts,
A posture humbler far and more downcast;
While Father Pain instructs us in the arts
Of praying, hunger is the worthiest fast.
We find ourselves where tongues cannot wage war
On silence (farther, mystics never flew)
But on the common wings of what we are,
Borne on the wings of what we bear, toward You,
Oh Word, in whom our wordiness dissolves,
When we have not a prayer except ourselves.

[12] From Vassar Miller, *Wage War on Silence* (Middletown, Conn.: Wesleyan University Press, 1963), p. 3. "Without Ceremony" is © 1958 by Vassar Miller.

But at least it intimates the redemptive nature of poetry, which raises the pain of life onto the level of beauty and intensifies the joy of life into a sacrament.

To give the joy and pain of life a new meaning is also to sanctify it. I see poetry, or my poetry at least, as setting the disparate events of time into a pattern. Somebody has said that *Hamlet* would be only a sordid tale of lust and murder had not Shakespeare touched it with his genius. King Lear would be merely another senile, selfish man had not Shakespeare exalted him to the level of poetry. I regard the most wretched of days as not wholly wasted when I have dragged it from the desert of disorder with a poem. Certainly, when I wrote "Love's Eschatology" I was not thinking of poetry, but with a poem we do indeed "view all for the first time forever/through the lens of the last," the hour of the new humanity.[13]

Poets, by their very nature, must have this vision. Why else would they be in love with everything, even with the bad? It is because the light forever shines through the darkness. I have forged this theory of poetry from the realities of my own life.

"Loneliness"[14]

So deep is this silence
that the insects, the birds,
the talk of the neighbors in the distance,
the whir of the traffic, the music
are only its voices
and do not contradict it.

So deep is this crying
that the silence, the hush,
the quiet, the stillness, the not speaking,
the never hearing a word
are only the surge
of its innumerable waters.

---

[13] Miller, *My Bones Being Wiser, op. cit.,* p. 72.

[14] From Vassar Miller, *Wage War on Silence* (Middletown, Conn.: Wesleyan University Press, 1963), p. 3. "Loneliness" is © 1963 by Vassar Miller.

This silence, this crying,
O my God, is my country
with Yours the sole footstep besides my own.
Save me amid its landscapes
so terrible, strange
I am almost in love with them!

Yet a poem about loneliness would not be possible if the poet writing it were not aware of its opposite. Hence, a poet has to share a Christian vision of life, whether he knows it or not, because he sits over against the chaos of his own experience and out of its nothingness makes a poem, redeems it by giving it meaning, and gives it meaning simply by writing it.

I frankly cannot affirm that the new Adam, the new humanity, is fully awake in my poetry yet. I doubt that he ever will be. I doubt that he will ever be alive in anybody's poetry for the simple reason that he has not appeared in the world except in Christ. Poets know this fact and that is why no poet worth his salt makes his poetry out of nothing but sweetness and light.

All the same my bones are wiser, as the title of my last book implies, if only because they are older. Any poet's bones are wiser, since he knows better than his more practical contemporaries not only that all religion is not conducted in the churches (which has been said so often that it is too easy to say), but also that the real business of living is not carried on in the banks. And that assertion no nonpoet can endure, including myself. I say myself, because every poet contains a nonpoet, just as every nonpoet conceals a poet. So every Christian has a sinner within him, and every sinner hides a Christian. A famous evangelist criticized the Gloria in Excelsis because in the midst of its praises it allows the plaintive cry "Lord, have mercy upon us." The evangelist showed a deplorable lack of poetic insight, which forever perceives the ambiguity of life. The title poem of my new book may at least show this much perception.

My answer to the final question seems, then, almost too obvious to put into words.

IV

Is there a species of criticism which you agree with?

I agree with that species of criticism which can grasp the intention of a given poet and point it out to the discerning reader.
I become disgusted with any critic who would force the poet into
a preconceived mold, who, for instance, would try to make a
Freudian or a Jungian, or for that matter a Catholic or a Protestant, out of Shakespeare. I grow downright angry with the critic
who would stop a poet after every other word to ask him what
he means. Such a critic analyzes a poem away, like the college
professor who is interested only in tracing Shakespeare's sources.
I had such a professor, who once asked a gangling, lazy student
to trace the origin of the fairies in *A Midsummer Night's Dream*.
The big, drowsy student roused himself long enough from his
nap to grumble, "I dunno. Looks like Shakespeare could have
had some ideas for himself." The boy proceeded to go back to
sleep, but not before his casual remark had proved him pro-
founder than many a pedant.

I have even had disputes with people over the question of to
which persons some of my poems were written. A good critic
knows that whenever a poet dedicates a poem to a friend, he
always has somebody else looking over his shoulder, that somebody else being himself, everybody he has ever really known, and
God. That is why, incidentally, I some time ago resolved to dedi-
cate my books only to my small nephews and whatever nieces
may be in the offing. The young cannot protest and their parents
are too busy to discover whether they should make any protest in
their name. By addressing my poems to the innocent care of children, I can safely give the risky gift of my love to everybody.

11 TOWARDS AN OPEN UNIVERSE

Robert Duncan

I was born January 7, 1919, in the hour before dawn, in the depth of winter at the end of a war. When I think of the hour, from their obscurity the tree at the window, the patterned curtain, the table and chair, the bowl of golden glass upon the chest of drawers are just emerging into view. Sleeping and waking fuse, things seen in an inner light mingle with things searched out by eyes that are still dim. Day "breaks," we say, and the light floods out over the land. The shining planets and the great stars, the galaxies beyond us, grow invisible in light of our sun.

The imagination of this cosmos is as immediate to me as the imagination of my household or my self, for I have taken my being in what I know of the sun and of the magnitude of the cosmos, as I have taken my being in what I know of domestic things. In the coda of the poem "Apprehensions," the "First Poem" calls upon the birth of life itself in the primal waters and may call upon my birth hour:

> It is the earth turning
> that lifts our shores from the dark
> into the cold light of morning,
> eastward turning,
>
> and that returns us from the sun's burning
> into passages of twilight and doubt,
> dim reveries and gawdy effects.
> The sun is the everlasting center of what we know,
> a steady radiance.

The changes of light in which we dwell,
colors among colors that come and go,
are in the earth's turning.

Angels of light! raptures of early morning!
your figures gather what they look like
out of what cells once knew of dawn,
first stages of love that in the water thrived.

So we think of sperm
as spark-fluid, many-millioned,
in light of the occult egg striking
doctrine.
          Twined angels of dark,
hornd master-reminders of from-where!
your snake- or animal-red eyes
store the fire's glare.

O flames! O reservoirs![1]

   In the very beginnings of life, in the source of our cadences,
with the first pulse of the blood in the egg then, the changes of
night and day must have been there. So that in the configuration
of the living, hidden in the exchanging orders of the chromosome
sequences from which we have our nature, the first nature, child
of deep waters and of night and day, sleeping and waking, remains.
   We are, all the many expressions of living matter, grand-
children of Gaia, Earth, and Uranus, the Heavens. Late born, for
the moon and ocean came before. The sea was our first mother
and the sun our father, so our sciences picture the chemistry of
the living as beginning in the alembic of the primal sea quickened by rays of the sun and even, beyond, by radiations of the
cosmos at large. Tide-flow under the sun and moon of the sea,
systole and diastole of the heart, these rhythms lie deep in our

   [1] The lines from "Apprehensions" (© 1962 Evergreen Review) are reprinted
with the permission of Charles Scribner's Sons from *Roots and Branches* by
Robert Duncan.

experience and when we let them take over our speech there is a monotonous rapture of persistent regular stresses and waves of lines breaking rhyme after rhyme. There have been poets for whom this rise and fall, the mothering swell and ebb, was all. Amoebic intelligences, dwelling in the memorial of tidal voice, they arouse in our awake minds a spell, so that we let our awareness go in the urgent wave of the verse. The rhyming lines and the repeating meters persuade us. To evoke night and day or the ancient hypnosis of the sea is to evoke our powerful longing to fall back into periodic structure, into the inertia of uncomplicated matter. Each of us, hungry with life, rises from the cast of seed, having just this unique identity or experience created in the dance of chromosomes, and having in that identity a time; each lives and falls back at last into the chemistry of death.

Our consciousness, and the poem as a supreme effort of consciousness, comes in a dancing organization between personal and cosmic identity. What gnosis of the ancients transcends in mystery the notion Schrödinger brings us of an aperiodic structure in *What Is Life?*: ". . . the more and more complicated organic molecule in which every atom, and every group of atoms, plays an individual role, not entirely equivalent to that of others."[2] *"Living matter evades the decay to equilibrium,"* Schrödinger titles a section of his essay of 1944. "When is a piece of matter said to be alive?" he asks, and answers: "When it goes on 'doing something,' moving, exchanging material with its environment."

What interests me here is that this picture of an intricately articulated structure, a form that maintains a disequilibrium or lifetime—whatever it means to the biophysicist—to the poet means that life is by its nature orderly and that the poem might follow the primary processes of thought and feeling, the immediate impulse of psychic life. As I start here, first with night and day, then with a genesis of life, and would go forward to the genesis and nature of consciousness, my mind balks at the complication. It is not that we are far afield from the poem. Each poet seeks to commune with creation, with the divine world; that is to say, he seeks the most *real* form in language. But this most

2 *What Is Life?* (Cambridge, Eng.: Cambridge University Press, 1944, 1956), p. 60.

real is something we apprehend; the poem, the creation of the poem, is itself our primary experience of it.

We work toward the Truth of things. Keats's ecstatic "Beauty is truth, truth beauty" rises from the sureness of poetic intuition or of recognition, our instant knowing of fitness as we work in the poem, where the descriptive or analytic mind would falter. Here the true is beautiful as an arrow flies from its bow with exact aim. Dirac in "The Physicist's Picture of Nature" tells us: "It is more important to have beauty in one's equations than to have them fit experiment."[3] What is at issue here is that the truth does not lie outside the art. For the experimenter it is more important to have beauty in one's experiments than to have them fit mathematics.

The most real, the truth, the beauty of the poem is a configuration, but also a happening in language, that leads back into or on towards the beauty of the universe itself. I am but part of the whole of what I am, and wherever I seek to understand I fail what I know. In the poem "Atlantis" I had this sense of the fabulous as an intuition of the real:

> The long shadow thrown from this single ob-
> struction to its own light!
> Thought flies out from the old scars of the sea
> as if to land. Flocks that are longings
> come in to shake over the deep water.
>
> It's prodigies held in time's amber
> old destructions
> and the theme of revival the heart asks for.
> The past and future are
> full of disasters, splendors
> shaken to earth, seas rising to overshadow
> shores and roaring in.[4]

Beauty strikes us and may be fearful, as there is great beauty in each step as Oedipus seeks the heart of tragedy, his moment of

3 *Scientific American* (May 1963), p. 47.
4 From Robert Duncan, *The Opening of the Field* (New York: Grove Press, 1960). © 1960 by Robert Duncan.

truth, as he tears out his eyes, and sees at last. But this is a heroic and dramatic gesture and may obscure what I would get at. For in our common human suffering, in loss and longing, an intuition of poetic truth may arise. In the poem "A Storm of White" I spoke from my grief, let grief have its voice, in the loss of a cat, a beloved person of my household. He had died of pneumonia within a few weeks of our moving to a house on the coast north of San Francisco.

A Storm of White[5]

<pre>
                neither
        sky nor earth, without horizon,   it's
              a-
        nother tossing, continually in-
                breaking

        boundary of white
            foaming in gull-white weather
        luminous in dull white,   and trees
            ghosts of blackness or verdure
        that here are
            dark whites in storm.

        White white white   like
            a boundary in death advancing
        that is our life,   that's love,
            line upon line
        breaking in radiance, so soft- so dim-
            ly glaring, dominating.

        "What it would mean to us if
            he died," a friend writes of one she loves
        and that she feels she'll
            outlive those about her.

            The line of outliving
            in this storm   bounding
        obscurity from obscurity,   the foaming
</pre>

---

5 From Robert Duncan, *The Opening of the Field* (New York: Grove Press, 1960). © 1960 by Robert Duncan.

—as if half the universe
(neither sky nor earth, with
    horizon)   were forever

breaking into being another half,
    obscurity   flaring into a surf
upon an answering obscurity.

O dear gray cat that died in this cold,
  you were born on my chest
    six years ago.

The sea of ghosts dances. It does not
    send your little shadow to us.
I do not understand this
empty place in our happiness.

Another friend writes in a poem
(received today, March 25th 58)

  "Death also
can still propose the old labors."

It is not that poetry imitates but that poetry enacts in its order the order of first things, as just here in this consciousness, they may exist, and the poet desires to penetrate the seeming of style and subject matter to that most real where there is no form that is not content, no content that is not form. "A change of cadence," so the early Imagists realized, "means a new idea." But idea means something seen, a new image: here it is the Way, in which action, vision, and thought have their identity.

In the turn and return, the strophe and antistrophe, the prose and the versus of the choral mode are remembered the alternations of night and day and the systole and diastole of the heart, and in the exchange of opposites, the indwelling of one in the other, dance and poetry emerge as ways of knowing. Heraclitus wrote the opposites or alternates large and imagined them as phases of a dynamic unity: "God is day, night, winter, summer, war, peace, satiety, hunger, and undergoes alteration in the way that fire, when it is mixed with spices is named according to the scent of each of them."

The Christian Hippolytus accuses Heraclitus of teaching "that the created world becomes maker and creator of itself." The Greek word for "created" being *poieitos* and for "creator" *poieiteis,* the created world is a poem and the creator a poet.

We begin to imagine a cosmos in which the poet and the poem are one in a moving process, not only here the given Creation and the Exodus or Fall, but also here the immanence of the Creator in Creation. The most real is given and we have fallen away, but the most real is in the falling revealing itself in what is happening. Between the god *in* the story and the god *of* the story, the form, the realization of what is happening, stirs the poet. To answer that call, to become the poet, means to be aware of creation, creature, and creator coinherent in the one event. There is not only the immanence of God, His indwelling, but there is also the imminence of God, His impending occurrence. In the expectancy of the poem, grief and fear seem necessary to the revelation of Beauty.

Central to and defining the poetics I am trying to suggest here is the conviction that the order man may contrive or impose upon the things about him or upon his own language is trivial beside the divine order or natural order he may discover in them. To see, to hear, to feel or taste—this sensory intelligence that seems so immediate to us as to be simple and given—comes about in a formal organization so complicated that it remains obscure to our investigation in all but its crudest aspects. To be alive itself is a form involving organization in time and space, continuity and body, that exceeds clearly our conscious design. "It is by avoiding the rapid decay into the inert state of 'equilibrium,' that an organism appears so enigmatic," Schrödinger writes, "so much so, that from the earliest times of human thought some special nonphysical or supernatural force was claimed to be operative in the organism."[6]

There is not a phase of our experience that is meaningless, not a phrase of our communication that is meaningless. We do not make things meaningful, but in our making we work towards an awareness of meaning; poetry reveals itself to us as we obey the orders that appear in our work. In writing I do not organize

6 Schrödinger, *op. cit.,* p. 70.

words but follow my consciousness of—but it is also a desire that goes towards—orders in the play of forms and meanings toward poetic form. This play is like the play of actors upon a stage. Becoming conscious, becoming aware of the order of what is happening is the full responsibility of the poet. The poem that always seems to us such a highly organized event is in its very individuality ("idiocy" the classical Greek would have said), in its uniqueness, crude indeed compared with the subtlety of organization which in the range of contemporary linguistic analysis the study of syntax, morphology, etymology, psychology reveals in the language at large from which the poem is derived. The materials of the poem—the vowels and consonants—are already structured in their resonance, we have only to listen and to cooperate with the music we hear. The storehouse of human experience in words is resonant too, and we have but to listen to the reverberations of our first thought in the reservoir of communal meanings to strike such depths as touch upon the center of man's nature.

Man's nature? Man's speech? Carlyle in his essay "The Hero as Poet" saw the inherent music of our common speech:

> All speech, even the commonest speech, has something of song in it: not a parish in the world but has its parish-accent;— the rhythm or *tune* to which the people there *sing* what they have to say! Accent is a kind of chanting; all men have accent of their own,—though they only *notice* that of others. Observe too how all passionate language does of itself become musical. All deep things are Song. It seems somehow the very central essence of us, Song; as if all the rest were but wrappages and hulls! The primal element of us; of us, and of all things. The Greeks fabled of Sphere-Harmonies; it was the feeling they had of the inner structure of Nature; that the soul of all her voices and utterances was perfect music. Poetry, therefore, we will call *musical* thought. The Poet is he who *thinks* in that manner. See deep enough, and you see musically; the heart of Nature *being* everywhere music, if you can only reach it.[7]

This music of men's speech that has its verity in the music of the inner structure of Nature is clearly related to that beauty of

---

[7] *Heroes and Hero-Worship* (1840).

mathematics that Schrödinger and Dirac feel relates to the beauty of the inner structure of the physical universe.

The dancer comes into the dance when he loses his consciousness of his own initiative, what *he* is doing, feeling, or thinking, and enters the consciousness of the dance's initiative, taking feeling and thought there. The self-consciousness is not lost in a void but in the transcendent consciousness of the dance. "Night and Day address each other in their swift course, crossing the great brazen threshold," Hesiod sings in his *Theogony;* "the one will go inside, the other comes out." As consciousness is intensified, all the exciting weave of sensory impression, the illustration of time and space, are "lost" as the personality is "lost"; in focus we see only the dancer. We are aware only in the split second in which the dance is present. This presentation, our immediate consciousness, the threshold that is called both *here-and-now* and *eternity,* is an exposure in which, perilously, identity is shared in resonance between the person and the cosmos.

In 1950, with his essay "Projective Verse,"[8] Charles Olson called for a new consideration of form in the poem where the poet as he worked had to be "instant by instant, aware."

And if you also set up as a poet, USE USE USE the process at all points, in any given poem always, always one perception must must must MOVE, INSTANTER, ON ANOTHER!

In the poem this instant was the attention of "the HEAD, by way of the EAR, to the SYLLABLE." The mind was not to be diverted by what it wanted to say but to attend to what was happening immediately in the poem.

With this warning, to those who would try: to step back here to this place of the elements and minims of language is to engage speech where it is least careless and least logical.

At the same time the poem demanded a quickening of "the HEART, by way of the BREATH, to the LINE." Here Olson too was thinking of the dance:

Is it not the PLAY of a mind we are after, is it not that that shows whether a mind is there at all? . . . And the threshing floor for the dance? Is it anything but the LINE?

8 *Projective Verse* (New York: Token Press, 1959).

This play of heart and mind we see as the play of life itself in the extension of our language as life plays in the extension of our lifetime upon the threshold of consciousness between what man is and his Cosmos—the very fire of Heraclitus upon the hearth where the imagination of what man is and what the cosmos is burns. Our gods are many as our times are many, they are the cast and events of one play. There is only this one time; there is only this one god.

If the sea is first mother of the living, the sun is first father, and fire is his element. Here too death and life, the heat of our blood and the light of our mind, in one reality. That I have seen in poems as the fire upon the hearth, the genius of the household, as if the secret of our warmth and companionship were hidden in a wrathful flame.

Food for Fire, Food for Thought[9]

góod wood
that all fiery youth burst forth from winter,
go to sleep in the poem.
Who will remember the green flame,
thy heart's amber?

Language obeyd flares tongues in obscure matter.

We trace faces in clouds: they drift apart,
palaces of air —the sun dying down
sets them on fire;

descry shadows on the flood from its dazzling mood,
or at its shores read runes upon the sand
from sea-spume.

This is what I wanted for the last poem,
a loosening of conventions and return to open form.

9 From Robert Duncan, *The Opening of the Field* (New York: Grove Press, 1960). © 1960 by Robert Duncan.

Leonardo saw figures that were stains upon a wall.
Let the apparitions containd in the ground
    play as they will.

You have carried a branch of tomorrow into the room.
Its fragrance has awakend me —no,

    it was the sound of a fire on the hearth,
    leapt up where you bankt it, sparks of delight.
      Now I return the thought

    to the red glow, that might-be-magical blood,
    palaces of heat in the fire's mouth

—*"If you look you will see the salamander"*—
    to the very elements that attend us,
    fairies of the fire, the radiant crawling.

That was a long time ago.
No, they were never really there,
    tho once I saw— did I stare
    into the heart of desire burning
    and see a radiant man? like those
    fancy cities from fire into fire falling?

We are close enough to childhood, so easily purged
of what we thought we were to be,

    flamey threads of firstness go out from your touch,

    flickers of unlikely heat
    at the edge of our belief bud forth.

    There is an emotion, a realization, but it is also a world and a
self, that impends in the first stirrings of a poem. In a poem like
"A Storm of White" or "Food for Fire, Food for Thought," the
voice may seem to rise directly from or to the incoming breakers
that had become a moving whiteness into which I stared or the

flickering light and shadow cast upon a wall by a fire on the hearth I had forgotten, waking in the night, still close enough to the sleeping mind that I dreamed in what was happening. In "A Poem Beginning with a Line by Pindar," the germ of the poem quickened as I was reading one evening the *Pythian Odes* translated by H. T. Wade-Grey and C. M. Bowra. I have an affinity with Pindar, but here it was my inability to understand that began the work or it was the work beginning that proposed the words I was reading in such a way that they no longer belonged to Pindar's *Pythian I:* "The light foot hears you, and the brightness begins." In Pindar it is the harp of Apollo that the light foot of the dancer hears, but something had intruded, a higher reality for me, and it was the harp that heard the dancer. "Who is it that goes there?" the song cried out.

I had mistaken the light foot for Hermes the Thief, who might be called The Light Foot, light-fingered, light-tongued. The Homeric Hymns tell us that he devised the harp of Apollo and was first in the magic, the deceit, of song. But as Thoth, he is Truth, patron of poets. The infant Hermes, child of Zeus and the lady Maia—Alexandrian gnostics of the second century saw Zeus as the One God and the lady as Maya, name and personification of the Buddha's mother and also of the Great Illusion—this genius of childhood in his story resolves: "I too will enter upon the rite that Apollo has. If my father will not give it me, I will seek—and I am able—to be a prince of robbers." First crossing the threshold of the Sun, he steals a tortoise. "Living, you shall be a spell against mischievous witchcraft," he says: "but if you die, then you shall make sweetest song." Then staring at the shell, he conceives song's instrument: "As a swift thought darts through the heart of a man when thronging cares haunt him, or as bright glances flash from the eye, so glorious Hermes planned both thought and deed at once."[10]

The poet is such a child in us. And the poem, the instrument of music that he makes from men's speech, has such a hunger to live, to be true, as mathematics has. Numbers and words were both things of a spell. To dream true, to figure true, to come true. Here poetry is the life of the language and must be in-

[10] *The Homeric Hymns,* Hugh Evelyn-Whik, trans. (Cambridge: Loeb Library, 1908).

carnate in a body of words, condensed to have strength, phrases that are sinews, lines that may be tense or relaxed as the mind moves. Charles Olson in his essays toward a physiology of consciousness has made us aware that not only heart and brain and the sensory skin but all the internal organs, the totality of the body is involved in the act of a poem, so that the organization of words, an invisible body, bears the imprint of the physical man, the finest imprint that we feel in our own bodies as a tonic consonance and dissonance, a being-in-tune, a search for the as yet missing scale. Remembering Schrödinger's sense that the principle of life lies in its evasion of equilibrium, I think too of Goethe's Faust, whose principle lies in his discontent, not only in his search but also in his search beyond whatever answer he can know. Our engagement with knowing, with craft and lore, our demand for truth is not to reach a conclusion but to keep our exposure to what we do not know, to confront our wish and our need beyond habit and capability, beyond what we can take for granted, at the borderline, the light finger-tip or thought-tip where impulse and novelty spring.

This exposed, open form ("Projective Verse," Olson named it in poetry) began to appear in the 1940's. With the *Pisan Cantos* of Ezra Pound and *Paterson* of William Carlos Williams, with the *Symphony in Three Movements* of Stravinsky, I began to be aware of the possibility that the locus of form might be in the immediate minim of the work, and that one might concentrate upon the sound and meaning present where one was, and derive melody and story from impulse not from plan. I was not alone, for other poets—Louis Zukofsky, Charles Olson, Denise Levertov, Robert Creeley—following seriously the work of Pound and Williams, became aware, as I was, that what they had mastered opened out upon a new art where they were first ones working. In music John Cage, Pierre Boulez, or Karlheinz Stockhausen seem in the same way to realize that Stravinsky, Schonberg, and Webern stand like doors, mastering what music was, opening out upon what music must be.

It is a changing aesthetic, but it is also a changing sense of life. Perhaps we recognize as never before in man's history that not only our own personal consciousness but also the inner structure of the universe itself has only this immediate event in which to be realized. Atomic physics has brought us to the threshold of such a—I know not whether to call it certainty or doubt.

The other sense that underlies the new form is one that men have come to again and again in their most intense or deepest vision, that the Kingdom is here, that we have only now in which to live—that the universe has only now in which to live. "The present contains all that there is," Whitehead says in *The Aims of Education:*

> It is holy ground; for it is the past, and it is the future. . . . The communion of saints is a great and inspiring assemblage, but it has only one possible hall of meeting, and that is the present; and the mere lapse of time through which any particular group of saints must travel to reach that meeting-place, makes very little difference.[11]

11 *The Aims of Education* (1929).

12 THE EXPERIENCE OF POETRY IN A SCIENTIFIC AGE

May Swenson

What is the experience of poetry? Choosing to analyze this experience for myself after an engrossment of many years, I see it based in a craving to get through the curtains of things as they *appear*, to things as they *are*, and then into the larger, wilder space of things as they *are becoming*. This ambition involves a paradox: an instinctive belief in the senses as exquisite tools for this investigation and, at the same time, a suspicion about their crudeness. They may furnish easy deceptions or partial distortions:

> Hold a dandelion and look at the sun.
> Two spheres are side by side.
> Each has a yellow ruff.
>
> Eye, you tell a lie,
> that Near is Large, that Far is Small.
> There must be other deceits. . . .

W. B. Yeats called poetry "the thinking of the body" and said: "It bids us touch and taste and hear and see the world, and shrinks from . . . every abstract thing, from all that is of the brain only—from all that is not a fountain jetting from the entire hopes, memories, and sensations of the body."[1] But sometimes one gets the inkling that there are extrasenses as yet nameless,

[1] W. B. Yeats, *Essays and Introductions* (New York: Macmillan, 1961), p. 292.

within the apperceptive system, if only one could differentiate them and identify their organs.

Not to be fully aroused to the potentialities of one's senses means to walk the flat ground of appearances, to take given designations for granted, to accept without a second look the name or category of a thing for the thing itself. On that ground all feelings and notions are borrowed, are secondhand. The poetic experience, by contrast, is one of constant curiosity, skepticism, and testing—astonishment, disillusionment, renewed discovery, re-illumination. It amounts to a virtual compulsion to probe with the senses into the complex actuality of all things, outside and inside the self, and to determine relationships between them.

Aroused to the potentialities and delights of the senses and the evaluating intellect and using them daily, the poet, however, comes eventually to their limits and notices that their findings are not enough—often fall short of yielding the total, all-comprehensive pattern that he seeks. A complete and *firm* apprehension of the Whole tantalizingly eludes him—although he receives mirages of it now and then which he projects into his work. He is not so separate from every man as not to be fooled by tricks of perspective, seduced by the obvious, or bogged down in old and comfortable myths.

The limitations of our minds and sensorial equipment partly stem from the brevity of our physical lives. Stendhal somewhere says that man is like a fly born in the summer morning and dead by afternoon. How can he understand the word "night"? If he were allowed five more hours he would see and understand what night is. But unlike the fly, man is sorely conscious of the vastness of the unknown beyond his consciousness. The poet, tracing the edge of a great shadow whose outline shifts and varies, proving there is an invisible moving source of light behind, hopes (naively, in view of his ephemerality) to reach and touch the foot of that solid whatever-it-is that casts the shadow. If sometimes it seems he does touch it, it is only to be faced with a more distant, even less accessible mystery. Because all is movement—expansion or contraction, rotation or revolution—all is breathing change.

The experience of poetry is to suppose that there is a moon of the psyche, let us say, whose illuminated half is familiar to our ordinary eye, but which has another hemisphere which is dark;

and that poetry can discover this *other side,* that its thrust can take us toward it. Poetry is used to make maps of that globe, which to the "naked eye" appears disk-like and one-dimensional, seems to "rise" and "set" rather than to orbit; which remains distant and merely a "dead" object until, in the vehicle of poetry and with the speed of poetic light, we approach it. It then enlarges and reveals its surprising topography, becomes a world. And *passing around* it, our senses undergo dilation; there is a transformation of perception by means of this realization of *the round.*

Miniature as we are in the gigantic body of the cosmos, we have somehow an inbuilt craving to get our pincers of perception around the whole of it, to incorporate infinitude and set up comprehensible models of it within our little minds. Poetry tries to do this in its fashion. Science tries it more demonstrably. The impulses of the scientist and the poet, it seems to me, are parallel, although their instruments, methods, and effects are quite divergent. Contrasts between science and poetry are easily illustrated by such apparent opposites as: Objective/Subjective, Reason/Intuition, Fact/Essence—or let me boldly say: Material/Spiritual. However, a point of contiguity between them is that poet and scientist both use *language* to communicate their findings.

The scientific investigator works as one of a team, as a rule. He works with formulae or with objective facts which are classified and reported as nakedly as possible so as to convey, in each instance, a single, specific, unambiguous meaning. The poet works alone, handling concrete sensual particulars, as well as their invisible and intangible essences, with the tools of intuitive perception; he then presents his discoveries wrapped in metaphor, metrical patterns, and often multifarious symbols. The scientist has an actual moon under observation—one he soon hopes to have under manipulation—although no robot or human explorer has yet succeeded in getting to it. "Until one does," I read in *The Saturday Review,* "scientists cannot tell whether the lunar surface is packed hard, porous, or buried deep in dust." And, "because of fuel limitations of the rockets that will orbit the moon and lower a ferryboat to the lunar surface, moon landings must be held within 5 degrees north and south of the moon's equator and within 45 degrees east and west of the moon's central meridian. Within this narrow zone of safety, flat lands must be found to receive the spaceships from earth."

My moon is not in the sky, but within my psyche. More or less subliminal, it orbits within the psyche of every man, a symbol both of the always-known and the never-to-be-known. I do not try to land on that moon. To do so would be to choose lunacy. But in 1958 I wrote a poem called "Landing on the Moon," that outlines, in its first three stanzas, a capsule history of the moon's psychic pull on man from primitive times to the present. The two concluding stanzas speculate as to whether it is well for man to succumb, literally, to that hypnotism and let himself be drawn up onto the moon:

Landing on the Moon[2]

When in the mask of night there shone that cut,
we were riddled. A probe reached down
and stroked some nerve in us,
the glint of a wizard's eye, of silver,
slanted out of the mask of the unknown—
pit of riddles, the scratch-marked sky.

When, albino bowl on cloth of jet,
it spilled its virile rays,
our eyes enlarged, our blood reared with the waves.
We craved its secret, but unreachable
it held away from us, chilly and frail.
Distance kept it magnate. Enigma made it white.

When we learned to read it with our rod,
reflected light revealed
a lead mirror, a bruised shield
seamed with scars and shadow-soiled.
A half-faced sycophant, its glitter borrowed,
rode around our throne.

2 "Landing on the Moon" (© 1958 The Nation Associates, Inc.) is re-printed with the permission of Charles Scribner's Sons from *To Mix with Time* by May Swenson.

On the moon there shines earth light
as moonlight shines upon the earth ...
If on its obsidian we set our weightless foot,
and sniff no wind, and lick no rain
and feel no gauze between us and the Fire,
will we trot its grassless skull, sick for the homelike shade?

Naked to the earth-beam we will be,
who have arrived to map an apparition,
who walk upon the forehead of a myth.
Can flesh rub with symbol? If our ball
be iron, and not light, our earliest wish
eclipses. Dare we land upon a dream?

Psychologically, then physically, what will happen to man made
to mount the moon—the moon being his first wobbling step in a
march to the stars? To either extinction or mutation? In an eon
or two, will he have *become* a rocket and a robot combined?
Maybe. Yet, whether it is well for him or not, I think man will
probably colonize the moon, eventually infiltrate the solar system,
and go beyond. It may be his destiny. But he may have to pay for
it with a transformation amounting to an evolutionary replace-
ment of his species by some other creature-thing, *Homo me-
chanicus.*

I confess to being envious, in a way, of the astronaut. Though
only in my imagination, where I can make him a hero and a lone
adventurer. What an array of absolutely new sensations is handed
him, like a Christmas paintbox; what an incomparable toy, his
capsule with its console of magic dials, gauges, buttons, and sig-
nal lights; and what a knight in shining plastic he is in his silver
suit. To escape the earth-ball, its tug, and one's own heaviness!
To dare the great vacuum and, weightless, be tossed—a moon
oneself—around the great roulette wheel with the planets! But,
in actuality, could I bear that claustrophobia in a steel womb,
attached to that formidable placenta by a synthetic umbilical,
dependent on a mechanical nipple for my breath of air?

In Space there is so little space. And who but a preconditioned,
tranquilized, denerved, desensualized, automatically responding

"test-subject" could stand for long that swaddling as in a rigid iron lung? Not only freedom of movement and of action, but freedom to think an aberrant thought or do an individual impulsive deed must be forfeited, it seems to me. Hooked to the indispensable members of his team by the paraphernalia of intercommunication, the astronaut, I imagine, must learn to forget what solitude, what privacy tastes like. His very heartbeat becomes public, his body and brain an encephalograph, a fluoroscope, a radio, a video screen. First trained to become a piece of equipment; next, perhaps born so. (Sometimes I long to remember my life as a cephalopod under the sea, and cannot.)

But let me go back to a consideration of the poetic method and its effects, compared to the scientific.

For the poet, Self is a universe, and he is embarked on a conquest of Inner Space. From the outside, in this accelerated age, our consciousness is being bombarded with the effects of rapid change and upheaval. It's as if we could *see* the earth shift and change while we walk on it. Familiar Space and Time have hooked together and we have Spacetime. Matter has split into uncountable explosive bits and become Energy. On the one hand —and virtually with the same engine—man prepares to fly to the stars, while on the other he seems intent on annihilating himself along with his sole perch in the universe. There is the temptation sometimes to stuff up the "doors of perception" and regress to that long-ago world that was flat—that was static and secure, since it rested immovably on the back of a turtle! Because the poet's precreative condition must be an emptiness, a solitude, a stillness close to inertia. It is a condition of alert passivity, with blankness behind and before him, while he is centered within the present moment, expectant only of the vividness to come, slowly or suddenly, with the combustion of sensations and impressions gathered and stored beforehand from his active life.

The method is the opposite of analytic industry spurred by communal effort (teamwork) proceeding according to prearranged outline, operating upon the material from the outside. Rather than grasping it a piece at a time, construction-wise, the poet seats himself *within* his subject, at its axis, so that, equidistant from all points of its circumference, he can apprehend its potential form as an immediate whole. This is the organic technique, allowing the growth from within, from the initial seeds of attention, until, as Rilke put it: "All space becomes a fruit around those kernels." I speak here of poetry in its conception; obviously there is an industrious and conscious work of building to be done before the body of a poem is complete.

Science and poetry are alike, or allied, it seems to me, in their largest and main target—to investigate any and all phenomena of existence beyond the flat surface of appearances. The products, as well as the methods of these two processes are very different—not in their relative value—but in the particular uses that they have for their "consumers." Each has a separate role and concern toward the expansion of human consciousness and experience. Poetry has a psychic use. Along with the other arts it is a depository for, and a dispenser of, such psychic realizations as wonder, beauty, surprise, joy, awe, revelation—as well as fear, disgust, perplexity, anxiety, pain, despair. It provides an input and an outlet for all the complex, powerful, fleeting grains and rays of sensation in the human organism. It is a quickener of experience, and it renews the archetypes and icons necessary to the human spirit, by means of which personality is nurtured and formed.

"The world is poetical intrinsically," Aldous Huxley has written, "and what it means is simply itself. Its significance is the enormous mystery of its existence and of our awareness of its existence." Who or what are we? Why are we? And what are we becoming? What is the relationship between man and the universe? Those are questions that ached in the mind of the first poet. They can be said to have created the first poet and to be first source of the art of poetry. Does the fact of our consciousness, unique and seemingly miraculous among all of nature's creatures, *a priori* indicate a superconsciousness shaping and manipulating the cosmos?

How is it that *with* our minds we can explore our own minds? And can we develop a technique to explore Mind—that aspect of the universe we might postulate exists in addition to its mere structural organization? Maybe such a Mind is not yet in existence, but in process; maybe our nervous systems and cortexes are early evidence of its future evolution. As Huxley reports in *Literature and Science,* psychologists know a great deal, but as yet they "have no recognized hypothesis to account for the apparent interaction of mind and matter in a simple act of consciousness." Nor is there even a firm hypothesis to explain the operation of memory. But atomic physics (the most exact of the sciences) is uncovering a factual foundation for many intuitions of existentialist poets and philosophers. According to a statement by physicist Werner Heisenberg, cited by Huxley, for the first time in the history of the planet man approaches a willingness to admit that he is alone with himself "without a partner and without an adversary."[3] This I believe to be an intuitive hunch, not only of the poet or philosopher, but of every thinking man when in moments of extremity he is forced face-to-face with his own soul. Huxley puts it that "man is in process of becoming his own Providence, his own Cataclysm, his own Saviour, and his own invading horde of Martians." And he adds: "In the realm of pure science the same discovery—that he is alone with himself—awaits him as he progressively refines his analysis of matter."[4] Modern science, according to Heisenberg,

> shows us that we can no longer regard the building blocks of matter, which were considered originally to be the ultimate objective reality, as being things-in-themselves . . . Knowledge of atoms and their movements in themselves—that is to say, *independent of our observation*—is no longer the aim of research; rather we now find ourselves from the very start in the midst of a dialogue between nature and man, a dialogue of which science is only one part, so much so that the conventional division of the world into subject and object, into inner world and outer world, into body and soul, is no longer applicable and raises difficulties. For the sciences of nature, the subject matter of research is no longer nature in itself, but nature subjected to human questioning, and to this extent man, once again, meets only with himself.

From reflection on a statement such as this, one can almost reach the spooky conclusion that all that we conceive as objective and under examination of our sensorial and intellectual equipment, is really subjective and a projection of our own heads! How

[3] Aldous Huxley, *Literature and Science* (New York: Harper & Row, 1963), p. 75–76.
[4] *Ibid.*, p. 75.

far significant or how far absurd, I still wonder, is this poem, called "The Universe," that I wrote in 1961:

The Universe[5]

What
is it about,
the universe,
the universe
about
us stretching out? We within our brains within it think
we must unspin the laws that spin it. We think
why because
we think
because.
Because
we think
we think
the universe
about
us.
But does it think
the universe?
Then what
about?
About
us? If not, must there be cause
in the universe?
Must it have laws? And what
if the universe
is *not about*
us? Then what?
What
is it about
and what
about
us?

[5] "The Universe" (© 1963 *The Hudson Review, Inc.*) is reprinted by permission of Charles Scribner's Sons from *To Mix with Time* by May Swenson.

In 1665 or thereabouts, the American poet Edward Taylor wrote a remarkable poem trying to penetrate into the origin of the universe. A portion of it reads as follows:

> Infinity, when all things it beheld,
> In Nothing, and of Nothing all did build,
> Upon what Base was fixt the Lath, wherein
> He turn'd this Globe, and riggalld it so trim?
> Who blew the Bellows of his Furnace Vast?
> Or held the Mould wherein the world was Cast?
> Who laid its Corner Stone? Or whose Command?
> Where stand the Pillars upon which it stands?
> Who Lac'de and Fillitted the earth so fine,
> With Rivers like Green Ribbons Smaragdine?
> Who made the Sea's its selvedge, and its locks
> Like a Quilt Ball within a Silver Box?
> Who Spread its Canopy? Or Curtains Spun?
> Who in this Bowling Alley bowld the Sun?
> . . .
> Who? who did this, or who is he? Why, know
> It's Only Might Almighty this did doe.[6]

It's interesting that Edward Taylor should have made Infinity, that great abstraction, the protagonist of his poem—even though he refers to it as "he"—and his expression "It's Only Might Almighty this did doe" (i.e., Energy) sounds like an intuition prefiguring a finding of modern science rather than reflecting (as he no doubt consciously intended) a God-centered metaphysics of the seventeenth century.

The poet's universe had better be centered within the present; it had better not install itself (and stall itself) in anachronisms either conceptual or expressionistic. Because the poet, I believe, should be in the vanguard of his time. He can, in his unique way, be a synthesizer and synchronizer of the many components and elements of a great new pattern emergent in the investigations of biologists, psychologists, anthropologists, astronomers, physicists,

6 From T. H. Johnson, ed., *Poetical Works of Edward Taylor* (New Jersey: Princeton University Press, 1943). "The Preface" is © 1939 Rockland Editions; © 1943 Princeton University Press; reprinted by permission of Princeton University Press.

et al. The poet's material has always been nature—human and otherwise—all objects and aspects of our outer environment as well as the "climate of the soul" and the "theater of the emotions." The poet is the great antispecialist. Still possible in our overorganized, compartmentalized culture and still needed is the work and the *play* of the artist. As a free-floating agent, medium, and conduit—a kind of "divining rod"—he may pass anywhere—over, into, around, or *through* the multifold fabric of experience and present the results of his singular discoveries and delights to fellow-searchers, fellow-beholders.

The *play* of the artist is psychologically very important. As the philosopher Huizinga in *Homo Ludens* has written:

> . . . in acknowledging play you acknowledge mind, for whatever else play is, it is not matter. Even in the animal world it bursts the bounds of the physically existent. From the point of view of a world wholly determined by the operation of blind forces, play would be altogether superfluous. Play only becomes possible, thinkable, and understandable when an influx of mind breaks down the absolute determinism of the cosmos.[7]

I said earlier that a point of contiguity between the poet and the scientist is that both employ *language* to communicate what they find. At this point there is also a crucial departure, for language is not only a tool in poetry, it is its very being. In a poem, subject is not presented by means of language but language is the thing presented with the aid of subject. Being merely instrumental, a scientific exposition can be restated in various ways without a loss of end-effect; when new facts render its message obsolete, such expositions are replaced and forgotten. But tamper with, or reconstruct the tissue of a poem and you deal death to its cells and molecules. The poet reaches for a vision of reality that is whole, seamless, and undivided; if he succeeds in that, his product need not suffer obsolescence. True art combines the properties of change *and* endurance.

What is it in poetry, beyond subject, beyond *what* is being said, that is given? The management of language for the poem must be such as to capture and fix the essence of the immediate experience—the sensation, illumination, *extra dimension*—that the

[7] (Boston: Beacon, 1955), p. 3.

poet felt when the impulse for the poem (the emotion or psychic mental discovery that engendered it) fell upon him. It must be such that the receiver of the poem recapitulates, as it were physically, the same illumination because it relates to, or fuses with, a vision within himself, dormant and dark until the moment the beam of the poem strikes into him. In the handling of his material, which is language, metaphor is to the poet what the equation is to the mathematician.

In one of his essays on art, published as long ago as 1919, Ezra Pound said:

> We might come to believe that the thing that matters in art is a sort of energy, something more or less like electricity or radioactivity, a force transfusing, welding, and unifying . . . The thing that counts is Good Writing. And good writing is perfect control. It is quite easy to control a thing that has in it no energy—provided that it be not too heavy and that you do not wish to make it *move* . . .

Discussing the origins of language, Pound said:

> The whole thing is an evolution. In the beginning simple words were enough: Food; water; fire. Both prose and poetry are but an extension of language. Man desires to communicate with his fellows. And he desires an ever increasingly complicated communication. Gesture serves up to a point. Symbols may serve. But when you desire something not present to the eye or when you desire to communicate ideas, you must have recourse to speech. Gradually you wish to communicate something less bare and ambiguous than *ideas.* You wish to communicate an idea *and* its modifications, an idea *and* a crowd of its effects, atmospheres, contradictions . . .

> Words and their sense must be such as fit the emotion. Or, from the other side, ideas, or fragments of ideas, the emotion *and* concomitant emotions, must be in harmony, they must form an organism . . .

> Poetry is a centaur. The thinking word-arranging, clarifying faculty must move and leap with the energizing, sentient, musical faculties.[8]

[8] T. S. Eliot, ed., *Literary Essays of Ezra Pound* (New York: New Directions, 1954), pp. 49–52.

At one time, wishing to clarify to myself the distinction between poetry and other modes of expression, I put down these notes:

Poetry doesn't tell; it shows. Prose tells.
Poetry is not philosophy; poetry makes things be, right now.
Not an idea, but a happening.
It is not music, but it sounds while showing.
It is mobile; it is a thing taking place—active, interactive,
in a place.
It is not thought; it has to do with senses and muscles.
It is not dancing, but it moves while it remains.

. . . And it is not science. But the experience of poetry is animated with the insatiable curiosity of science. The universe, inside and out, is properly its laboratory. More plain than ever before is the potent fact that we are human particles in a culture of living change. We must either master the Great Whirl or become victims of it. Science is unavoidably reshaping our environment and in the future will prominently influence the next development of individual man and his species. Art, more intimately, deals with and forms the emotional and spiritual climate of our experience. Poetry can help man to stay human.

13 ON MY OWN WORK

Richard Wilbur

Since the second World War, the American people have come to accept the poetry reading as a legitimate and frequently satisfying kind of artistic performance. Prior to the 1940's there were, to be sure, a few vivid or beloved figures to whom our audiences were glad to listen: Robert Frost, with his New England wit and accent; Carl Sandburg with his guitar; Edna Millay in her white dress; Vachel Lindsay with his camp-meeting style and his tambourines. But the public attitude toward the verse recital has now so matured that any poet, whether or not he qualifies as a platform personality, is likely to find himself on a platform several times a year. Sometimes it will be in a university auditorium, sometimes in an art gallery or community center, sometimes in a night club or coffee house. The audience may be ten or twenty; or it may be hundreds, even thousands; what matters is that it is now there.

The presence of all these listening faces has already, I think, affected the social posture of the American poet. He shows somewhat less of the conventional romantic defiance, somewhat less of the bitterness of the wallflower; he is increasingly disposed to think of himself as a citizen, who may have a certain critical and expressive office to perform in the community. It goes without saying that this new attitude—or shall I say this revival of an old attitude—has been encouraged by the late President Kennedy's readiness to acknowledge and affirm the dignity of the arts.

I may misinterpret these phenomena, or make too much of them; but let us suppose that I am right and that there really is an increased responsiveness to poetry in America. Our poets will run certain risks, of course, in responding to that responsiveness. It would be too bad if large audiences in the Middle West, and occasional courtesies from Washington, inclined any poet to adjust his work to fancied demands—to become a defender of conventional pieties, or an apologist for official policy, or an entertainer, or (worst of all) a stingless gadfly, one of those public performers who shock their audience in just the way it wants to be shocked.

There are risks of corruption, then, in becoming a poet-citizen rather than an alienated artist, but I myself would consider them risks well taken, because it seems to me that poetry is sterile unless it arises from a sense of community or, at least, from the hope of community. I think this is true even in America, where beneath so much surface homogeneity there lies a radical commitment to diversity and to the toleration of dissent. We are not a settled and monolithic nation; we are not really one culture, and we offer our artists no Byzantine advantages. Yet the incoherence of America need not enforce a stance of alienation in the poet; rather it may be seen as placing on him a peculiar imaginative burden, and committing him perhaps to something like Yeats' long and loyal quarrel with his native Ireland.

But let me turn back from these large assertions to the subject with which I began: the poetry reading. Very often, at these affairs, the actual reading of poems will be preceded or followed by a question period, during which the audience is invited to interrogate the poet about his art. This is not unusual, of course, in other countries; I have seen Yevgeny Yevtushenko, at a poetry reading in Moscow, cheerfully and patiently replying to the questions of his hearers. But the idea of the poet's accountability to his audience is axiomatic in Russia, as it is not here; and I must confess that question periods are sometimes a strain on my good citizenship. For one thing, I feel (as most poets do) that what I have to say has best been said in my poems, and that in discussing or expounding them I necessarily dilute and falsify. For another thing, I feel a certain mistrust of the desire to be well-informed; it strikes me that far too many people are anxious to substitute ideas about poetry for the experience of possessing some poem in itself.

And yet I do try to answer people's questions, and with good will, reminding myself that no true poem can die of being talked about, that the lover of poetry may also be critically informed, and that after all one should be gratified by any show of interest.

For me, the hardest questions to answer are always those which bear broadly, rather than specifically, on my own work. I am sometimes asked, for example, whether I feel that my poems have greatly changed in style or attitude—whether I see myself as having passed through distinct periods of development. At such times I always feel envious of poets more willful and deliberate than I can manage to be. I envy Ezra Pound, whose whole literary performance may be seen as a series of conscious prescriptions for the health of the arts or of society. I envy Dr. Williams, with his explicit and developing aesthetic theories and his dogged metrical experiments. I envy Yeats, whose every collection of verse had a forceful, and I suspect forcible, unity of idea.

Such poets are always able to say what their intentions have been, and when and how their productions have changed in character. That I can make few such statements makes me seem irresponsible, no doubt, and passive; though a kinder word might be "spontaneous." The unit of my poetry, as I experience it, is not the *Collected Poems* which I may some day publish; nor is it the individual volume, nor the sequence or group within the volume; it is the single poem. Every poem of mine is autonomous, or feels so to me in the writing, and consists of an effort to exhaust my present sense of the subject. It is for this reason that a poem sometimes takes me years to finish. No poem of mine is ever undertaken as a technical experiment; the form which it takes, whether conventional or innovating, develops naturally as the poem develops, as a part of the utterance. Nor does my poem ever begin as the statement of a fully grasped idea; I think inside my lines and the thought must get where it can amongst the moods and sounds and gravitating particulars which are appearing there. Robert Frost once said that a poem's beginning is like falling in love, and I feel about the matter as he did: when we fall in love, we are powerfully drawn by something, but we do not yet know what it means.

I am not, in short, a programmatic poet; I have never set about to write in this way or that. The best I can do, therefore, in answer to the question I have quoted, is to back off and play the critic to myself. If I do that, I find myself in slight disagreement with the friendly British reviewer who declared that my later poems don't much differ from the early ones. I think they do. My first poems were written in answer to the inner and outer disorders of the second World War and they helped me, as poems should, to take ahold of raw events and convert them, provisionally, into experience. At the same time I think that they may at moments have taken refuge from events in language itself—in word-play, in the coinage of new words, in a certain preciosity. At any rate, my writing is now plainer and more straightforward than it used to be. An adverse critic, considering the same evidence, might say that my language has simply grown dull; I can only hope that he would not be right.

Another change in my work has been a partial shift from the ironic meditative lyric toward the dramatic poem. Most American poets of my generation were taught to admire the English Metaphysical poets of the seventeenth century and such contemporary masters of irony as John Crowe Ransom. We were led by our teachers and by the critics whom we read to feel that the most adequate and convincing poetry is that which accommodates mixed feelings, clashing ideas, and incongruous images. Poetry could not be honest, we thought, unless it began by acknowledging the full discordancy of modern life and consciousness.

I still believe that to be a true view of poetry, and therefore I can still stand behind the poem I am about to read you, the title of which is "A Baroque Wall-Fountain in the Villa Schiarra." It is, in the first place, a minutely descriptive poem, in which I portray a wall-fountain in one of the public gardens of Rome, and then proceed across town to describe the celebrated fountains in St. Peter's Square. At the same time the poem presents, by way of its contrasting fountains, a clash between the ideas of pleasure and joy, of acceptance and transcendence.

A Baroque Wall-Fountain in the Villa Schiarra[1]

> Under the bronze crown
> Too big for the head of the stone cherub whose feet

---

[1] From Richard Wilbur, *Things of This World* (New York: Harcourt, Brace & World, 1956). © by Richard Wilbur; reprinted by permission of Harcourt, Brace & World, Inc.

A serpent has begun to eat,
Sweet water brims a cockle and braids down

Past spattered mosses, breaks
On the tipped edge of a second shell, and fills
The massive third below. It spills
In threads then from the scalloped rim, and makes

A scrim or summery tent
For a faun-menage and their familiar goose.
Happy in all that ragged, loose
Collapse of water, its effortless descent

And flatteries of spray,
The stocky god upholds the shell with ease,
Watching, about his shaggy knees,
The goatish innocence of his babes at play;

His fauness all the while
Leans forward, slightly, into a clambering mesh
Of water-lights, her sparkling flesh
In a saecular ecstasy, her blinded smile

Bent on the sand floor
Of the trefoil pool, where ripple-shadows come
And go in swift reticulum,
More addling to the eye than wine, and more

Interminable to thought
Than pleasure's calculus. Yet since this all
Is pleasure, flash, and waterfall,
Must it not be too simple? Are we not

More intricately expressed
In the plain fountains that Maderna set
Before St. Peter's—the main jet
Struggling aloft until it seems at rest

In the act of rising, until
The very wish of water is reversed,

That heaviness borne up to burst
In a clear, high, cavorting head, to fill

With blaze, and then in gauze
Delays, in a gnatlike shimmering, in a fine
Illumined version of itself, decline,
And patter on the stones its own applause?

If that is what men are
Or should be, if those water-saints display
The pattern of our areté,
What of these showered fauns in their bizarre,

Spangled, and plunging house?
They are at rest in fullness of desire
For what is given, they do not tire
Of the smart of the sun, the pleasant water-douse

And riddled pool below,
Reproving our disgust and our ennui
With humble insatiety.
Francis, perhaps, who lay in sister snow

Before the wealthy gate
Freezing and praising, might have seen in this
No trifle, but a shade of bliss—
That land of tolerable flowers, that state

As near and far as grass
Where eyes become the sunlight, and the hand
Is worthy of water: the dreamt land
Toward which all hungers leap, all pleasures pass.

It may be that the poem I have just read arrives at some sort
of reconciliation between the claims of pleasure and joy, acceptance and transcendence; but what one hears in most of it is a
single meditative voice balancing argument and counterargu-
ment, feeling and counterfeeling. I now want to read you a
somewhat later poem on very much the same subject, in which

there are two distinct voices speaking, both of them dramatic. The title of the poem is "Two Voices in a Meadow," and the speakers are a milkweed and a stone. The milkweed speaks first:

> Anonymous as cherubs
> Over the crib of God,
> White seeds are floating
> Out of my burst pod.
> What power had I
> Before I learned to yield?
> Shatter me, great wind:
> I shall possess the field.

And now the stone speaks:

> As casual as cow-dung
> Under the crib of God,
> I lie where chance would have me,
> Up to the ears in sod.
> Why should I move? To move
> Befits a light desire.
> The sill of Heaven would founder,
> Did such as I aspire.[2]

The virtue of the ironic meditative poem is that the poet speaks out of his whole nature, acknowledging the contradictions which inhere in life. The limitation of such a poem is that the atmosphere of contradiction can stifle passion and conduce to a bland evasiveness. The virtue of the dramatic poem is that, while it may not represent the whole self of the poet, it can (like the love song, hymn, or curse) give free expression to some one compelling mood or attitude. The fact is that we are not always divided in spirit and that we sometimes yield utterly to a feeling or idea. Each of these kinds of poem, then, has its own truth to life and without abandoning the first, I have lately been writing more and more of the second.

[2] From Richard Wilbur, *Advice to a Prophet and Other Poems* (New York: Harcourt, Brace & World, 1961). "Two Voices in a Meadow" is © 1957 by Richard Wilbur.

Another question often asked of the poets of my generation is where they stand in relation to the revolution in American poetry which is said to have begun in the second decade of this century. I think that there truly *was* a revolution then, in poetry as in the arts generally, and if one looks at poetry anthologies of the year 1900 one can see that a revolution was called for—a revolution against trivial formalism, dead rhetoric, and genteel subject matter. The revolution was not a concerted one and there was little agreement on objectives; nor is there now any universal agreement as to what, in that revolution, was most constructive. But certainly it has been of lasting importance that Robinson and Frost chose to enliven traditional meters with the rhythms of colloquial speech; that Sandburg and others insisted on slang and on the brute facts of the urban and industrial scene; and that Pound and Eliot sophisticated American verse by introducing techniques from other literatures, and by reviving and revising our sense of literary tradition.

All of these contributions were inclusive and enlarging in character; but there were also, of course, experiments and movements of a reductive nature, in which one aspect of poetry was stressed at the expense of others. I think of Gertrude Stein's apparent efforts to reduce words to pure sound; I think of the typographical poems of Cummings, which—however engaging—sacrificed the ear to the eye; I think of the free-verse movement, which sought to purify poetry of all but organic rhythms; of the Imagist insistence that ideas be implicit in description, rather than abstractly stated; of the efforts of some poets to abandon logical progression and to write in quasimusical form.

We have seen, in this century, a number of the arts entrapped in reductive theories: music, some have said, is merely sound in time; architecture is nothing but the provision of areas for living or working; painting is only the arrangement of line and color on a plane surface. All these definitions are true enough, except for those words *merely* and *only* and *nothing but*, which imply that to go beyond the bare fundamentals of any art is to risk impurity. There have been, as I've said, a number of reductive approaches to poetry in this century, but somehow American poetry has never fallen into such a condition as we now find in American painting, where for the most part one must choose between the solipsism of Abstract Expressionism and the empty objectivity of so-called pop art.

My own position on poetry, if I have to have one, is that it should include every resource which can be made to work. Aristotle, as you may remember, argued that drama is the highest of the arts because it contains more means and elements than any other. I'm not sure that Aristotle is right about the pre-eminence of drama, but I do share his feeling that an art should contain as much as it can and still be itself. As a poet, my relationship to the revolution in question is that I am the grateful inheritor of all that my talent can employ, but that I will not accept any limitations or prohibitions or exclude anything in the name of purity. So far as possible, I try to play the whole instrument.

Let me illustrate, if I may, by presenting another poem of mine. If I understand this poem rightly, it has a free and organic rhythm: that is to say, its movement arises naturally from the emotion and from the things and actions described. At the same time, the lines are metrical and disposed in stanzas. The subject matter is both exalted and vulgar. There is, I should think, sufficient description to satisfy an Imagist, but there is also a certain amount of statement; my hope is that the statement seems to grow inevitably out of the situation described. The language of the poem is at one moment elevated and at the next colloquial or slangy: for example, the imposing word "omnipresence" occurs not far from the undignified word "hunks." A critic would find in this poem certain patterns of sound, but those patterns of sound do not constitute an abstract music; they are meant, at any rate, to be inseparable from what is being said, a subordinate aspect of the poem's meaning.

The title of the poem is a quotation from St. Augustine: "Love Calls Us to the Things of This World." You must imagine the poem as occurring at perhaps seven-thirty in the morning; the scene is a bedroom high up in a city apartment building; outside the bedroom window, the first laundry of the day is being yanked across the sky and one has been awakened by the squeaking pulleys of the laundry-line:

168

"Love Calls Us to the Things of This World"[3]

The eyes open to a cry of pulleys,
And spirited from sleep, the astounded soul
Hangs for a moment bodiless and simple
As false dawn.
                 Outside the open window
The morning air is all awash with angels.

  Some are in bed-sheets, some are in blouses,
Some are in smocks: but truly there they are.
Now they are rising together in calm swells
Of halcyon feeling, filling whatever they wear
With the deep joy of their impersonal breathing;

  Now they are flying in place, conveying
The terrible speed of their omnipresence, moving
And staying like white water; and now of a sudden
They swoon down into so rapt a quiet
That nobody seems to be there.
                  The soul shrinks

  From all that it is about to remember,
From the punctual rape of every blessed day,
And cries,
          "Oh, let there be nothing on earth but laundry,
Nothing but rosy hands in the rising steam
And clear dances done in the sight of heaven."

  Yet, as the sun acknowledges
With a warm look the world's hunks and colors,
The soul descends once more in bitter love
To accept the waking body, saying now
In a changed voice as the man yawns and rises,

[3] From Richard Wilbur, *Things of This World* (New York: Harcourt, Brace & World, 1956). © 1956 by Richard Wilbur; reprinted by permission of Harcourt, Brace & World.

"Bring them down from their ruddy gallows;
Let there be clean linen for the backs of thieves;
Let lovers go fresh and sweet to be undone,
And the heaviest nuns walk in a pure floating
Of dark habits,
              keeping their difficult balance."

I have already stated that each of my poems, as I write it, seems to me unique; complete; quite unrelated to anything else I have done. But when I play the critic to my work, as I am doing now, it isn't hard to see that the poems have a number of persistent concerns. The three poems I have included here all have to do (a critic might say) with the proper relation between the tangible world and the intuitions of the spirit. The poems assume that such intuitions are, or may be, true; they incline, however, to favor a spirituality which is not abstracted, not dissociated and world-renouncing. A good part of my work could, I suppose, be understood as a public quarrel with the aesthetics of Edgar Allan Poe.

But enough of that: the ideas of any poet, when reduced to prose statements, sound banal, and mine are no exception. Let me close by making a few observations on the poet's relationship to ideas. Madame Furtseva, the Soviet Minister of Culture, said recently that in her country the leaders of the state are thought to understand the world better than the artists do, and that Soviet artists therefore look to their political leaders for the ideas which they are to express and the goals toward which their art is to inspire the people. How rigorously that theory is applied in the Soviet Union I do not know, but I am sure that I would find it oppressive if it were applied to me. I should not care to limit my poetic thought to politics and economics, which are not, after all, the whole of reality; I should not like to be forbidden that honesty which comes of the admission of doubts, contradictions, and reservations; and if the leaders of my state behaved viciously, as leaders sometimes do, I should like to feel entitled to protest rather than justify.

I don't think poetry can be healthy if it derives its attitudes from any authority. On the other hand, I don't think that society should look to poetry for new philosophies, new religions, and synoptic intellectual structures. That demand has been made repeatedly during the past century, ever since Matthew Arnold, and when poets have taken it seriously the result has been, at best, something like Hart Crane's magnificent botch of a poem, *The Bridge*. Poets are often intelligent men and they are entitled to their thoughts; but intellectual pioneering and the construction of new thought-systems are not their special function. Aeschylus' *Oresteia* was not a contribution to Athenian legal theory; Dante's *Commedia* gave us no new theology; and Shakespeare's history-plays added no fresh concepts to the political thought of his age.

What poetry does with ideas is to redeem them from abstraction and submerge them in sensibility; it embodies them in persons and things and surrounds them with a weather of feeling; it thereby tests the ability of any ideas to consort with human nature in its contemporary condition. Is it possible, for example, to speak intelligibly of angels in the modern world? Will the psyche of the modern reader consent to be called a soul? The poem which I have just presented was a test of those questions.

14 SOME OF MY BEGINNING . . . AND WHAT I FEEL RIGHT NOW

Gregory Corso

Poetry and the poet are inseparable—I cannot write about poetry without writing about the poet. In fact I, as poet, am the poetry I write. I did not know how to write a poem when I felt I wanted to be a poet. I was thirteen years old and I was alone in the world —no mother, and my father was at war. I belonged to the streets and no school did I attend: to exist I stole minor things and to sleep I slept on the rooftops and in the subways of the city, the big wild city of New York during World War II in 1943. I went through a strange hell that year and I guess it is just such hells that give birth to the poet. There swelled in me at the time some inexpressible joy and sorrow; I wanted to tell the whole world about it, but just didn't know how.

If I had remained on the streets I might not have known how. I was sent to prison. I truly don't feel that my life was *ill-directed*, if it was I who ill-directed it, and that is sheer nonsense—my direction has always been goodly, no matter what the clime realm situation. What would seem to most as a great injustice—being sent to prison in my seventeenth year, where I was the youngest inmate, rather than to a boy's reformatory, if such had to be— proved to be one of the greatest things that ever happened to me.

In prison I was not hampered by the undeveloped and oft-times silly consciousness of youth; in prison I had to deal with men, all kinds of men, caught in a single fate; and with time, three years of it. In that time I read many great books and spoke to many amazing minds—men who had spent years on Death Row and had been reprieved—one can never forget talking to such souls. One man told me "Boy, don't you serve time, let time serve you." So it did; time, so often so cruel, was kind and beneficial to me. When I left, I left there a young man, educated in the ways of men at their worst and at their best. For this reason I am unable to say anything really bad about prison. I do not say prison is a good place—far from it. For the middle-aged and old, it is a breathing coffin—any door locked against a man is a sad business. But I am me and it is not my fashion to dislike a dislikable thing when that thing has, in its strange way, been beneficial to me. Sometimes hell is a good place—if it proves to one that because it exists, so must its opposite, heaven, exist. And what was that heaven? Poetry.

I did not write poems about prison or prison men. I wrote about the world outside because I was once again outside with the world. I was of the world, not of prison. In prison I only learned, I did not write. If one must climb a ladder to reach a height and from that height see, then it were best to write about what you see and not about how you climbed. Prison to me was such a ladder.

A saving grace and a disturbing handicap it is to speak from the top of your head, putting all trust in your self as truthsayer. I write from the top of my head and to write so means to write honestly, but it almost means to write clumsily. No poet likes to be clumsy. But I decided to heck with it, as long as it allows me to speak the truth. If the poet's mind is shapely then his poem will come out shapely.

My first poem I remember only slightly; I have no copy of it; I lost it with hundreds of others, none of which I remember, in a bus terminal in Miami Beach, Florida, of all places. I had them in a suitcase—that's all I used to carry with me on my frequent itineraries, one big sole suitcase in which I would have a shirt and a suit, all crumpled up, amidst a deluge of poems. I never went back to claim that suitcase. But years later I went to the president of the bus company and he said they had probably been destroyed. So much for my early works. I never felt badly about it because I felt myself to be inexhaustible—like I had a great big supply of this stuff called poetry. The only care I took, and maybe not even that so well, was not to lose the poet. As long as I had the poet I would have the poems.

Even when I traveled throughout Europe during these last five years I still carried with me one suitcase, and still the same contents, fifty poems to one pair of underwear. Many times when passing customs I would have to open my suitcase and all the customs' man would see would be poems, poems, poems. Only a diplomat arrives with so many papers—surely by my looks and much traveled-in clothes I looked like no diplomat. So what else could I be but a spy, or a poet, or both. A poet is a spy, but not the political kind. He's everybody's spy, he spies for everybody and reports to everybody. Keats claimed he was God's spy. Since I believe in man, that makes me mankind's spy. Anyway I never really had any trouble with the border customs, except that it was always kind of difficult to close the suitcase. I would have it packed down real tight, so when I had to open it in the train compartment, which was usually crowded, the poems would jump up like a jack-in-the-box and fly everywhichway, which was a kind of drag—so I tried traveling without them and that proved to be not such a good idea because I then lost them; I think I have lost more poems than I have at hand. The best thing that could have happened to me and to the poems was my getting a publisher. As soon as I had finished a batch of them, I would send it off to my New York publisher. In that way the poems were saved.

From the time I was a child to the time I left prison I was a poet, but one who did not write any poems. When I left prison I began to write very much and maybe they were not any good— I'd like to think that was the reason for my losing them. I began to take care not to lose my poems when I wrote less. Somehow I felt, in the beginning, that it was too easy to write poetry; that even though most critics hail poetry as being one of the most difficult arts, I couldn't believe it so. As I say, I found it too easy to write this great big difficult thing. But the time came when I could only write one or two poems a month, a time when it became really hard to put down on paper what I wanted to express from the heart. It is those poems, the ones that took sweat and laborious joy to create, which remain.

The distribution of poetry among poets is a fair distribution; and the understanding of poetry is, today, more distinguished and distributed than ever before. It makes no difference whether a poem is abundantly distributed or not; as long as it holds the truth and power of the poet's advanced consciousness it will, whether understood or not, whether accepted or not, reach the main and general consciousness of mankind in time and thereby benefit it. Such is the poem's magic and this is the true mystery of poetry—its ability to advance and better the lot of men's minds.

There is a reason for the poem, for the poet—just as there was a reason for the navigator-explorer, the sea, the ship, and the discovery. Someone must "Christopher-Columbus" the mind, the great expanse of the consciousness, and this the poet does. But unlike Columbus who discovered a new world, a world that was there, the poet must make a new world—it is not there until he himself puts it there. He must put it there and discover it for all peoples and time. When I have had the self-insight to realize that what I had written was like a key to an unwritten door, I wrote that door, and when I opened it, what lay behind such a door? Nothing. Nothing, unless I put something there. I know that I shall not find anything not for the looking, I know that I must *create* the room of my truth's desire; and then, and only then, may I enter and dwell in peace and joy. For if the poet is at peace and with joy then, rest assured, all humankind is. But all humankind is not at peace, is not joyous, and never has it been—will it ever be? Can such a humankind come about? I am able to imagine it, but I do not think it is possible. All peoples are not one people. Some will be happy and some will be unhappy, and vice versa. To have the whole world happy and yet have a rope that can hang you . . . tells me that as long as there is death there will be unhappiness. Sorrow, like death, is inevitable. This is our fate. As for sorrow, the only thing we can do about it is try to make others happy; and as for death, the only thing we can do about that is to prevent it from going mad. This is the main concern of the poet of today. He has accepted the inevitable. He must now learn how best to live with it.

And yet the comedy is that everyone seems to be living with it with a better heart and spirit than the poet. Such is the case, here in America.

I feel it is a comedy that I am a poet in such a world as the world is today. Even though I feel that words like "modern" and "contemporary" are illusory words and that all peoples are of one time and one spirit, I am left with the odd feeling that in this world a poet may write a perfect poem but he may not perfect himself. He is secondary to the poem. Let the poet suffer, but do not let the poem suffer nor have it suffer us. I say this is a sad comedy because whatever light the poet may have to offer, he— and not the poem—offers it. The light comes from the poet, not from the poem. The poet gives it to the poem and the poem gives it to man. In America we honor poetry, not poets.

I am the substance of my poetry. If you honor poetry, you honor me; if you damn me, you damn poetry. I am the poetry I write. I live it, joy it, suffer it, and I wish all that is great and wonderful in it for myself and for all, and no poem have I written that was not, in one way or another, akin to me as is my flesh. Everything I know I know from man, and books, and myself— and since books are the issue of man, and since I myself am a man, it then goes to say that the whole business of poetry is in the hands of man. Poetry is nothing without man. The world is a tough place to live in and for the poet it can be unbearable. In all this spin of human endeavor the poet-man is fated to dwell on the outskirts of humankind. The poet more than any other figure in all of human time is the only being unstained by dark, monstrous, unforgivable deeds—and yet he lives as though he were exiled from life by life. It is a lonely, laborious, unrewarding place—that necessary outskirt. No, the poet is not the happiest of people, indeed he could well be the least happy.

I doubt that the poets of yesteryear had as hard and as awkward a time as does the poet today and I doubt the poet today will have had it as hard and as awkward as the poet to come. It is the poet, now, and not the poem, that must become a work of art—that must be lovely and perfect. The times demand that the poet—that is, man—be as true as a poem. And this is happening. Poets are their poems.

I'd say these poets are extremely different from the poets of old, first, because of their stress on the psyche rather than on the poem. They wholly believe that if the poet's being is of a good shape so the poem will be of a good shape. It is impossible for a crooked poet to create a straight poem. And second, the poet today has to cope with a changing world and a changing common consciousness; he has to deal with the unpoetic rather than the poetic; this goes completely contrary to his entire make-up, his whole being; yet he must himself change or else die. He sees the world changing and he realizes he must change with it if he is to survive. This is his new and difficult and heavy state—the process is all too clear: the world is changing therefore man must change, and the poet, who sooner than most becomes aware of the changing, must blow the trumpet.

The poet today does not really want to sing about trees. I once saw myself doting upon tree-poetry with my time; I had to deny such poetry because a far more desperate poetry beckoned. I recall some "nature" poets taunting me with: "But trees are so beautiful and, indeed, far grander than man." I pounded my fist on a wooden table and said: "This is what man does to trees."

Today in America there are many poets; all have something to say, some say it badly and some say it excellently, and yet all speak of love of goodness and of hopes of universal individual freedom; all are indicative of a new consciousness, a new age; they seem to represent both dusk and dawn. Today as in no other time in human history the poet is face to face with the world about him, at times at odds and at times fully with it. He sees himself, and sees how others see him, and both eyes seldom meet. The poet cries for a change in society, not for himself but for all peoples; yet he and not the people is the one in need of the change. There seems to be no society for the poet. In America the poet is something of a joke; and then again, something of a rebel, if he happens to step on an old toe of society. No one owns society and the poet most certainly would be the last to claim to; but he can, more than anyone in that society, bring about a change within it. He can do this, but fate would have it even then that he would be unable to enter that changed society. He is doomed to live on its fringe. The fault lies with no one. The poet is of his own world; it is the best that life can offer him and it should be sufficient—it should be, but it is not.

I feel that in the future many many poets will blossom forth— the poetic spirit will spread and reach toward all; it will show itself not in words—the written poem—but rather in man's being and in the deeds he enacts. If this should come about it will then be necessary for both worlds, the world of the poet and the world that belongs to everybody, to join and become a possibility. A handful of poets in every country in the world can and have always been able to live in the world as well as in their own world; and whether by chance, or by will, or by fate, it was not the people but the poet, who did not wish his world to be infringed upon. But when such humankind becomes manifold, when all are embraced by the poetic spirit, by a world of poets, not by the written word but by deed and thought and beauty, then society will have no recourse but to become suitable for them and for itself. I feel man is headed in such a direction; he is fated and due to become aware of and knowledgeable about his time; his good intelligence and compassion will enable him to cope with almost all the bothersome, distracting difficulties that may arise—and when he becomes so, "poet" will not be his name, but it will be his victory.

Man will change, and so will the poet—he too is in need of change because he too is far from perfect—in fact there are many poets who are downright messes. In America especially—where the poet is more likely to be bereft of respect and honor. Respect and honor is something almost every being wants—indeed, demands. The sad thing about respect and honor in America is that it takes money to have them; therefore the American poet who wishes respect and honor is defeated before he starts, because money is a very difficult thing to obtain, and for a poet it is almost virtually impossible. A fool and his money are soon parted, but a poet and money never even meet to be parted. And that old muse's tale about poets writing better when they are famished and ill-housed is downright idiocy.

I think of the poet because I know full well that the poem is nothing without the poet, that there would be no poetry were there no poets. Everything today seems to work against the poet; he is always in danger of being wiped out. The way the poet is treated today, I doubt that any future poet would want to be a poet—not if he has anything on the ball. First of all, given his extreme sensitivity and even if he is less sensitive, he would not accept the stigma of being classified as some kind of character or rebel because he is a poet. His intelligence would not want the insult of cheap publicity (if he happens to be controversial)— movie stars wish it because it brings them popularity and money. To the poet it brings nothing but destructive popularity without the sad recompense of gold. The poet, unlike the popular star or

178

singer, is not an entertainer. I relate mostly to my own country, America, where I hold that if it were not for poetry, for that generation of poetry that I am a part of, America would be a pretty square business. As it was, it was the poets who took that stifling squareness out of it.

I do not pity the poet of America today or yesterday because if ever there was an American poet's cry, it was never for freedom. The poet in America is free to do anything he can or hopes to regarding the state of poetry and his own state of being a poet. If the poet feels he is in a lousy state then it is up to the poet alone to change that state—not his poetic state, because all the poets of the world and of history have always been free; if a poet needs help in his poetic state then he is alone, nobody can help him. It is in his human state, the poet as a human being, that he may be mixed up and uncertain and ofttimes ill-treated and hurt. The poet does not suffer his poetry, he suffers his humanity—it is his humanity I am concerned with. I feel it is treated ungraciously, stupidly, and sometimes dangerously.

I do not say that if a country does extend respect and honor to its poets that it will have poets. Many countries I have been to, countries known for their respectful treatment of the artist, were clearly lacking in poets. My concern is not just with American poets but with the poets of the world because a poet is first of all a universal being—that is why it is impossible for a true poet to be nationalistic. To write poems for the state and not from his heart is death to the poet.

So I contend that the state of the poet on earth today is lousy. In America he is looked upon as something strangely averse to the American way of life; in Russia he is unable to sing his song —he must sing for the state and no poet can sing a song not his; in Europe he is exhausted; in Asia he doesn't exist; the dark cloud of uncertainty prevails over all. And this necessary agent, once the agent of beauty, is now the recipient of certainty. That is why the poet must be. The world is uncertain; the poet is striving toward certainty.

The world is changing; and what makes for uncertainty is that the world is aware that it is changing. To not know that the world is changing is to be certain of a world, familiar and old, a world that is no longer—the past always seems safer than the future because we know the past; we don't know the future. Gone is the certainty of yesterday's world, a world molded once by new ideas and ways, soon to become familiar and decadent, old and dying. The ideas and ways of yesterday are dead. The world now seems to sit back and to ask: "Okay, now what? What next?" Nobody knows; nobody can know; one can only hope or predict or try to make what is hoped for and predicted a reality. I feel that it takes uncertainty to get to what is certain. A smart man knows that no one can be certain about life, especially the changing life of the present—to be thus certain is to be presumptuous and ill-visioned; it is against the nature of life. Today man is at a level with the world; the world goes on and it needs man to help it go on, not for the world's sake but for man's sake, because the world will always go on—man is the only thing in danger of not continuing. He is stuck in the world; he can't get out without dying, so he is able to take the reins of the world and direct. He has no other choice, if he wants to continue on, that is. And so the world goes on; life goes on and death goes on, and poets come and go, and death comes before life, and poetry comes after life, and everything, yes, everything is changing. Man is changing, seas and mountains are changing, dresses and cars are changing. It has always been so, but it has not always been like it is today. Today we are fully aware of the changing process in and around us—we are close to it, and for the first time in human history we are wholly uncertain of what will come of it all. . . .

The world is getting bigger while getting smaller, as it diminishes via rocket speed it expands via human thought, via our consciousness. There are no more lands to explore, to conquer—Christopher Columbus must now traverse the sea of the mind and who can doubt he'll not discover some kind of wondrous continent there? Once this new mental territory is found and opened up, people will most assuredly migrate there and settle there and build. The wonderful human mind has long ago been to the moon—we are our own rockets; and the bigger the rocket the farther the journey; so the wider the expanse of the mind the greater our possibility to learn and enjoy the adventures it holds for us. But one cannot take this maturing consciousness of peoples for granted. Man still suffers; his compassion, his broken heart cries out "O God" perhaps to no God—man seems to be a god-minded creature without a god. He knows the cause of his uncertain predicament; he knows that it is man who torments man; that it is not life that is bad or sad but man that is bad, sad. All know that it is man who operates the cannon, the vise-boot, the electrode; everything imagined about hell is imagined by man; it was man drove the tank, fired the bullet—men are killed more often by men than by anything else. The human plague is always on. It is man who makes death a lousy, stinking business, who makes death fearsome and a sorry thing for all. We must all die but it is how we die that counts. The crowded world clamors for birth control, yet death control seems to be more our fashion. Death has never been the property of man.

We are a great, fast, learning, growing people, and with all the death thrown at us, by us, somehow we manage to strive toward peace with some kind of dignity and love.

So I will conclude with the feeling that the poet today must be unlike the poet; he cannot be a discriminator between heart and soul, flesh and spirit, beauty and ugliness, truth and untruth. He stands merely as a man, a man who feels that he is but the guardian of the human consciousness and that when he dies there will be another poet to take his relay, in order that consciousness grow ever more perfect, and man ever more human, and life ever more total. . . .

15 A FRAME FOR POETRY

William Jay Smith

I

William Plomer, a poet I much admire, has spoken of himself as a "solitary prospector" on the poetic scene, and the term is one that might apply to a number of writers in the vast, uneven literary expanse that is America. I, for my part, have staked out my claims, and legitimate claims in the area of lyric poetry I believe them to be; they may appear modest only because unannounced in gaudy and sprawling letters. I hate sloppiness of any sort and although I have belonged to no school, the fact that I can write a proper sentence places me, in the eyes of the recent resurgent literary bushmen, inevitably with the "academic" poets. In actuality, I have been associated with colleges only in recent years and then mostly on a part-time basis; and I deplore the way poetry is discussed in most classrooms. There is a vast amount of dull patter that passes for poetry today, both in and out of the academy; but the worst offenders are those "new" poets who go on interminably about their free-wheeling "poetics" derived from Williams and Pound. These self-expressionists had been quietly mimeographing their efforts for years (indeed, they themselves existed in a limbo of mimeography), but now that they have broken into print, their pretension is boundless. There is much dull talk about poetry of late; and although it can only briefly obscure the merits of good poems, it can unfortunately foster and promote many dull ones.

II

Variety in poetry, as in any art, is everything. It is the spice without which the cooking is glutinous and unpalatable. To repeat oneself *ad infinitum,* as even some extremely talented modern poets do, seems to me like locking oneself up with stale, unpleasant odors in the kitchen. I have always believed in Jean Cocteau's dictum that the artist should find out what he can do and then do something else. The poet should always be venturing, trying out new things. One doesn't want experimentation for its own sake, the sense of the freakish doctor surrounded by retorts in the laboratory, but one does want the poet who is willing time after time to risk everything and play for the highest stakes. The poet must be constantly exploring, going out on a limb. This does not mean the continual development of wholly new styles, but rather the enlargement and expansion of one's basic style. It means putting out new shoots, growing as a tree grows up and out, feeding more and more on light and air. The following poem, "Tulip," seems to me to have something to say in this connection. The tulip, that favorite flower in the gardens of the mathematicians and philosophers of the eighteenth century, came originally from Persia (the word means "turban") and entered Europe by way of Constantinople. It became so famous that there developed the phenomenon of tulipmania when tulip bulbs were prized more highly than jewels. The tulip is, of course, the most metallic appearing of flowers, and one of its chief characteristics is that it has no scent.

Tulip[1]

A slender goblet wreathed in flame,
From Istanbul the flower came
And brought its beauty, and its name.

Now as I lift it up, that fire
Sweeps on from dome to golden spire
Until the East is all aflame:

By curving petals held entire
In cup of ceremonial fire,
Magnificence within a frame.

[1] From William Jay Smith, *Poems 1947–1957* (Boston: Atlantic Monthly Press-Little, Brown, 1957).

Poetry for me should be continually expanding within its frame. Humor is itself a form of expansion; laughter, as Max Beerbohm said, is "but a joyous surrender." I have been drawn to light verse because of a firm belief that humor is one of America's greatest and most enduring characteristics. Children's poetry, with its wide use of stanza forms and the range of its nonsense, has been for me a liberating influence, giving me a chance to explore in a light vein themes that I have developed and expanded in adult work.

III

Some poems rise like mushrooms, full-grown, mysterious, complete in every detail, and one wonders from whence they have sprung. "The Peacock of Java" is for me such a poem, although it may seem otherwise in view of the facts of its composition.

The Peacock of Java[2]

I thought of the mariners of Solomon,
Who, on one of their long voyages, came
    On that rare bird, the Peacock
    Of Java, which brings, even
To the tree of heaven, heaven.

How struggling upward through the dark
    Lianas, they beheld the tree,
    And in the tree, the fan
That would become a king's embroidery.

How they turned and on the quiet
    Water then set sail
    For home, the peacock's tail
Committed to the legends of the sea.

I remember not long after the war copying out from a bird book at the Houghton Farm in Mountainville, New York, where I was

2 From William Jay Smith, *Celebration at Dark* (New York: Farrar, Straus & Giroux, 1950). Copyright 1950 by William Jay Smith; reprinted by permission of the publisher, Farrar, Straus & Giroux, Inc.

then staying, the facts about the peacock and Solomon's mariners. I do not have the quotation now to refer to it; it reposes, along with the original typescript of the poem, in the Lamont Library at Harvard. I had the impression at the time that the reference might in some way be useful in connection with a group of poems on which I was then working that had to do with the Pacific. Some time later in New York, without referring to the piece I had copied out, I wrote the poem right off in a few minutes. The only word that gave me trouble was the first one in the last line. It took me a while to settle on "committed," which I now think is absolutely right and one of the best touches in the poem. When I had written down the piece as it stands, I still had the vague feeling that it was somehow incomplete and part of a longer work. But I realized later the reason for this. The poem clearly was concerned in some way with the years I had spent in the Pacific, but not with Java, where I had never been. In trying to locate to my own satisfaction what had given rise to the poem, I concluded that the experience itself had been omitted, or rather transformed, entirely and had to do with a peacock only metaphorically.

While I was liaison officer on board a French ship attached to the South Pacific fleet, we were requested by the French Admiralty to make a tour of the islands of the New Hebrides. We were received wherever we went with great excitement by French planters who in some cases had not seen a French ship, nor often any of their metropolitan countrymen, for twenty-five years or more. On one island we trekked at length through what seemed impenetrable jungle, and finally, as we approached the plantation, the vegetation began to clear and the rotting bittersweet smell of copra and the other overrich odors of a tropical farm greeted our nostrils. As we emerged on the clearing, there rose, in a green circle before the low-lying plantation house, a superb traveler's tree, the great radiating fan of its branches flung up against a blazing sky. This marvelous sight made us all reflect on the appropriateness of the tree's name; it provided a rich and wonderful welcome. I thought of that vision afterward and of the remainder of that day and that journey, and wanted to put it all down in some way. Years later I concluded that perhaps I had in "The Peacock of Java."

"Galileo Galilei" is one of my favorite poems by reason, I think, of the curious circumstances of its composition:

Galileo Galilei[3]

Comes to knock and knock again
At a small secluded doorway
In the ordinary brain.

Into light the world is turning,
And the clocks are set for six;
And the chimney pots are smoking,
And the golden candlesticks.

Apple trees are bent and breaking,
And the heat is not the sun's;
And the Minotaur is waking,
And the streets are cattle runs.

Galileo Galilei,
In a flowing, scarlet robe,
While the stars go down the river
With the turning, turning globe,

Kneels before a black Madonna
And the angels cluster round
With grave, uplifted faces
Which reflect the shaken ground

And the orchard which is burning,
And the hills which take the light;
And the candles which have melted
On the altars of the night.

Galileo Galilei
Comes to knock and knock again
At a small secluded doorway
In the ordinary brain.

In Oxford in 1947 an acquaintance of mine told me one morning that he had awoken the previous night and found that the peculiar happenings of his dream had suggested to him the lines of a poem. He began to write them down, but he could not get beyond the opening:

> Galileo Galilei
> Comes to knock and knock again
> At a small secluded doorway
> In the ordinary brain.

I noted the lines down, and forgot about them until that same night when I found myself unable to sleep. I got up and wrote the poem down more or less as it now appears.

This may all sound suspect—*à la* "Kubla Khan"—but it did really happen. The lines I now realize appealed to me particularly because I had just returned from my first trip to Florence, where I had been staying with friends in Pian dei Giullari, just around the corner from the house in which Galileo was living when Milton came to visit him. I was aware in writing the poem of many impressions of Italy, and of the movement of a kind of *mandala*, the dance of a priest around the altar.

In any case, I was rather pleased with what I had done and showed the result the next morning to my friend. He said indignantly that what I had written had nothing whatever to do with what he had had in mind. *Tant pis*, I replied, then he could certainly not expect to get credit for the lines. He agreed that they were now mine; and we have not met since.

Oddly enough, those readers who have admired the poem have all commented on its strange dreamlike quality.

Poems grow out of dreams but dreams are often dreamt with one's eyes wide open. Once in St. Louis, when on leave during the war, I was driving past a building that I knew well (I had passed it hundreds of times without ever giving it much thought). It was a school for the blind, run by the Sisters of Mercy. I had just heard that there was a power failure in this part of the city, and as I drove by, looking out at the sign: "School for the Blind," I realized in a flash that this failure meant absolutely nothing to those whose eyes were already permanently sealed. The line came to me—one of those *données* on which we all subsist and for which we thank the gods:

> The lights have gone out in the School for the Blind.

It traveled with me for a long time, that line, circling in the back of my head. I felt instinctively that I had the beginning of a poem. It was there: I had the rhythm, I had the title, "The Failure of Power." I felt the strength of some mysterious force pulling me forward, but I did not yet have the words. I remember, thinking back on it, of the story of the painter Degas excitedly taking some poems he had written to the poet Mallarmé. Degas had tried to put into them all his delight in dancers and race horses and when Mallarmé hesitated to give his approval, the painter protested that he had, after all, started the poems with very good ideas in mind. Mallarmé's rejoinder was, of course, that poems are written with words, not with ideas. In any case, the few words that I did have—not yet an idea even—traveled with me for some time, until I sat down one night in Noumea, New Caledonia after an afternoon visit to a leper colony above the city and wrote out the poem—with its title changed, rightly I think, to "Miserere."

Miserere[4]

The lights have gone out in the School for the Blind,
  And all the shades are drawn.
  Sisters of Mercy move over the lawn.

Sisters of Mercy move into the mind
  With steps that are swifter than any;
  Light on each pupil is perched like a penny.

The lights have gone out in the School for the Blind;
  The flare on the runway dies,
  And the murderer waits with dancing eyes.

4 From William Jay Smith, *Celebration at Dark* (New York: Farrar, Straus & Giroux, 1950). Copyright 1950 by William Jay Smith; reprinted by permission of the publisher, Farrar, Straus & Giroux, Inc.

The murderer waits in his quiet mind,
    While Night, a Negress nun,
    A Sister of Mercy, sweeps over the sun.

What I have been attempting to say about the peculiar genesis of poetry is something like what Charles Causley said recently— that all works of art must have their mystery, and although poems *can* be taken apart like clocks, when they are put back together they may still not be *explained*. They retain, they give off, as Garcia Lorca said every great work of art must, their *sonidos negros,* dark sounds.[5] This, it seems to me, is the resonance that all great poetry possesses—that unfathomable mystery of the psyche that we can approach only with reverence and love.

IV

Poetry for me always begins with the particular, and I can generalize only from my own experience. One of my poems that has become an anthology piece may serve as a peculiar and particular example of how poems—mine, at least—get written:

American Primitive[6]

Look at him there in his stovepipe hat,
His high-top shoes, and his handsome collar;
Only my Daddy could look like that,
And I love my Daddy like he loves his Dollar.

The screen door bangs, and it sounds so funny—
There he is in a shower of gold;
His pockets are stuffed with folding money,
His lips are blue, and his hands feel cold.

He hangs in the hall by his black cravat,
The ladies faint, and the children holler:

[5] *Dawn and Dusk,* "Poems of Our Time" (New York: Franklin Watts, 1963), p. 11.
[6] From William Jay Smith, *Poems 1947–1957* (New York: Atlantic Monthly Press-Little, Brown, 1957).

Only my Daddy could look like that,
And I love my Daddy like he loves his **Dollar**.

A poet friend remarked to me once that this was one of my
poems that he most admired and that it must have been a delight
to write it right off, as I so clearly had done. It was indeed a delight
to write it right off—as it now stands—after working on it at odd
moments for a period of five years. I cannot recall how many
versions I put down during this period, most of them discarded.
I knew exactly where I wanted to get to; the problem was getting
there, and getting there with directness and *élan*—and without
fuss. I had in mind a Mississippi River guitar tune—absolutely
mechanical in its rhythm—an out-and-out child's innocent un-
adorned view of horror—horror with the resonant twang of
strings to it. In its original version, the poem was very much
longer. There were a good many little ballad bits, of which this
is an example:

I fear the feel of frozen steel,
I fear the scarlet dagger;
But more than these I fear the eel,
I fear the carpetbagger.

I had indeed the vision of the carpetbagger who had made his
money in some suspect manner; and with the sunlight and the
screen door I wish to suggest the large, open, airy Southern house
that I remembered from childhood. The most difficult line for me
to get in the poem was the one that now seems the simplest, and
it is the turning point:

He hangs in the hall by his black cravat.

Poetry is all in verbs, in verbs and nouns, and it seems to me it is
all here in the verb "hangs." I have frequently been asked to discuss this poem with gradeschool children and, although it may
appear a macabre choice on the part of the teacher, I have discovered that children respond to it without hesitation. They
understand that a child is speaking and that the father has
hanged himself for some reason involving money. College stu-

dents, on the other hand, have often found this piece bewildering; they have lost the down-to-earth metaphorical approach of childhood and cannot follow the simple words to their unexpected conclusion. I think that I scarcely need add that although "American Primitive" is a bitter poem in the tradition of Edwin Arlington Robinson's "Richard Cory," it is certainly not intended as my sole view of the American scene.

V

My recent work has evolved in many ways and if I have in the past been attracted by the short poem—the lyric in which spirit is compressed—the fire in the brazier, to which Marianne Moore referred in speaking of the poems of Louise Bogan—I have been no less drawn to the opposite side of the coin, the long poem with the long line, slowly expanding, drawing the inner fire upward and outward. The danger of the long free-verse line is naturally a lapse into loose echoes of Whitman, but one must take the risk; one must break up the frame to make of the fractured frame a wholly new and different one. Poems must continually expand and contract, and I like to think of the lines in a long poem of this sort as akin to the pleats in an accordion—each intact and trim but ready to open out resonantly to its full proportion. In conclusion then, I offer a poem that I hope illustrates in larger ways those qualities in verse that I have stressed and to which in any presentation of reality I feel one must return:

The Tin Can[7]

One very good thing I have learned from writer friends in Japan is that when you have a lot of work to do, especially writing, the best thing is to take yourself off and hide away. The Japanese have a word for this, the *kanzume*, or the "tin can," which means about what we would mean by the "lock-up." When someone gets off by himself to concentrate, they say, "he has gone into the tin can."

> Herbert Passin, "The Mountain Hermitage:
> Pages from a Japanese Notebook," *Encounter*, August 1957

[7] Reprinted from *Poetry* (September 1963). Copyright 1964 by William Jay Smith.

I

I have gone into the tin can: not in late spring, fleeing a stewing, meat-and-fish smelling city of paper houses,

Not when wisteria hangs, a purple cloud, robbing the pines of their color, have I sought out the gray plain, the indeterminate outer edge of a determined world,

Not to an inn nestling astride a waterfall where two mountains meet and the misty indecisiveness of Japanese ink-drawn pines frames the afternoon, providing from a sheer bluff an adequate view of infinity,

But here to the tin can in mid-winter: to a sagging New England farmhouse in the rock-rooted mountains, where wind rifles the cracks,

Here surrounded by cross-hatched, tumbling stone walls, where the snow plow with its broad orange side-thrust has outlined a rutted road,

Where the dimly cracked gray bowl of the sky rests firmly on the valley and gum-thick clouds pour out at the edges,

Where in the hooded afternoon a pock-marked, porcupine-quilled landscape fills with snow-swirls, and the tin can settles in the snow.

I have gone into the tin can, head high, resolute, ready to confront the horrible, black underside of the world.

Snow-murmur! Wind-dip! Heart-rage! It is now my duty to record, to enumerate, to set down the sounds, smells, meanings of this place. . . .

How begin? With the red eye of the chocolate-brown rhinoceros? With the triple-serrated teeth of the pencil-fed monster with bright fluted ears and whirling black tail? . . .

There is a skittering and scrambling in the can: a trickle of sand and sawdust from a sack, wet leaves blown back, cracks spreading along the wall.

There is the chitter and clatter of keys, a smudge of pencils, a smear of time. . . .

Stippled heaven! Snow-ruffle! Garnet-grove! Black water winding through snow-wounds! Ripple-roost!

Will the wilds wake? Will the words work? Will the rattle and rustle subside? Will the words rise?

A bluejay flashes by a window, the stripes of his tail, chevrons torn from a non-com's sleeve; and in the afternoon the snow begins.

First: a hush—pit-stillness, black accent of hemlocks up and down the mountain, mist in the valley thickening and deepening until it breaks

And the snow already fallen swirls up to meet the snow descending—sky-darkening, still-deepening, sky-hooded and whirling, flakes flying,

Houses settling sidewise in the drifts—winds wedging, snow-choked road lost, still-winding, earth white-star-carpeted, still-wheeling;

And in the tin can the same still, paper-white, damp emptiness.

II

A door opens—is it a door?—and a woman walks by in the tin can watering tropical plants that jut from the wall or spring from the floor, their leaves great green famished mouths,—

Feeding the fish, distributing specks to the seahorses in their tank and meat to the turtle on his wet pillow;

Cats curling about her legs, she pats the dogs and caresses the heads of the children, and the children open their green mouths and grow upward toward the sunlight like plants.

A door opens: a woman walks by, and through her bobbing, mud-colored glass watches the movements of my pencil,

And a record turns, a black hemstitched whirlpool, and the woman wheels off in a trance of drum beats, screaming of need and nothingness and money;

And money like wet leaves piles around my ankles, and I am sickened by its smell. . . .

Snow-madness! Leaf-mania! Green parabolas! In the tin can there is no morning of revelation, no afternoon of appraisal, no evening of enchantment.

In the tin can a small boy in a nightmare kicks one leg from his bed overturning a glowing iron stove, and in seconds fire sweeps through a city of tin cans.

I wake thinking of the boy, and all about me are the smoking ruins of cigarettes; and the ashes descend through the half-extinguished afternoon with the smell of burning flesh. . . .

A weasel waddles along in a kind of trotting walk; a mole inches up through darkness, his blind trail, the workings of consciousness.

In the tin can I hear a murmur of voices speaking of life in other tin cans, of death sifting through them.

A vision of bodies blasted on the black earth; and I think of those photographs my father kept from the Nicaraguan Insurrection, was it? —that we played with as children on a sun-spotted floor—

Brown bodies spread out over the jungle floor, the figures beside them wide-eyed and bewildered, toy soldiers in ridiculous stances in a meaningless world;

I think of the photographs rubbed vinegar-brown in the sunlight; and of how we placed them around us, lined our toy fortress with them,

And talked to one another through tin-can telephones, while from out the photographs the jungle's green arm tapped our small brown shoulders.

III

The tin can is circling with beasts: dogs howl in the night, cats sidle through slats in the tin, wet field mice hanging from their mouths;

I step in the morning over the entrails of rodents lying like spun jewels on the carpet, offerings to the dark gods.

And the dogs rise from their corners, their dirt-crusted rag beds, smelling of snow, sniffing the roots, digging the floor, and begin again to circle the can. . . .

Bright flashes of morning! Blue snow-peaks! Fog smoking the valleys! Angels lighting the rubble: Children skating on a blue pond! Deer stepping delicately down through the pines! . . .

And always the face, the woman's face, brooding over all, rising from the earth beside me, disembodied; always the woman clean and classic as sunlight, moving about the room, sifting the dirt, watering the shadowy flowers, polishing the spotted tin.

I hear her speak softly; and there she is again beside me; and again the face turns, a small bat-face and the lips draw back in a red wound and shriek; and the room is filled with a smell of mould and money. . . .

The woman turns, the bat-face again a woman's face blue
with shrieking, and the woman walks to the end of the
corridor, climbs a broad white stairway. . . .

Leaf-fringe! Sky-tingle! Cloud-clatter! Earth-blaze! All my
underworld crumbles; and I am left with the one brooding face, no face; with bat-wings folding the black air
into a shroud.

IV

When am I to emerge? Dirt falls; eyes blur; memory con-
founds; multiple voices move furred and batlike round
my ears; and then no sound—

Only the grating of a pencil over a page—an army of ant
words swarming up to consciousness.

When will they break through to a bright remembered
world, up through the top of the tin?

Snow-swirl—hemlocks hunching toward the window—gray-
black shadow cutting over black, fan shaken over fan. . . .

From here the windows open their white mouths to swallow
the wind-driven snow.

And I remember salmon sky, fine-boned sunsets sweeping the
spiny mountains; and I have seen the snow

In banks driven back from the road, the black edges scraggly
and bearded, the snowbanks under the birches like milk
from buckets overturned and frozen. . . .

Will the words rise? Will the poem radiate with morning?
Here where I see nothing, I have seen the Cyclops-eye
ballooning over a frozen world,

The wide fringe of eyelashes opening on all existence, the single glazed dazzle of the eye watching,

And I have lived with my eyes—watching the watching eye, the eyeball swiveling in nothingness, a huge black moon in egg-white immensity,

And I have seen the edges of the tin can fold in around it.

V

O bodies my body has known! Bodies my body has touched and remembered—in beds, in baths, in streams, on fields and streets—will you remember?

Sweet vision of flesh known and loved, lusted after, cherished, repulsed, forgotten and remembered, will you remember my body buried now and forgotten? . . .

In childhood we played for hours in the sun on a dump near a cannery; and the long thin ribbons of tin rippled round us, and we ran by the railroad track and into the back yard behind the asparagus and through the feathers of green our bodies touched and the strips of tin radiated their rainbows of light—

And our bodies were spiraled with tin and wondrous with light—

Now out of darkness here from the tin can, through snow-swirl and wind-dazzle, let the tin ribbons ride again and range in new-found freedom;

Let the tin rip and rustle in the wind; let the green leaves rise and rift the wondrous windows, leaving behind the raging women, and the sickening mould of money, rust, and rubble. . . .

And the words clean-spun and spiraling orbit that swift-seeing, unseen immensity that will never be contained!

197

16 POETRY AS DISCOVERY

Reed Whittemore

I think of poetry as a thing of the mind and tend to judge it, at least in part, by the qualities of mind it displays. There is nothing revolutionary about this doctrine, yet it's an unpopular one these days. The poet begins by trying not to be taken for a philosopher or a scientist and ends up contentedly being described as irrational and ignorant. I prefer to be described as a rational beast or at least one exhibiting rational tendencies. This is only to say that the properties of mind I most admire are the daytime properties—those that get us to the store or shop and back, and put us on the radio discussing poetry or arguing about communism and democracy. Most of my poems, therefore, tend to deal primarily with the daytime part of the mind, that is, the prosaic part; only occasionally do they deal directly with the nighttime self, as in this poem where the daytime and nighttime selves are set up against each other. It is called "The Girl Friend," and the girl friend is a nighttime acquaintance whose name, rather ironically, is Sylvia (a more straightforward poet than I would call her Ulalume, perhaps, or Madame Blavatsky).

The Girl Friend[1]

Waking was wisdom, ungodly, civil,
Wrapped in the shawl of the commonplace.
There he could let his wilderness
Tame itself in a breakfast haze and stroll

[1] From *An American Takes a Walk* (Minneapolis: University of Minnesota Press, 1956). "The Girl Friend" is copyright 1956 by Reed Whittemore.

Lazily out of context
Through kindly halls and offices
Of faith and flabby flesh and the morning comics.
But at night, ah, in old General Terror's tenement,
It was winter.
Winter and war and the two together,
Troops in a grey cloud marching, December
And guns, messkits and snow,
Tacked like a gothic print on his wall of sleep.

Reality?
Who was Sylvia? What was she? Could anyone
Balked and foiled in the soft mist
Of days and blood and nights and blood
And all that marching, marching
Answer? Not he; so the questions
Pounced in the twilight at him as he padded
Softly, softly,
Sleeping, waking,
Towards what in fire or cloud or bush or whirlwind
Would be Sylvia all right,
Sylvia.

I say this is an unrepresentative poem of mine and I think it is.
Yet it may serve to introduce the problem of how the poetic pre-
tender to reason, like me, struggles to mediate between his selves;
or, to put it differently, how he thinks. For he *does* think—he
doesn't just feel, despite a good deal of propaganda to the contrary—but unlike more prosaic thinkers, or even unlike himself
when he is at work in a prosaic form like a lecture or essay, he
tends to think subversively about the limitations of thought. His
meditations betray him, leading him to discover the insufficiencies
of his own meditations, his own art, his own rhetoric.

One can imagine other more consoling forms of poetic meditation, of course (I am talking about a kind which leads the poet
inexorably into despondency). There are the happy lyrics ("God's
in his heaven, all's right with the world") and the epic orderings
like *The Odyssey* and *The Divine Comedy;* but this depressing
form I cultivate is a very common one, one respected by poets

with great rational prowess like Shakespeare or Donne—or, in modern times, Gerard Manley Hopkins, Wallace Stevens, W. H. Auden. Indeed the short-poem genre in which poets mostly perform nowadays is itself ironically most suitable for meditations about our rational insufficiency as meditators. Extended, discursive meditations simply cannot be conducted in it. It is like a syllogism in that it so isolates a problem spatially and temporally that it simply cannot carry all the burdens of a complex mind.

As a poet given to writing short poems according to the modern practice I have been impressed by the insufficiencies of the short-poem art for about twenty-five years; yet I have gone on writing short poems and I suspect that my reputation as a poet, if I have any, is almost entirely based on a few short poems. I find the genre a congenial one in which to deal with my own insufficiencies, among which is my own rational incapacity to work things out, order them logically, on a big scale. Here is a poem with such a complaint, a poem which summarizes my sentiments after I had experienced a series of failures to make for myself an extended or full statement, that is, a coherent, unified book.

Preface to an Unwritten Text[2]

Words of thanks and caution to the many
Teachers, students, authors, friends and loves
Whose words and writings made me, and who led me
From the errors that my work disproves;

And to the academic centers of complexity,
Without whose constant services my premises,
For better or for worse, were never scholarly;
And to my mother and my father and my nemesis,

I am grateful.
But all these I disjoin
From all that here is hateful.
The text which does not follow is my own.

2 From *An American Takes a Walk* (Minneapolis: University of Minnesota Press, 1956). "Preface to an Unwritten Text" is copyright 1947 by *The New Yorker* magazine.

And here is another on the same general theme, recounting the same discovery of personal limits.

After Some Day of Decision[3]

He doesn't know when it was that the last door closed,
But now it is closed for good. What he is doing
He will continue to do, and what he has not done
Will not be done. He can relax,
Letting a law of Newton's lay his tracks.

He is relieved. In the past the future was always
Troublesome, he being caught
In an onward and upward tradition. Not any more.
Now all the frontiers are closed where he could be other
Then what he has been, which is no bother.

It is called settling down. The time between waking
And sleeping shrinks, the days run together,
And all that was messily tentative, shaky and new
Is quietly stored away, that he may pursue
What, having been tried, is now his true.

And so forth. Stanza by stanza. If there is any
Slightest complaint he might possibly make
Against having made for his weary head such a bed,
It is merely that sometimes in it, as he was bred,
He dreams of being tried and pronounced—"Dead."

My complaints, however, have not always been against myself. I assume that my condition is not an unusual one among poets, though perhaps I have made more of insufficiency than some of my contemporaries. Here is a small lyrical blast against some empty lyricism in our time:

3 From *An American Takes a Walk* (Minneapolis: University of Minnesota Press, 1956). "After Some Day of Decision" is copyright 1956 by Reed Whittemore.

The Line of an American Poet[4]

That American Poet's future
Is bright because he began
With the know-how of Ford and Chrysler
And the faith of American Can.

He fathomed success's secret
And stuck to his P's and Q's,
And urged himself, over and over,
To produce and produce and produce.

His very first works were cleverly
Built, and the market boomed.
Some of the world's most critical
Consumers looked, and consumed.

Lines off his line became smoother
And smoother as more and more
Know-how came in the window
And verses rolled out the door.

Now everyone in the market
Knows his new works are sure
To be just as the country wants them:
Uniform, safe and pure.

It may seem that I am being perverse here, constantly celebrating insufficiency in myself and in others. How can I, as a professed rationalist, defend such defeatist activities rationally? I don't think I can. The writing of a short poem is an impulsive, unreasoned act in many respects; its origins are more probably to be found in some dark mental cave than in the daytime mind. One does what one does; the process is automatic, primitive, as I have tried to indicate in the following poem, an imaginary ex-

---

[4] From *An American Takes a Walk* (Minneapolis: University of Minnesota Press, 1956). "The Line of an American Poet" is copyright 1956 by Reed Whittemore.

cerpt from a writer's diary in a week of sterility. Here I am simply describing the necessity I feel to write something even when I have nothing to write about.

A Week of Doodle[5]

This kind of thing (these lines) might be likened to those
Hobbies with hammers and drills
Practiced in all the best basements by men who'd dispose
Of some of a long day's cache of bills and ills

In the evening. Manual therapy.
Even physicians practice it. It is approved.
The mind is soothed by the hand as the hand pounds a rickety
Chair or table together; violently soothed,

As, in this instance, this unregenerate mind
Seeks to dispose of some of its winter's reverses
By letting this ink in this pen in this clumsy hand
Make (for this mind) these verses.

Literature itself is frequently described as essentially irrational. For example, many comparisons have been drawn between the properties of literature and the religious or magical rites of savages (thus the traditional view of literature as an imitation of life may be looked at quite simply as a late form of homeopathic magic, the practitioners of which assume that one may act upon the real world or a part thereof by acting upon a constructed image of that world). And surely short poems like those I have been reading tend to sustain such a thesis. Yet you will remember that I began this talk by asserting that I personally think of poetry as a thing of the mind and tend to judge it by the qualities of mind it displays.

Since I am too advanced a being to think I can destroy my enemy by sticking pins in his picture, a contradiction is clearly at work here which I will not straighten out—for the mind, I have been saying, has contradictory elements in it—but I would nonetheless like to defend literature from the suggestions which

[5] From *An American Takes a Walk* (Minneapolis: University of Minnesota Press, 1956). "A Week of Doodle" is copyright 1956 by Reed Whittemore.

seem to accompany descriptions of its irrationality, mainly the suggestion that in being irrational literature is somehow different from, or more primitive than, other human activities. My point is that literature is not a bit unique in its irrationality. To play chess or bridge or football, to attend Mass on Sunday and take communion, to observe birthdays and fourths or fourteenths of July—all these are *also* primitive, irrational rites if one pleases to be anthropological about them; what we find to be primitive is something we think we ought somehow to have outgrown.

If we abandon here the words with unfortunate connotations, like irrationality and primitiveness, we will be better off. Let us ask instead what perpetuates these games—for games they are— as popular actions for human beings. Why do we like to work within fourteen lines, or one hundred yards of green turf, or to agree that a bishop should move only on diagonals? The answers will not come readily, but surely they will have something to do with the great practical advantage bestowed upon the mind by such arbitrary limitations. The whole concept of mental concentration is rooted here and surely not many persons would wish to suggest that the capacity to concentrate is merely a primitive mental property.

The writing of a short poem is a characteristic act of concentration and is perfectly analogous to the playing of a game of chess up to the point at which the poet has, as it were, achieved reasonable mastery of the verbal and prosodic rules of the game, a mastery which any number of bad poets have achieved. At that point, however, chess and poetry move apart and as they do so, poetry rather oddly begins to demonstrate a clear superiority to chess as a mental game. The chess master, to *be* a chess master, need not be a master of anything beyond his sixty-four squares (though he may become a great general on the side); but the poet, while he may become a master of prosody and all sorts of verbal gambits, is not even really a poet until he has done *more* than achieve such mastery.

I am referring to the dimensions of the game of poetry, as distinguished from chess. Mastery of the game of poetry would seem to include the capacity to evaluate—which is to mediate intelligently about—the game itself, as well as play it. The common words for this capacity are wisdom and understanding.

I think it can be discovered of almost all great poems that they demonstrate a kind of wisdom *about* the game being played. One can hardly imagine the comparable situation in chess—the chess master perhaps removing his own king's head with a penknife and saying, "alas, poor Claudius?"—yet poetry seems to demand this of its practitioners, to demand as part of the game that they stand outside of the game and look at it with the perspective that concentration upon the game itself tends to deny them. This is the inwardness of poetry I have been trying to describe; it leads to all sorts of depressing discoveries, such as the inadequacy of words as tokens for the playing of the game, or the dubious integrity of the roles or positions in the game which various "pieces" adopt. Chess players can ill afford to make such discoveries (they are apt to stop playing), but poets can ill afford not to make them.

These discoveries, as I have said, lead poets into melancholy swiftly. Shakespeare's heroes get terribly depressed about their own rhetoric; and Shakespeare himself, where we find or think we find him, seems constantly to be mumbling about the inadequacies of his stage, his dramatic form, his heroes' powers. These discoveries are, in other words, antigame discoveries and they may take many forms. My own discoveries (though I am not trying to compare myself with Shakespeare here except insofar as we are practitioners of the same game) tend to emerge indirectly in mock-heroics, which are themselves antigame by nature. In the mock-heroics genre the poet overplays the game to demonstrate that the game, or part of it, is absurd. Thus I have a number of heroes in my poems whose heroic properties tend to be canceled out by their own stupidity or by the senselessness of the matters they are delighted to be heroic about. Here is a poem about a familiar American "hero."

The Man Who Can Do It Himself[6]

This must be done in narrative form. Imagine
A boy with the world before him,
Blond hair, blue eyes,
And the rest of the paraphernalia for light, culture and joy,

[6] From *The Self-Made Man* (New York: Macmillan, 1959). "The Man Who Can Do It Himself" is copyright 1959 by Reed Whittemore.

A wife in the best part of town
And a pretty home
(Which he'd built himself)
And a good name in a sound business, and friends
(Who had built themselves), so that
Our boy could be sure forever or nearly that nothing
Or nearly nothing
Except perhaps war and the fall-out
Would presume to unbuild his self-made, blue-blond destiny—
Imagine this, if you please, and then
Cast your envious eyes upon his other
And multiple parts: a workshop
Equipped with a lathe, a vise and hundreds of Stanley hammers
As well as a studio, a bar and some hi-fi tweeters—
All of this
Used up to the hilt by our hero who was,
If there ever was,
A kind of green-thumb character who could
Make what he wanted at will, a table, a fortune—
Are you not jealous?
                    Well,
Hear this. He took some
Rags, last week, he had oiled himself, a match,
And his wife, tweeters, the works, and when he had
Got it all going good with his green thumb,
He jumped in himself with a guitar he had constructed
Out of a packing box, a cat, that sort of thing,
And he strummed upon it, and sat him down to sing:

> Do it yourself, fol-de-rol, fol-de-rol;
> Be your own man and fate.
> Do it yourself, fol-de-rol, fol-de-rol;
> Don't wait, and wait, and wait.

Whatever the merits of this rather bitter piece, I think it can be said to be an instance of a poet playing a rhetorical, narrative game—that is, telling a familiar American success story—with the intention of showing the game up. There is little direct meditation by the poet; the comments he makes are implicit in the resolution he devised for the story. This procedure—a procedure some students find simply a perverse artistic way of *concealing* the thought they think they are supposed to carry away from the poem—this procedure pretty uniformly characterizes poetic meditations and may indeed be the reason why poetry is so commonly thought of as nonmeditative, nonthoughtful.

The poet, even while criticizing the game, is obliged to keep playing it, which means that his meditations may not be, as it were, idle meditations, meditations detached from any personal predicament or feeling. A common way of putting this is to say that poetry is an art in which matters are presented rather than discussed, rendered rather than talked about; and I take exception to this rendering principle only in asserting that it too is a product of the mind, of meditation, not a product of some wholly different factory, like the spleen. I do not think that a poem can merely discuss its matter, and in fact object to the following poem because the meditative element is too clearly, too explicitly present in it; I am directly commenting upon the absurdity of the actions of the "heroes" involved:

A Projection[7]

I wish they would hurry up their trip to Mars,
Those rocket gentlemen.
We have been waiting too long; the fictions of little men
And canals,
And of planting and raising flags and opening markets
For beads, cheap watches, perfume and plastic jewelry—
All these begin to be tedious; what we need now
Is the real thing, a thoroughly bang-up voyage
Of discovery.

Led by Admiral Byrd
In the Nina, Pinta and Santa Maria
With a crew of one hundred experts
In physics, geology, war and creative writing,
The expedition should sail with a five-year supply of

> Pemmican, Jello, Moxie,
> Warm woollen socks and jars of Gramma's preserves.
> Think of them out there,
> An ocean of space before them, using no compass,
> Guiding themselves by speculative equations,
> Looking,
> Looking into the night and thinking now
> There are no days, no seasons, time
> Is only on watches,
>   and landing on Venus
> Through some slight error,
> Bearing
> Proclamations of friendship,
> Declarations of interstellar faith,
> Acknowledgments of American supremacy,
> And advertising matter.
>
> I wonder,
> Out in the pitch of space, having worlds enough,
> If the walled-up, balled-up self could from its alley
> Sally.
> I wish they would make provisions for this,
> Those rocket gentlemen.

This happens to have been one of my more popular poems. Anthologists looking for verses about contemporary problems or looking for verses with a clear (and hopefully constructive) thought or two in them, keep asking for permission to reprint it. Yet I have put it here, though I rather like parts of it, largely to illustrate what seems to me to be a defective form of poetic meditation. I don't object to the meditations themselves, but to the superior, impersonal vantage point I adopt for expressing them. Who am I to set myself up as immune to the foolishness of the rocket gentlemen? The quality of poetic thought cannot be considered in isolation from its originator.

The scientist or mathematician, like the bridge player or chess player, takes a good bit of pride in conjuring up thoughts which are detachable from his own ego: syllogisms, equations, and the like. But the poet cannot do this; it is the peculiarity of his art that he must display himself in conjunction with the thought he expresses. And to make such a display he must first—here is the joker—know who he is.

To find one's self, to know one's self—these are perhaps the major quests of most poetic meditation. The poet thinks of himself as Achilles for a bit and then decides that no, he is more like Caspar Milquetoast. Or he blusters forth with some magnificent proposal for bringing order and justice to his kingdom, then discovers that not only is he incapable of carrying through such a proposal but also that he has no kingdom—and so on. Most of the tragic heroes in poetic drama become tragic figures as a result of their failures of self-perception. Even Satan's trouble in *Paradise Lost* could be described as a great big misunderstanding from the beginning about his identity (Milton and God both keep asking him the question: who do you think you are anyway?).

Why does a poet—particularly a dramatic poet—project himself into so many different characters if not for the purpose of estimating his own relationship to these figures? Sometimes his estimates are conclusive: Browning decides he likes Fra Lippo Lippi or Rabbi Ben Ezra terribly well (he thus, in the psychiatrist's phrase, identifies with them). Sometimes they are inconclusive: I doubt that Melville ever made up his mind about Ahab; Ahab's mystery was in effect the mystery of Melville's self. But in all such projections the quest *motif*—quest for self-discovery—would seem to be present. And I am inclined to think that this quest is the underlying quality of poetic meditation which distinguishes it from other kinds of meditation.

In a great many short poems this quest is deviously and diffidently undertaken. The poet, for example, may undertake a sort of character sketch in which he describes someone who is deficient in understanding and thereby indicates that he, the poet, has gone further on the path to understanding than has his character. A good many instances of this might be cited—E. A. Robinson's poem about Miniver Cheevy is a familiar example in which Robinson emerges as a more understanding person than Miniver Cheevy, but more understanding largely because he has mastered Miniver Cheevy. Similarly, in the following short and frivolous sketch of the North Wind I suppose that I could be said to be trying to rid myself of some of the qualities of the North Wind.

North Wind[8]

If one should meet the North Wind in the flesh,
Would he be blustery? I don't think so.
I see in my mind's eye a kind of failure,
Dickensian, mousy, a shuffler, living alone
In a London flat, descending for meals,
Sitting the evenings out in the parlor with puzzles,
And then padding up to his cold bare room at bedtime
To lie awake in the dark in the windless hours
Muttering, "Boreas, Boreas, I am Boreas—
D'ye hear?"

But sometimes of course the quest is described quite directly and the poet comes up explicitly with certain discoveries about himself, almost uniformly melancholy. I suppose some of Robert Frost's poems might be cited here, for example, the poem in which he discovers desert places within himself and is suitably depressed. He cannot, after all, do very much about those desert places, unless the act of discovering them and writing a poem about them be regarded as doing something. In such instances poetry would seem to serve the function of prayer or the confessional and we, the audience, are moved by the poetry to the extent that it makes a discovery about us too, and then utters our own prayer, makes our confession for us.

Let me conclude with a sort of confessional poem of my own, though hardly a solemn one. The first discovery in the poem is of someone *not* myself, someone in my own profession—or perhaps I should say racket—who does all the things of which I disapprove. The second discovery in the poem is that I am describing myself after all. Who is this person? Well, he is a literary lecturer on tour—a person who is too glib, too ready to make easy generalizations about poetry and culture.

The Cultural Conference[9]

The author, critic and cultural messenger (me?)
Comes to the cultural conference with snap-on tie,
Two shirts and a briefcase; and in between drinks
Holds forth for a week on the state of the state
Of letters—
          that is, takes stock.
He finds science doing its best and wishes that artists
Would pay some attention to thermodynamics.
He doubts that our age will go down in the books for its verse,
But hopes for the novel. He thinks there is room
For a new vital form of some sort—the novella?—
And wonders if any mass culture, even our own,
Can really sustain a high art, thinking that paperbacks
Help. Lastly he knows it is late and the room is stuffy,
But if anyone really wishes to, he would be more than. Thereupon,
Asked if he thinks that the modern poets are difficult,
Or that writers should be depressing, defeatist or dirty,
He smiles, looks at his watch, hunches over the lectern
And recites (for another half hour) (with lengthy asides)
Passages out of the Great Tradition from Chaucer
To (with suitably deprecatory sniffles) himself, *simply to show*
—Uh, would the lady repeat the question? Thereupon
She does and he firmly agrees and everyone breaks up
And the week goes insanely on and he leaves at the end of it
Alone on a plane for home where, arriving, he'll take
Another week, of a cultural silence profound,
Getting used to the hardship of having himself (me) around.

[9] From *The Fascination of the Abomination* (New York: Macmillan, 1963). "The Cultural Conference" is copyright 1963 by Reed Whittemore.

17

TOWARD A CLASSICAL MODERNITY AND A MODERN CLASSICISM

Theodore Weiss

Coming to New York in 1938 from a town in Pennsylvania to study literature at Columbia University released in me a spate of what I then believed to be poetry. This no doubt constituted a reaction in part to the multiple pressures of the city, a feverish attempt at survival as an individual. Meantime, my reading led to a rapidly growing admiration for Homer, at once the most telling revelation for me of things as they are, of the underlying cold war life is, and in the person of Odysseus the happiest, most reassuring confrontation of that war. What better antidote to the perils of a present, self-intoxicated for its unexampled capacity for change? What better reminder of that which because it is essential—as long as man remains man—may in a turmoiled time be ignored or at least regarded as insignificant?

In those years Odysseus more than fancifully occupied me. Curious past the most daring cosmonaut, a curiosity that helped to embroil him in devastating as well as all-seductive adventures, he never forgot his own beloved land, his own deeply rooted being. What is America, the modern world, I thought, but the latest leg of his travels, the inland journey predicted for him. I reveled in the strange conditions his curiosity would discover here; yet I was confident that they, by the miracle of his manhood, would only further reinforce his nature as Odysseus.

Through its title *The Catch* my first book was supposed to suggest the haul as of fish that the poems comprised and the round or a song to be repeated—that is, the poems in their echoing of each other thematically and otherwise. In general the book meant to explore the diverse ways we are caught: in *this* time,

this place, *this* occasion, in war as in the warrings of peace, in
nature as in our natures, and in the designs the past set going.
So the rigors of the modern world, engrossed in its distractions,
struck me as an intriguing setting for another hero, but one, unlike Odysseus, committed to a different, "better" world—Christ,
especially as he undertook the flesh and found it, in himself as in
men's response to him, for its awing dailiness almost too convincing. "A Commonplace" seeks to catch him in the midst of this
racking dilemma.

A Commonplace

as the silly shepherds
after their first radiant scare—
sheep and cattle at their munching
with the winter
              bent yet spin-
ning lilies—forgot . . . hunched
puttering over our benighted star,
we lose track of tears.

See him stamped there,
come down into the commonplace who let himself be stabled
in the blood.
           His walk
brought sea, salt, fish, bread
of his body. Yet within his memory,
each breath travail,

did loiterings of his past,
in sleep perhaps, cajole him: pride,
when as a child he confounded
the learned elders;
             lust:
touched by a woman long possessed,
he knew his virtue troubled
in him:
           or pain itself, simple-
minded pain, did it perhaps reduce

him to the pulse of immediately
suffering man?
O the garden
of agony, so dry it drank his blood,
grew in him, till he cried with a man
mouth and a man mortality . . .

but the garden had its malt as well.
For the shepherds, far inland, blood-
warmed, the star faded into a stone
their cattle sucked for salt.

Meantime, taken though I was by the modern scene and
poetry's remarkable attempts to deal with it, I increasingly re-
gretted poetry's surrender of immense sectors of the world to
prose, most of all to the novel, which often so eroded the terri-
tories occupied that they seemed spoiled for poetry forever. Certain older poets did win me for their impressive grappling with
such problems: Yeats' affirmation of the heroic spirit and Pound's
and Eliot's efforts to recover some part of the epical. So William
Carlos Williams delighted me with his Odyssean ability to remain
human, whole-man-alive, among most forbidding contemporary
conditions. By his busy doctoring of necessity he became a master
of the improvisational; but though he achieved exceptional immediacy, frequently he courted the improvisational's dangers:
brokenness, incompleteness. I dreamed, as Cezanne had said of
the Impressionists, of employing Williams' virtues in work solid
as the art of museums.

Such feelings led me to that poetic form, seemingly least likely
now, the long poem. Direct narrative appeared impossible. Yet
elements of it, I believed, could be combined with our new techniques. "Shades of Caesar" was the first long poem I felt realized
enough to venture into print. It focuses on a particular place,
responded to for its own attractions and for the reverberations in
it still of the historical (the Indians, the Dutch settlers, the Hudson River flowing into the misty past), the mythical and the
spiritual (Greek and Roman thought and Christian dogma as reflected in a little Hudson Valley college, originally a Christian
seminary, but more recently a center of experiment in education).

All this climaxes in the rise and fall of modern dictators, Mussolini particularly as ironically highlighted by a greater predecessor, Caesar.

My second book, in contradistinction to *The Catch,* emphasizes the basic American sense of going out, the various ways of meeting the dilemmas of our day. This pioneering spirit, however, has brought in its train a feeling of uprootedness, of being lost in the boundless desert of time and space. Gradually the book organized itself around the theme of the homelessness of our time; I found it brilliantly exampled in America itself, this continent with its extraordinary mixture of savage climates and landscapes, its vastness, frightening indeed to men usually fled from smaller, man-sized worlds. Against the desperate modern struggle to subdue nature through technology I posed a number of worthies, outlanders like Thoreau and the nineteenth century American painter Albert Ryder, who were, in their personal stands, heroic replies to, if not solutions of, the outrages unleashed.

The poem "Barracks Apt. 14" has to do with one of a series of housing units, thrown up during World War II, officially temporary, yet used long after; a fairly typical American makeshift arrangement, it reflects a sense as well of life's ruggedness through the makeshift, something like a continuation of the early pioneering spirit. At the end, however, the overwhelming fecundity of nature itself is acknowledged.

Barracks Apt. 14[1]

All must be used:

this clay whisky jug, bearing
a lamp-shade; the four brown pears,
lying ruggedly among each other
in the wicker basket; the cactus
in its pot; and the orange berries,
old now as they dangle from their twigs
as though badly hung there.

These as well as the silence,
the young women reading Aristotle

[1] From *Outlanders* (New York: Macmillan, 1960). "Barracks Apt. 14" is copyright © 1957 by Theodore Weiss.

with difficulty, and the little girl
in the next room, voluble in bed:
"I'm talking in my sleep . . . laughing
in my sleep . . . waking in my sleep,"

all are parts hopeful, possible,
expecting their place in the song;
more appealing because parts
that must harmonize into something
that rewards them for being, rewards
with what they are.

      Do this and do
till suddenly the scampering field
you would catch, the shiny crows
just out of reach, the pears
through which a brown tide breaks,
and the cactus you cannot cling to
long like that thorny Aristotle
suddenly, turning, turn on you

as meaning, the ultimate greenness
they have all the time been seeking
in the very flight they held
before you. No matter what you do,
at last you will be overwhelmed,
the distance will be broken,

    the music will confound you.

"The Fire at Alexandria" starts banteringly. But destruction, a culture ravaged, with its intense overtones for us, is confronted, as is the precariousness of the rare and the precious, the terrible, swift ease with which the best man has thought and done can be obliterated. At the same time in splendor's kinship at its core with the very fiery element that destroys it, the poem implies, not so much hope, but past it exuberant identification with that force and its renewing powers.

The Fire at Alexandria[2]

Imagine it, a Sophocles complete,
the lost epic of Homer, including no doubt
his notes, his journals, and his observations
on blindness. But what occupies me most,
with the greatest hurt of grandeur, are those
magnificent authors, kept in scholarly rows,
whose names we have no passing record of:
scrolls unrolling Aphrodite like Cleopatra
bundled in a rug, the spoils of love.

Crated masterpieces on the wharf,
and never opened, somehow started first.
And then, as though by imitation, the library
took. One book seemed to inspire another,
to remind it of the flame enclosed
within its papyrus like a drowsy torch.
The fire, roused perhaps by what it read,
its reedy song, raged Dionysian, a band
of Corybantes, down the halls now headlong.

The scribes, despite the volumes wept
unable to douse the witty conflagration—
spicy too as Sappho, coiling, melted
with her girls: the Nile no less, reflecting,
burned—saw splendor fled, a day consummate
in twilit ardencies. Troy at its climax
(towers finally topless) could not have been
more awesome, not though the aromatic house
of Priam mortised the passionate moment.

Now whenever I look into a flame,
I try to catch a single countenance:
Cleopatra, winking out from every joint;
Tiresias eye to eye; a magnitude, long lost,
restored to the sky and the stars he once

2 From *Outlanders* (New York: Macmillan, 1960). "The Fire at Alexandria" is copyright © 1959 by Theodore Weiss; reprinted with permission of The Macmillan Company.

struck unsuspected parts of into words.
Fire, and I see them resurrected.
madly crackling perfect birds, the world
lit up as by a golden school, the flashings
of the fathoms of set eyes.

Then, to go with our difficulties as far as I can, in "A Trip through Yucatan" I try, by using our many languages as the main metaphor, to explore, something of the mystery our lives are as we travel through them—tourists all, never more so than today. I chose Yucatan because it is ancient, most mysterious America, yet not so remote from our mysteries as it would seem. I chose it also for our desire to sound, like archaeologists, the secrets of our own lives and worlds as well as each other. The poem's poet-interpreter, supposedly the priest of language, leaps about, not so much to make fundamental sense now as to hide the fragmentation from the others. Words themselves, bent on their own pleasures and destinies, are unruly enough. Add to this the defiance of objects and circumstances and we see the quandary we are in, no one more so than the artist, especially sensitive because of his gifts and training to this collapse. Yet at the end, by his accepting things as they are, in the middle of this very jungle state he knows serenity, belongingness.

A Trip through Yucatan[3]

You have, in a sense,
been through it all; each experience
has known you, like a Swiss clock
in the middle of the room, forcing
all things to its rickety breathing.

Abruptly then the one out
that you see—rather than swinging
in and out, forever, on a crazy
and precarious stick, pretending
to be another hour, another place,

[3] From *Outlanders* (New York: Macmillan, 1960). "A Trip through Yucatan" is © 1957 by Theodore Weiss; reprinted with permission of The Macmillan Company.

one of you for one time, another
for the next, and never meeting—
the one out is a break-down.
Then all things can, with a sigh,
forget you . . .

yet after days
of snow, too swiftly falling to be
accounted for, in the middle of it
a moon appears, absurdly beautiful
and warm . . .
like the dinner-
party you have just come from where
the speaker assured you your French
accent reminded him of his trip
through Yucatan:
a group
of Americans, a few Spaniards,
and several French, all insisting
they understood each other's speech;
only he, interpreting, knew the truth.

Madly, the epitome of tact,
he hopped about from one to the next,
trying to keep their ignorances
from them . . . I have stopped jumping;
and moon-wise, in a sense, arises

that last implacable light-
heartedness, like emerging mid-jungle
into a jubilant calm, a clearing
of florid birds and plumaged flowers
that set the feastday of the storm.

Serenity and the sense of belonging, the loss of these, have
much to do with the book's one long monologue, "The Generations." It presents an old woman, resolute in her Christian funda-
mentalism as ever, working over her garden and thoughts of her
sons. Despite her unceasing efforts, all—even the promising

youngest—have gone their errant way. As she recalls moments most oppressive in their reality, she undergoes an almost literal redoing, so passionately does she live in the Bible, of the terrible expulsion from the first garden. She is engulfed by a sense of failure and futility. Yet in that very moment of anguished revelation, even as she recognizes her prominent part in the destructiveness, her nature's fixedness reasserts itself. And bent as ever, as if in furious prayer, she continues her weeding.

Such a poem reflects my desire to pass on beyond the lyrical. The dramatic monologue as developed by Browning has long attracted me in the conviction that poetry can and must renew its older, larger interests in people and a world past the poet's self-preoccupation. The encouragement to confession that psychoanalysis and the chaos of the world at large have given many writers, a feverish absorption in the minute particulars of their own subjectivity, may have its effectiveness. But just as the confession often remains raw (the present moment tends to prefer it so, to confuse the raw with the real, the true), so it occasionally comes to little more than a gossiping about, a stripping of, oneself in public.

My next book, *Gunsight,* one long poem, as it seeks to extend the dramatic monologue, to enrich it with modern poetry's accomplishments, tries to put those accomplishments to more ambitious uses. The poem's central figure, a young American soldier wounded in World War II, undergoes a major operation. At the poem's opening he is in spirit almost as paralyzed as he is in body. As the anesthesia takes effect, he descends into his own hell; he becomes the theater to a flock of memories, each clamoring for his attention which has till now been denied. In fragmentary scene after scene, summoned by each voice, in seemingly free association, he relives much of his painful past from childhood on. But bit by bit progress is made, and gradually, as these harrowing experiences are endured, the possibility of some understanding, as well as of the renewal of his will, is held out.

Meanwhile, during the years spent on *Gunsight,* other shorter poems (and a group of monologues beyond them) have been collecting. These are on the way to becoming a volume called *The Medium.* The title and the poems have to do with language— whatever its distortions and seductions and whether it be words, paint, or notes—as it makes our lives possible, ordering them and enabling us to live with each other and with the objects, known and unknown, of the world. At the same time some of the poems concentrate on the resources—the secret, vibrant life—of language itself, as on the endless transactions between it and the world and ourselves. Beyond that I find myself frequently turning to the notion of ourselves as a medium, though for who knows what purpose and used by who knows whom.

So I wish to acknowledge the hardships man undergoes whatever the shape, time, and place—or medium—he happens to be in. "A Dab of Color," dedicated to Ralph Ellison, a distinguished American novelist, proposes by way of art what an abysmal difference a mere drop of color can make in the human scene.

A Dab of Color

For R.E.

By dint of color
in his skin
that nature, unrelenting
innovator, dabbled in
(it marked him

off better than fences
can) a wind began,
a winter that companion-
ately and forever
went with him.
                    O never
twit the artist, never
call him ivory-tower
scholar, bent
on anything but sense.

He knows—for he has
learned from nature—
that a little dab
of color, aptly mixed,
makes all the difference.

Finally, in "Out of Your Hands" I pay homage to William Carlos Williams. In many ways the most indigenous of America's recent poets, perhaps Whitman's worthiest successor, he was occupied with the poor, the suffering, the cast-off. Utterly honest and open before the modern scene, he proved profoundly reassuring, especially to younger poets, in his capacity to deal with American phenomena on their own terms. It is his love, his deeply identifying sympathy, fortified by an unblinking dedication to the truth, as well as his ability to remark poetry in the seemingly intractable, that particularly endears him. Poet par excellence though Williams was of the scrubby urban world, in "Out of Your Hands" I draw heavily on his translation of Theocritus' *Idyl I* to stress the fundamentally pastoral, not to say classical, nature of his work.

Out of Your Hands

On receiving W. C. Williams' Theocritus, June 5, 1953

> Though you regret it,
> out of your hands it must go,
> this manuscript your letter calls
> "a unique copy" you would hate to lose,
> out of your hands still warm on it,
> loving with the best love,
>
> a bare mind, undaunted,
> inside the hands, and casting
> the familiar line, a child fished,
> a poem. How unique only those who seek
> to make as well, having staked out
> their pleasurable awareness
>
> in the clearing
> of your verse, can know. June
> now, the first sultry day, swept in
> on the back of last night's thunderous
> rain, a swollen glare, the morning
> looking as though its masons

just broke off.
And you, returning whence you
came, have mailed us *Idyl I,* after
your local hundreds, ground from which,
outlandish though it is, our world
has sprung: you, aging, know

that hungering still,
the virgin green—quick field
where crops nourish crops—growing
through practiced hands. Of the rugged
few equipt to face Priapus equally
with old Chronos, out of Libya

or wherever, you alone
among shrill horns, a traffic
shattering as war, midnoon's panic
raging, manage to keep the quiet music
going, freshets as of a deepdown
source; once more Pan, chase-

worn, exasperation only
reedy at his nostrils, finds
a spot where revelry, love and folly
know some ease. Despite your vigilance
the gifts come to you hardly goat,
shag-white, no firstling kid,

a delicate-fleshed
for being eaten before its milk
begins, you feed on bramble-berries,
make iron, refuse, yield. This is no less—
your hands not letting go except it,
naming, bless—must slip away.

Your voice informing,
worked like the cup Thyrsis won
for his sad song, your poems will stay,

will, passing through whatever hands,
retain the markings of your clean-
edged knife. A seasoned wine

poured in, sly winds,
involved in the curving ivy,
carved, flickering through yellow
flowers, sport their airs: April, May,
leading groves in frolic; alewives
too, tails flashing in the sea-

dark surge; and bees,
drunk in a rose—all garland-
ing a girl, thereon wreathing them,
a rite, for her, fairer than the gods
might dream, your mind's familiar.
There too a wrinkled fisherman

on a wrinkled rock,
mending lines, handling pipes
that these release their wood's chief
ingrained spell: one pair of hands
to do all things, pluck lasting
moods from time, the harmony

past need that makes
the need the more. Set to cast
now the thousandth time—his whole
heart in it—the mighty net. And near
this veteran, straddling a ruddy
vineyard wall, indifferent

to grape-roused foxes,
winter, and the Foe, greedily
fixed at his foot, a boy, plaiting
star-flower stalks around three reeds
into a cricket cage in intent,
wise and thoughtless joy.

18 THE POET TURNS ON HIMSELF

James Dickey

When I was in high school twenty-five years ago, I had courses in literature and memorized a number of poems, parts of which I can still remember, although I seldom do. From the class in poetry I went to another class in the basement of the high school, which was called Manual Training and purported to teach us how to work wood lathes, do a little light carpentry, weld, pour metals, and perform other similar tasks which I have not had occasion to repeat since that time. Then, however, I could not help being struck by the contrast between what we had been doing in the poetry class and the materials and skills—the means and the tangible results—of our work in Manual Training and, like every other American boy, I developed a strong bias in favor of learning how to *do* something, of being able to make something, of having at least in some degree a skill that paid off in "measurable entities."

To a certain extent I still have this prejudice, as I believe many American poets do: we are such a thoroughly pragmatic people that intangibles, such as spirit, "soul," or even good taste are always a little embarrassing to acknowledge or discuss. Yet even in my high school days I also began to be aware of a connection—a very disturbing and apparently necessary one—between words in a certain order and the events of my own life. When I was in the Service in the South Pacific shortly thereafter and first heard the phrase "sweat it out" applied in a context where I *was* sweating it out—an artillery barrage—there blazed up in my mind, for the first time fully there, the idea of perfectly expressive language, for sweating it out was exactly what we were doing under those palm logs: there was nothing else we could do. I believe I responded to this phrase neither more nor less strongly than the other men in that hole with me; it was a phrase all of us understood equally well, each with his own temperament, without the need for commentary.

From this incident and a few others like it stems my interest in language and in its peculiar use which we—or at least I—call poetry. Occasionally, very occasionally, I would hear another phrase in popular speech, in the argot of the army, in a fortunate sentence in a newspaper (sometimes even in a misprint) that seemed to me to have this same unforeseeable but *right* correlation between lived time—experience—and words, but it was only years later that I recognized, very slowly, that this quality I was seeking more and more was poetry. The realization came to me that the highest concentration of language employed in this way was in the work of those very writers who had seemed so utterly useless to me when I was forced to study them in high school.

I eased into poetry, over a course of many years, by some such route. As a writer of poetry I began comparatively late, around my twenty-fourth year. I came to poetry with no particular qualifications. I had begun to suspect, however, that there is a poet—or a kind of poet—buried in every human being like Ariel in his tree, and that the people whom we are pleased to call poets are only those who have felt the need and contrived the means to release this spirit from its prison. As soon as I began writing I knew that I had the need, but that the means were not immediately forthcoming. I knew nothing whatever of poetic technique, of metrics, prosody, stanzaic construction, and to a certain extent I still consider those things—all the things that Herbert Read calls "the bag of monkey-tricks of English poetry"—as secondary to something else which I can only define, using one of the words I most despised in my younger days, as the spirit of poetry: the individually imaginative or visionary quality.

The first poem I wrote that had anything good in it—anything that I had seen for myself—was, I think, a description of football players dressing in a locker room. It seemed to me that their body-hair was *dry*—very dry-looking—and I put this into the poem, although against my better judgment, since it was a decidedly unbeautiful detail and at that time I wanted very much to write "beautiful" poems. When I looked at what I had put down on paper, I could see immediately that this line, poor as it was, had a quality of observation and of immediacy not to be found in the rest of the poem, which was derived from half a dozen other poets I had been reading. At that unlikely time I began to see what poetry would have to be for me and came by the idea that words, once placed in a certain order, will stay where they have been put and say what one tells them to say.

But what did I want to tell them to say? Very slowly I gravitated toward another idea which, like the other, has never left me: the belief in the inexhaustible fecundity of individual memory. I discovered that I had, as everyone has, a life and the memories engendered by it. When I examined these memories, I found that certain of them stood out in my mind and recurred to me at odd times, as if seeking something, perhaps some act of understanding, from me. Some recollections seemed more important than others, without my being able to tell why. Later, I saw that these incidents, the more important ones, were not only potential raw material for the kind of poetry I wanted to write, but were in fact the principal incidents in my life: those times when I felt most strongly and was most aware of the intense reality of the objects and people I moved among.

Recently I was delighted to read, in the work of a French poet, Patrice de la Tour du Pin, an account of this poet's similar conclusions. La Tour du Pin confirms in me the belief that the isolated episodes and incidents of a human life make up, in the end, a kind of sum, a continuous story with different episodes, and that these moments of natural responsiveness show what he is and in a sense explain him; in the case of a poet they are not so much what he writes but what he *is*. If I were to arrange my own poems in some such scheme, chronologizing them, they would form a sort of story of this kind, leading from childhood in the north of Georgia through high school with its athletics and wild motorcycle riding, through a beginning attempt at education in an agricultural college, through World War II and the Korean War as a flyer in a night-fighter squadron, through another beginning at college, this time completed, through various attempts at a valid love affair culminating in the single successful one known as "marriage," through two children, several deaths in the family, travels, reflections, and so on.

The poet as well as the man is always a little shocked—though he hopes that at forty his story is not near its conclusion—to find that his story will most likely never be told in any other way than that in which he is telling it, and that when he is gone it is the only story he will ever have. In the end, however, he will settle for that, for just those conditions: underlying everything he writes is the dual sense of being glad to be alive to write that particular poem and of outrage at the possibility of the loss of all the things that have meant much to him—outrage that these personal, valuable things could ever be definitively lost for anyone. Beneath his words is this sense of battling against universal dissolution, of the loss of all he and other men have been given as human beings, of all they have loved and been moved by.

All this I felt, though very dimly at the beginning. I had some things that I wanted to write about; I had certain ways of feeling about them: about war, about love and sex, about athletics, about being a Southerner, about hunting and flying and canoeing, about the flight of birds and the movement of animals and the feeling of swimming in the presence of fish. But there seemed to be no language for writing about these things in any way which would do them the kind of justice I believed they deserved. I read a lot of poets, trying to find something I could use. Though I responded strongly to many of these poems, there were a great many that I did not respond to at all, even though I felt I should. I responded to these, in fact, no more than I had done in high school; no more than I do now.

I was distressed at the license that many poets claimed for themselves and which, I thought, allowed a great deal of highly dubious material to be brought into poems. For the live feel and delivered personality of one good phrase there seemed to be hundreds of poems built out of literary lumber: hundreds of dead, period-style poems indistinguishable from one another, the fodder of classrooms. Very early in the game I knew I wanted to avoid writing like that, like those poems. I was then, without knowing it, involved in the question of style and with that I wrestled for a long time—am still wrestling.

I had in the beginning a strong dislike of rhyming poems, for the element of artificiality is one of the characteristics of poetry I most distrust, and I have always had trouble distinguishing between artificiality and the traditional modes and methods of verse; for a time I was convinced that craft and artifice were the same thing. At the same time I also had a secret suspicion that Whitman, Lawrence, the Imagists, and others were cheating, absolving themselves from the standing problems and difficulties of verse. But I found, unlike so many others, that the qualities of poems which seemed to me poetic—*essentially* poetic—were not in the least dependent on whether or not they occurred in poems which rhymed. I also discovered that the restrictions imposed by rhyme led me away from what I had intended to say. Other writers have since told me—citing Valéry and others—that significant discoveries are made through the attempt to satisfy such restrictions and that as often as not one ends up as a result with a better poem than one anticipated. Doubtless this is true and it is also true that certain poets, certain kinds of creative minds, are helped enormously by the support they receive from such sources. Nevertheless, such a practice did not seem right for me; I felt continually carried past my subject, carried around it, sometimes close to it but never in it in the way I wished to be in it.

I saw that I was faced with a kind of choice and that it was an important choice: should I continue to try to satisfy the conditions of rhyming English verse, or should I sacrifice rhyme and try to come to terms with my subjects in some other way? I decided to do the latter and have used rhyme in very few poems since. Although I didn't care for rhyme and the "packaged" quality which it gives even the best poems, I did care very much for meter, or at least rhythm. I have always liked strongly cadenced language and the sound of words in a line of verse is to me a very important part of its appeal. I read a good many manuals and textbooks and treatises on prosody, some of which were interesting, but none of them helped me to get the sound I wanted. Most of the material I read on metrics concluded that the systematic use of anapests and dactyls tends to monotony and I accepted this judgment on faith, and continued to try to work with the customary English iambic line.

Yet now and then I began to hear lines of verse, lines without words to them, that had what was to me a very compelling sound:

an unusual sound of urgency and passion, of grave conviction, of inevitability, of the same kind of drive and excitement that one hears in a good passage of slow jazz. I thought that perhaps if I kept listening to those sounds and found satisfactory words for them, this strong carrying rhythm might help restore to the poems something of the feeling of formal completeness that I had sacrificed when I decided against using rhyme, and at the same time it might allow the poems a certain sense of self-determination which the strait jacket of rhyme did not seem to me to allow. It was not until later that I thought to analyze the metrical basis of the sounds I kept hearing at odd times—when stopped at traffic lights, when waking in the early morning, when playing tennis or hunting in the woods of north Georgia—and discovered that they were anapestic.

I sat down at the typewriter one afternoon in an American business office and wrote:

> All dark is now no more.
> This forest is drawing a light.
> All Presences change into trees.
> One eye opens slowly without me.
> My sight is the same as the sun's . . .

I was very much excited by this, for it had something of what I wanted: a strange, incantatory sound, a simplicity that was direct without being thin, and a sense of imaginative urgency that I had never been able to get into verse before. It was something new for me; it satisfied and excited me at the same time and I abandoned work on everything else I was doing, including office work, to finish it. When I completed it I began to write other poems in the same way, starting with a subject—often very vaguely defined—and letting rhythms develop out of it, aided, no doubt, by years of guitar playing, and then supplying what I thought were the right words to inject the subject into the cadences that now seemed to be running in my mind endlessly, not stopping even when I was asleep. I saw at once—or rather I *heard* at once—when I began to have this kind of relationship to sound, language, and subject, that the anapest needn't always result in the monotonous, slugging, obtrusive singsong that it has in the poems of Edgar Allan Poe, Robert Service, Kipling, and others. I found that the anapest was as capable of interesting variation as any other kind of line; in fact, as the iamb itself.

Along with the rhythmical experiments, I also found that what I was working toward was a very stripped kind of simplicity in verse; what I really wanted to be able to do was to make effective *statements*. I began to use short lines, usually having three accents or beats, because I wanted to say one thing—hopefully, one memorable thing—in each line: one thing that would make its own kind of impression and would also connect with other single things, one per line, and so form a whole poem. In the poem I have been talking about, "Sleeping Out at Easter," I used this approach and used also a kind of refrain technique that, so far as I know, I invented for the occasion. In this, the last or refrain lines of the stanzas unite to make, themselves, a last stanza which sums up the attitude and action of the poem. It is a poem about Easter and a man who is sleeping in the back yard of his home the night before Easter. He wakes in a small grove of pine trees and finds that he is thinking of resurrection.

Sleeping Out at Easter[1]

All dark is now no more.
This forest is drawing a light.
All Presences change into trees.
One eye opens slowly without me.
My sight is the same as the sun's,
For this is the grave of the king,
Where the earth turns, waking a choir.
 All dark is now no more.

Birds speak, their voices beyond them.
A light has told them their song.
My animal eyes become human
As the Word rises out of the darkness
Where my right hand, buried beneath me,

---

[1] Reprinted with the permission of Charles Scribner's Sons from *Into the Stone and Other Poems*, by James Dickey (copyright © 1960, James Dickey), "Poets of Today VII."

Hoveringly tingles, with grasping
The source of all song at the root.
Birds sing, their voices beyond them.

Put down those seeds in your hand.
These trees have not yet been planted.
A light should come round the world,
Yet my army blanket is dark,
That shall sparkle with dew in the sun.
My magical shepherd's cloak
Is not yet alive on my flesh.
Put down those seeds in your hand.

In your palm is the secret of waking.
Unclasp your purple-nailed fingers
And the wood and the sunlight together
Shall spring, and make good the world.
The sounds in the air shall find bodies,
And a feather shall drift from the pine-top
You shall feel, with your long-buried hand.
In your palm is the secret of waking,

For the king's grave turns him to light.
A woman shall look through the window
And see me here, huddled and blazing.
My child, mouth open, still sleeping,
Hears the song in the egg of a bird.
The sun shall have told him that song
Of a father returning from darkness,
For the king's grave turns you to light.

All dark is now no more.
In your palm is the secret of waking.
Put down those seeds in your hand;/,
All Presences change into trees.
A feather shall drift from the pine-top.
The sun shall have told you this song,
For this is the grave of the king;/,
For the king's grave turns you to light.

Through this method and largely through this poem, I discovered that the simple declarative sentence, under certain circumstances and in certain contexts, had exactly the qualities I wanted my lines of poetry to have. As I wrote more poems of this kind, I was increasingly aware of two things. The first was that I liked poems which had a basis of narrative, that described or depicted an action, that moved through a period of time—usually short—and allowed the reader to bring into play his simple and fundamental interest in "what happens next," a curiosity that only narrative can supply and satisfy. I also discovered that I worked most fruitfully in cases in which there was no clear-cut distinction between what was actually happening and what was happening in the mind of a character in the poem. I meant to try to get a fusion of inner and outer states, of dream, fantasy, and illusion where everything partakes of the protagonist's mental processes and creates a single impression.

It was with some such intention as this that I wrote "The Lifeguard," in which a lifeguard at a summer camp for boys, after failing to rescue one of the children from drowning, hides in the boathouse and, in his delirium of grief and helplessness, comes to believe that he can walk out upon the water of the lake where the child drowned and raise him back up into life: that he can accomplish the most impossible of all human feats and the most desirable: undo what has been done.

The Lifeguard[2]

In a stable of boats I lie still,
From all sleeping children hidden.
The leap of a fish from its shadow
Makes the whole lake instantly tremble.
With my foot on the water, I feel
The moon outside

Take on the utmost of its power.
I rise and go out through the boats.
I set my broad sole upon silver,

2 From James Dickey, *Drowning with Others* (Middletown, Conn.: Wesleyan University Press, 1961). "The Lifeguard" is © 1961 by James Dickey.

233

On the skin of the sky, on the moonlight,
Stepping outward from earth onto water
In quest of the miracle

This village of children believed
That I could perform as I dived
For one who had sunk from my sight.
I saw his cropped haircut go under.
I leapt, and my steep body flashed
Once, in the sun.

Dark drew all the light from my eyes.
Like a man who explores his death
By the pull of his slow-moving shoulders,
I hung head down in the cold,
Wide-eyed, contained, and alone
Among the weeds,

And my fingertips turned into stone
From clutching immovable blackness.
Time after time I leapt upward
Exploding in breath, and fell back
From the change in the children's faces
At my defeat.

Beneath them I swam to the boathouse
With only my life in my arms
To wait for the lake to shine back
At the risen moon with such power
That my steps on the light of the ripples
Might be sustained.

Beneath me is nothing but brightness
Like the ghost of a snowfield in summer.
As I move toward the center of the lake,
Which is also the center of the moon,
I am thinking of how I may be
The savior of one

Who has already died in my care.
The dark trees fade from around me.
The moon's dust hovers together.
I call softly out, and the child's
Voice answers through blinding water.
Patiently, slowly,

He rises, dilating to break
The surface of stone with his forehead.
He is one I do not remember
Having ever seen in his life.
The ground I stand on is trembling
Upon his smile.

I wash the black mud from my hands.
On a light given off by the grave
I kneel in the quick of the moon
At the heart of a distant forest
And hold in my arms a child
Of water, water, water.

My second book, *Drowning with Others,* is made up of poems written in this manner: poems with a predominantly anapestic rhythm and dealing often with dream, hallucination, fantasy, the interaction of illusion and reality. My third book, *Helmets,* employed many of these same themes and approaches, but was less pronouncedly rhythmical and less hallucinatory. By this time I had begun to grow a little restive at the limitations of my method and was beginning also to dislike the way I had been handling the narrative elements. All my old reservations about the vitiating effects of artifice began to trouble me once more; I was afraid that I had simply substituted another set of conventions—of artifices—for those I had congratulated myself on discarding earlier. Although I still felt I had chosen rightly in aiming for simplicity of diction and the other qualities that attracted me, I felt in addition that I needed to move beyond these qualities as I had employed them, into other areas of diction, image, and subject matter.

I began to conceive of something I called—doubtless misleadingly—the "open" poem: a poem which would have none of the neatness of most of those poems we call "works of art" but would have the capacity to involve the reader in it, in all its imperfections and impurities, rather than offering him a (supposedly) perfected and perfect work for contemplation, judgment and evaluation. I was interested most of all in getting an optimum "presentational immediacy," a compulsiveness in the presentation of the matter of the poem that would cause the reader to forget literary judgments entirely and simply experience. I experimented with short lines some more and, eventually, with putting several of these together on the same physical plane to make up what I called the "split line," in which spaces between the word groups would take the place of punctuation. I wrote two longish poems using the split line; they were published as *Two Poems of the Air*. The first is "The Firebombing," and includes a section which attempts to depict the sensations of a pilot in an aircraft at night over the enemy's home country, in this case Japan.

The Firebombing[3]

There is then this re-entry
Into cloud, for the engines to ponder their sound.
In white dark the aircraft shrinks; Japan

Dilates around it like a thought.
Coming out, the one who is here is over
Land, passing over the all-night grainfields,
In dark paint over
The woods with one silver side,
Rice-water calm at all levels
Of the terraced hill.
                Enemy rivers and trees
Sliding off me like snakeskin,
Strips of vapor spooled from the engines
Going   invisible   passing   over   on

3 From *Buckdancer's Choice* (Middletown, Conn.: Wesleyan University Press, 1964). "The Firebombing" is © 1964 by James Dickey; reprinted by permission of Wesleyan University Press. Appeared originally in *Poetry*, "A Magazine of Verse."

Over   bridges   roads for night-walkers
Sunday night in the enemy's country   absolute
Calm   the moon's face   coming   slowly
About
       the inland sea
Slants   is woven with wire thread
Levels out   holds together like a quilt
Off the starboard wing   cloud flickers
At my glassed-off forehead   the moon's now and again
Uninterrupted face going forward
Over the waves in a glide-path.

Going   going with it. . . .

Of late my interest has been mainly in the conclusionless poem,
the open or ungeneralizing poem, the un-well-made poem. I hope
in the future to get the reader more and more into the actions
and happenings of the lines and require him less and less to
stand off and draw either aesthetic or moral judgments. If I am
successful in this, my themes will stand forth clearly enough: the
continuity of the human family, the necessity of both caused and
causeless joy, and the permanent interest of what the painter
John Marin called "the big basic forms"—rivers, mountains,
woods, clouds, oceans, and the creatures that live naturally among
them. The forfeited animal grace of human beings, occasionally
redeemed by athletes, interests me also, and the hunter's sense of
understanding with the hunted animal.

All poetry, I suspect, is nothing more or less than an attempt to
discover or invent conditions under which one can live with oneself. I have been called a mystic, a vitalist, a pantheist, an anti-
rationalist, and a good many other things. I have not been conscious of the applicability of any of these labels, although they
very well may all apply. At any rate, what I have always striven
for is to find some way to incarnate my best moments—those
which in memory are most persistent and obsessive. I find that
most of these moments have an element of danger, an element of
repose, and an element of joy. I should like now to develop a
writing instrument which would be capable of embodying these
moments and their attendant states of mind, and I would be most

pleased if readers came away from my poems not at all sure as to where the danger and the repose separate, where joy ends and longing begins. Strongly mixed emotions are what I usually have and what I usually remember from the events of my life. Strongly mixed, but giving the impression of being one emotion, impure and overwhelming—that is the condition I am seeking to impose on my readers, whoever they may be. The doing, of course, is another thing. I cannot really judge as to the success of that, or of the adequacy of my means. Those judgments I must leave to you.

19 ATTENTIVENESS AND OBEDIENCE

Howard Nemerov

When I agreed to act as editor of this collection of essays by some American poets on their art, I proposed to the contributors several questions that seemed to me of some interest, with the idea that these might form a sort of thematic center for the book. But because a poet's view of his own work is necessarily personal, I left it to the contributors to decide whether they would be stimulated by the questions, provoked by the questions, or so unaffected by the questions as to pay them no mind. As might have been anticipated, some of the contributors responded to the questions and others did not.

At that time, I did not contemplate being a contributor myself; but now that I find I am one, it seems only just that I thrash around for a while in this labyrinth of my own devising and try to describe my work with reference to those questions I so glibly asked without a thought of ever having to answer up myself.

I

Do you see your work as having essentially changed in character or style since you began?

In style, I hope and in part believe it has, for I began and for a long time remained imitative, and poems in my first books, not to mention the undergraduate work that preceded publication, show more than traces of admired modern masters—Eliot, Auden, Stevens, Cummings, Yeats. I think these reminiscences largely dropped away in later work; though as a corollary to that it should be said that I never consciously sought for what people

239

call "one's own voice," originality, a uniquely recognizable style; so far as anything like all that happened—I am uncertain how far that is—it happened more or less of itself, while I concentrated on writing this or that poem.

Stylistically, I began under the aegis of notions drawn, I suppose, chiefly from T. S. Eliot. Along with many other beginners, I learned to value irony, difficulty, erudition, and the Metaphysical style of composition after the example of John Donne. Again along with many others I learned from William Empson to value ambiguity; it was part of our purposeful labor, in those days, to fill our poems with somewhat studied puns which could be said to "work on several different levels," though often they did not work even on one. I think the direction of my development was away from all these things considered as technical devices; I now regard simplicity and the appearance of ease in the measure as primary values, and the detachment of a single thought from its ambiguous surroundings as a worthier object than the deliberate cultivation of ambiguity.

Yet more than a trick of the old rage remains; as, for example, coming across an abandoned railroad waiting room in which there was a clock with no hands, I came to see that clock somehow as the serpent himself, who initiated human time, and said of "the still mainspring,/Behind the even and the odd," that it "Hides in its coiled continuing/A venomous tense past tense." The difference in meaning, depending on whether you read the first "tense" as adjective or noun, seems to me to belong quite properly to the "tensions" developed by the poem as it reaches that conclusion.

So if character or attitude can be distinguished from style in a technical sense, there has perhaps been not so much change. Brought up to a poetry of irony, paradox, and wit as primary means of imagination, brought up to a view that did not always sharply divide the funny from the serious and even the sorrowful, I continue so, and have sometimes found it a strain to suffer critics gladly upon this issue in particular.

Given so much, however, of consistency in development, I think there have gradually appeared two marked changes in my poetry. The first has to do with the natural world, which I came to rather late, having been born and raised in the city. During the war and since, I have lived in the country, chiefly in Vermont, and while my relation to the landscape has been contemplative rather than practical, the landscape nevertheless has in large part taken over my poetry.

The second change is harder to speak of; it involves a growing consciousness of nature as responsive to language or, to put it the other way, of imagination as the agent of reality. This is a magical idea and not very much heard of these days even among poets —practically never among critics—but I am stuck with it. Trying to say this somewhat difficult idea, I come upon this: I do not now, if I ever did, consent to the common modern view of language as a system of conventional signs for the passive reception of experience, but tend ever more to see language as making an unknowably large part of a material world whose independent existence might be likened to that of the human unconscious, a sleep of causes, a chaos of the possible-impossible, responsive only to the wakening touch of desire and fear—that is, to spirit; that is, to the word.

To put this another way: having a dominantly aural imagination, I not so much look at nature as I listen to what it says. This is a mystery, at least in the sense that I cannot explain it—why should a phrase come to you out of the ground and seem to be exactly right? But the mystery appears to me as a poet's proper relation with things, a relation in which language, that accumulated wisdom and folly in which the living and the dead speak simultaneously, is a full partner and not merely a stenographer.

I once tried to say something of this more or less directly in a poem called "A Spell before Winter." It is about Vermont in late fall, when the conventional glory of the leaves is over and the tourists have gone home, and the land not only reveals itself in its true colors but also, in the figure of the poem, speaks:

A Spell before Winter[1]

After the red leaf and the gold have gone,
Brought down by the wind, then by hammering rain
Bruised and discolored, when October's flame

[1] From *The Next Room of Dream* (Chicago: University of Chicago Press, 1962), "A Spell before Winter" is copyright 1962 by Howard Nemerov; all rights reserved.

Goes blue to guttering in the cusp, this land
Sinks deeper into silence, darker into shade.
There is a knowledge in the look of things,
The old hills hunch before the north wind blows.

Now I can see certain simplicities
In the darkening rust and tarnish of the time,
And say over the certain simplicities,
The running water and the standing stone,
The yellow haze of the willow and the black
Smoke of the elm, the silver, silent light
Where suddenly, readying toward nightfall,
The sumac's candelabrum darkly flames.
And I speak to you now with the land's voice,
It is the cold, wild land that says to you
A knowledge glimmers in the sleep of things:
The old hills hunch before the north wind blows.

To see certain simplicities and to say over the certain simplicities—they are in a sense the same thing; a philosopher of language tells us that *see* and *say* come from the same root, "for to 'say' is to make someone else 'see' vicariously that which you have 'seen.' "

II

Is there, has there been, was there ever, a "revolution" in poetry, or is all that a matter of a few sleazy technical tricks? What is the relation of your work to this question, if there is a relation? Otherwise put: do you respond to such notions as The New Poetry, An American Language Distinct from English, The Collapse of Prosody, No Thoughts but in Things, The Battle between Academics and—What?—Others (A Fair Field Full of Mostly Corpses)?

Because I was the one to phrase this question, a certain surly sarcasm in the asking probably betrays at least the tone of my response and the somewhat distant attitude I take toward the theater in which these war games go on in what looks like continuous performances. But I shall elaborate a little.

I think there was a revolution in poetry, associated chiefly with Eliot and Pound; but maybe it is of the nature of revolutions or of the nature of history that their innovations should later come to look trivial or undistinguishable from technical tricks. I remain grateful to Eliot and Pound and the others, for winning for poets the freedom to do anything that seems to them necessary. Nowadays, if you want to write free verse, or "cadenced verse," or no particular verse at all, you can do it and no one will object so long as you don't write a manifesto proclaiming your courage and wits to (or against) the world. In fact it is also probable that no one will even notice what you are doing unless you write a manifesto, for if the "revolution" won freedom for poetry it also won for large parts of the world freedom from poetry. And why poets should still be found, fifty years later, fighting for that "freedom to experiment" as though they did not have it, is a mystery, but maybe one of the sillier mysteries.

It is also possible that the revolution produced, as revolutions will, some bad effects from which poetry can only with difficulty recover; introducing, among many other things, an extreme insistence on qualities rightly thought to be virtues in the then-obtaining situation—urbanity, consciousness, control, a certain dryness—its example may have cut poets off from great ranges of experience that begin and end in places deeper than consciousness can be happy in. So many people now concerned with the poetic art are obsessed with technique, even if the obsession is avowedly directed toward "liberation," that poetry sometimes appears as a technology, as though the "new idioms," announced with the regularity of new hair styles, were going to make obsolete everything that preceded them; which for a short, bad time they appear to do. One might put the point as a riddle: if poems are written by poets, idioms are written by guess who?

I tried to say something of this in a poem, "Lion & Honeycomb," whose title alludes to the riddle wherein Samson asked how from strength shall come forth sweetness. The speaker in this poem is a poet, discontented and somewhat angry with himself and with the other poets, too. It seems he has come to a place where he knows he has lost the way; all his art appears to him merely as *skill*, or technical virtuosity; he feels especially that he has lost the vital truth of poetry, the great wonder that first beckoned him into its enchanted realm. The process of the poem is the finding his way back to first things and if the poem succeeds, which isn't for me to say, the strength of his angry rejection at the beginning should resolve in the sweetness of the images he comes to at the end, the remembrance from childhood of two instances in particular, soap bubbles and skipping stones, where a certain gaiety, marvelousness, energy, maintained itself against gravity, even against possibility, in a hard world.

Lion & Honeycomb[2]

He didn't want to do it with skill,
He'd had enough of skill. If he never saw
Another villanelle, it would be too soon;
And the same went for sonnets. If it had been
Hard work learning to rime, it would be much
Harder learning not to. The time came
He had to ask himself, what did he want?
What did he want when he began
That idiot fiddling with the sounds of things?

He asked himself, poor moron, because he had
Nobody else to ask. The others went right on
Talking about form, talking about myth
And the (so help us) need for a modern idiom;
The verseballs among them kept counting syllables.

So there he was, this forty-year-old teen-ager
Dreaming preposterous mergers and divisions
Of vowels like water, consonants like rock
(While everybody kept discussing values
And the need for values), for words that would
Enter the silence and be there as a light.
So much coffee and so many cigarettes

Gone down the drain, gone up in smoke,
Just for the sake of getting something right
Once in a while, something that could stand
On its own flat feet to keep out windy time
And the worm, something that might simply be,
Not as the monument in the smoky rain
Grimly endures, but that would be
Only a moment's inviolable presence,
The moment before disaster, before the storm,
In its peculiar silence, an integer
Fixed in the middle of the fall of things,
Perfected and casual as, to a child's eye,
Soap bubbles are, and skipping stones.

It goes with all this that I have not much sympathy for either side of the perennial squabble about, most generally, form and content; as a great master said, when you look at a cow, do you see the form or the content of the cow? No Thoughts but in Things is a slogan having considerable pathos, a brave challenge. But people who try to follow it will find themselves either smuggling thoughts back in, or writing Imagist poetry over again. As for An American Language Distinct from English, if people want to write poems in that language, fine. But if they want to argue with you about it and the room hasn't got a door, you listen to what they have to say as patiently as possible and then ask them to say it over in American. Mostly these slogans amount to edicts decreeing that from now on you should walk on one foot only; when you have got that much of the message you needn't wait around to find out whether they mean the right or the left. The same master I quoted from a moment ago also said, perhaps to artists,

Great things are done when Men & Mountains meet;
This is not done by Jostling in the Street.

III

Does the question whether the world has changed during this century preoccupy you in poetry? Does your work appear to you

245

to envision the appearance of a new human nature, for better or
worse, or does it view the many and obvious changes as essentially
technological?

This is by all odds the hardest of the questions, for me. I am
not even certain now what I meant by it, and perhaps would not
have asked had I known a response would be demanded from
myself. Probably my secret thought was that the other poets, by
their answers, would somewhat illuminate the depths of the
question. But I shall have a go.

It sometimes seems to me as though our relations with the
Devil have reached that place, so near the end, where paradox
appears immediately in all phenomena, so that, for example, the
increase of life is the fated increase of mortal suffering, the multiplication of the means of communication is the multiplication of
meaninglessness, and so on. At the obsequies for the late President of the United States the "eternal flame" was extinguished by
holy water in the hands of children; in the material world that
may have been an unfortunate accident, but in the poetic world,
where one is compelled to listen to symbolic things, it appears
as possibly a final warning, a witty and indeed diabolical under-
lining of the dire assassination itself.

So if paradox and accenting the hidden side of the paradoxical
has always played such a part in my poetry, perhaps the seriousness of that view of life, its necessity even, may now begin to appear. The charge typically raised against my work by literary
critics has been that my poems are jokes, even bad jokes. I incline
to agree, insisting however that they are bad jokes, and even
terrible jokes, emerging from the nature of things as well as from
my propensity for coming at things a touch subversively and from
the blind side, or the dark side, the side everyone concerned with
"values" would just as soon forget. And a commitment to paradox, I think, is liable to be as serious as a commitment to anything whatever else. I shall try to put this in a plain relation with
my work in poetry.

In the first poem, "A Spell before Winter," I spoke of "the
running water and the standing stone." This distinction of imagery goes far and deep in my poetry and has assumed, over the
past seven years, the nature of an antithesis. Long before writing

that poem, I had observed in my work a growing preoccupation
with statues, with heroic monuments, as representing the rigid
domination of the past over present and future: stillness, death,
power, compacted into giant forms; the standing stone that looks
over the landscape assumes early in history a human face, a
frown, even a smile; becomes a god.

The thought of statues as representing a false, historical im-
morality seems clearly related to the scriptural prohibition
against the making of graven images; and the category in which
the statues finally come, which I generalized out as "effigies," may
include also photographs, mythological figures such as Santa
Claus, even mannequins in shop windows, or anything that tends
to confirm the mind in a habitual way of regarding the world,
which habitual way is, to be short with it, idolatry. There are
many examples in my work, and I have chosen one which repre-
sents newspapers, by a slight extension of the thought, as a sort of
verbal effigies, idolatrously confirming human beings day after
day in the habit of a mean delusion and compelling them to regard this mean delusion as their sole reality. I say this halfway
as a joke with the name of a newspaper, "The Daily Globe."

The Daily Globe[3]

Each day another installment of the old
Romance of Order brings to the breakfast table
The paper flowers of catastrophe.
One has this recurrent dream about the world.

Headlines declare the ambiguous oracles,
The comfortable old prophets mutter doom.
Man's greatest intellectual pleasure is
To repeat himself, yet somehow the daily globe

Rolls on, while the characters in comic strips
Prolong their slow, interminable lives
Beyond the segregated photographs
Of the girls that marry and the men that die.

(I might mention for the benefit of foreign audiences that in American newspapers the pictures on the obituary pages are almost exclusively of men, those on the matrimonial pages exclusively of girls).

It is the contention of my poetry very often that the world is increasingly, and with an increasing acceleration, dominated by habitual idolatry, by images for which my first representation was that of statues. The extension of the argument to television, for instance, is not difficult. So that, if my poetry does envision the appearance of a new human nature, it does so chiefly in sarcastic outrage, for that new human nature appears in the poetry merely as a totalitarian fixing of the old human nature, whose principal products have been anguish, war, and history.

As to the opposite attitude, and the image opposed. Well, if you do not take your notions of this world from newspapers you take your notions of this world from looking at this world and listening to what it seems to say. A great novelist, Thomas Mann, characterized the religious attitude as "attentiveness and obedience." His illustration of all that is *not* attentiveness and obedience is given in his story of Joseph, where he portrays the mean-spirited businessman Laban as having buried, according to ancient custom, his first born beneath the foundations of his house; unaware, so to speak, that the human spirit, with the divine spirit, had moved on from that old-fashioned idea of security. The image that has seemed to me most appropriate for this notion of "attentiveness and obedience" is the image—so dialectical, so subtle, so strange, and yet so evidently an emblem for human life and the life of the imagination—of a stream, a river, a waterfall, a fountain, or else of a still and deep reflecting pool. This image, of the form continuing in the changing material, belongs also to cloud and fire, and I once gave it a somewhat political shape in a despairing epigram: God loves (I said) the liberal thrice better than the conservative, for at the beginning he gave to the liberal the three realms of water, air, and fire, while to the conservative he gave only the earth.

Of the many appearances of this figure of water in my work, I have chosen one that seeks to set the nature of water in relation to human perception and human imagination.